For a Better Worldliness

For a Better Worldliness

Abraham Kuyper, Dietrich Bonhoeffer,
and Discipleship for the Common Good

BRANT M. HIMES

Foreword by Richard J. Mouw

PICKWICK Publications • Eugene, Oregon

FOR A BETTER WORLDLINESS
Abraham Kuyper, Dietrich Bonhoeffer, and Discipleship for the Common Good

Copyright © 2018 Brant M. Himes. All rights reserved. Except for brief quotations in critical publications or reviews, no part of this book may be reproduced in any manner without prior written permission from the publisher. Write: Permissions, Wipf and Stock Publishers, 199 W. 8th Ave., Suite 3, Eugene, OR 97401.

Pickwick Publications
An Imprint of Wipf and Stock Publishers
199 W. 8th Ave., Suite 3
Eugene, OR 97401

www.wipfandstock.com

PAPERBACK ISBN: 978-1-5326-3845-9
HARDCOVER ISBN: 978-1-5326-3846-6
EBOOK ISBN: 978-1-5326-3847-3

Cataloging-in-Publication data:

Names: Himes, Brant M., author | Mouw, Richard J., foreword

Title: For a better worldliness : Abraham Kuyper, Dietrich Bonhoeffer, and discipleship for the common good / by Brant M. Himes; foreword by Richard J. Mouw.

Description: Eugene, OR : Pickwick Publications, 2018 | Includes bibliographical references.

Identifiers: ISBN 978-1-5326-3845-9 (paperback) | ISBN 978-1-5326-3846-6 (hardcover) | ISBN 978-1-5326-3847-3 (ebook)

Subjects: LCSH: Kuyper, Abraham, 1837–1920. | Bonhoeffer, Dietrich, 1906–1945. | Christian life. | Common good. | Public interest.

Classification: LCC JC330.15 H48 2018 (print) | LCC JC330.15 (ebook)

Manufactured in the U.S.A.   09/26/18

For Jackie

To us it is only given . . . to bear our cross in joyful discipleship.
—Abraham Kuyper

Following Christ—what that really is, I'd like to know—it is not exhausted by our concept of faith.
—Dietrich Bonhoeffer

As he was walking along, he saw Levi son of Alphaeus sitting at the tax booth, and he said to him, "Follow me." And he got up and followed him.
—Mark 2:14

Contents

Foreword by Richard J. Mouw | ix
Preface | xiii
Acknowledgments | xv

Introduction | 1

Part 1—Abraham Kuyper's Theology of Discipleship: 1894–1905

CHAPTER 1
Locating a Framework for Discipleship, 1894–1898 | 17

CHAPTER 2
Discipleship in Politics, 1899–1905 | 59

Part 2—Dietrich Bonhoeffer's Theology of Discipleship: 1935–1945

CHAPTER 3
A Discipleship of Simple Obedience, 1935–1939 | 97

CHAPTER 4
Discipleship In and For the World, 1939–1945 | 130

Part 3—Discipleship for a Better Worldliness

CHAPTER 5
Discipleship for the Common Good in Kuyper and Bonhoeffer | 165

CONCLUSION
The Culmination of Discipleship | 199

Bibliography | 205

Foreword

—Richard J. Mouw

When someone from a campus where I was going to speak asked me for a phrase that would capture the theme of my forthcoming lectures, I proposed "public discipleship." The person responded with a request for something a little different. "Most of the people who might attend your talks would find it puzzling to put 'public' and 'discipleship' together," he said.

I hope they read Brant Himes's important book on that campus. The puzzles would disappear. This is a significant study of public discipleship—as a focus within what we have come to know in recent decades as "public theology."

Nor are the lessons of this book only designed for folks who still might find the notion of public discipleship puzzling. As someone who has explored that topic much for the past half-century, I gained some new insights from Brant Himes's study.

For one thing, Himes has made Dietrich Bonhoeffer *available* to me in new ways. Over the decades I have read and re-read key works by Bonhoeffer, and always with deep appreciation. But it typically has been with a sense of theological distance. We Calvinist types have tended to see him as speaking to us from a different theological camp. Or, actually, from two other camps, because it is not just the Lutherans who claim him as one of their own. Many of my Anabaptist friends also see Bonhoeffer as a like-minded theological pilgrim—so much so that they have felt a bit betrayed by his reported complicity in a plot to kill Hitler.

The shared theological "ownership" of Bonhoeffer by Lutherans and Anabaptists is grounded, of course, in Bonhoeffer's affinity for "two Kingdom" tensions. He was a servant of Christ's Kingdom who sensed a clear call to oppose, at the cost of his own life, a horribly malevolent manifestation of the earthly kingdom of the secular state.

When put in those terms, the contrast with Abraham Kuyper can appear rather stark. While Kuyper was, like Bonhoeffer, a trained theologian and influential churchman, he was also a political leader who not only led his party in the Dutch Parliament for decades, but even served a term as the nation's Prime Minister. It is not difficult to see how the two of them could be used as examples of opposing "types" in characterizing the relationship of "Christ" to "public life"—Bonhoeffer somewhere on the "against" to "in tension with" side of the spectrum, with Kuyper on the "transforming" (or at worst, the "of"!) end.

Brant Himes refuses to give into these too-easy characterizations. "For all their differences," he contends, "the outlook of both men were markedly similar." While they may have "employed different methods, emphasized different dogmas, and advocated for different outcomes, Kuyper and Bonhoeffer were really after the same thing." They shared a common conviction that "the Christian faith demanded clear and direct action in the public arena."

In order to establish this common ground, Himes must explore the concept of "discipleship" more deeply than is often the case in public theology discussions. When commentators on Bonhoeffer's theological ethics have propounded his well-known "cost of discipleship" theme, they have often focused primarily on the "cost" aspect—taking the notion of "discipleship" as a given. Since "disciple" is not a term that looms large in Kuyper's writings (except when he was referring to those who accompanied Jesus in his earthly ministry), it is important for Himes to probe the idea of discipleship as it applies to the career of a successful Dutch public leader. And, indeed, this counts for one of the major contributions of this study: the careful survey of scholarly treatments of the concept of discipleship as such.

As one who has devoted considerable attention in my own scholarship and teaching over the past half-century to Abraham Kuyper's thought, Brant Himes's study has provided for me new insights into Kuyper's public theology. Introducing Kuyper and Bonhoeffer to each other as conversation partners illuminates the way in which a deep commitment to Christ as the supreme Ruler over all principalities and powers can take shape in different social-political contexts.

During one of my visits to China in the 1990s I talked with a seminary student who was writing a paper for one of his courses on the relevance of Bonhoeffer's understanding of discipleship. "Chinese Christians need to study Bonhoeffer," he said. "He is a theologian who speaks directly to our experience!" A decade later I met with a Chinese scholar who was doing research on Kuyper's life and thought. With some passion he declared: "Kuyper is very important for China!"

I wish I could have handed each of them a copy of Brant Himes's book and encouraged them to read it together!

Preface

FOR A BETTER WORLDLINESS is not only a statement of Abraham Kuyper's and Dietrich Bonhoeffer's theological concept and historical practice of discipleship; it is also—and perhaps more importantly—a call to engage in the fullness of the Christian life here and now. While this book goes to great efforts to establish sound historical and theological insights specifically in regards to Kuyper and Bonhoeffer, there is a strong underlying current that these particular insights deeply matter to the life of discipleship in the world today.

Kuyper and Bonhoeffer scholars will find much to explore here, both within their individual fields and in dialogue with each other. But this book is not only for the specialists. Church leaders, other academics, and anyone interested in taking a deep dive into a history and theology of discipleship are all invited on a journey of discovery and application. While the book is situated squarely in the scholarship of historical theology, there are real insights and implications for the scholar and lay-reader alike.

Overall, this study aims to contribute to the larger discussion about how discipleship can take shape in the world today. In some contexts, "discipleship" is short-hand for ready-made church curriculum aimed at encouraging the development of a few personal disciplines. This is unfortunate because historically and biblically, discipleship is a life-altering holistic theological paradigm that impacts the very core of our being. A common challenge, then, is gaining a theological framework for understanding and articulating what such a holistic concept and practice of discipleship could look like.

This is where Kuyper and Bonhoeffer become invaluable theological companions and conversation partners. Through their different contexts and experiences, we can engage in an overarching discovery of key theological concepts and practices for discipleship. The result is not a list of things to do for discipleship; rather, we gain a much deeper and broader framework for how theology impacts belief, obedience, practice, and possibility. This framework recognizes that Jesus Christ came to live in the midst of this world in order to bring about its redemption. *For a better worldliness*, then, reminds us of Christ's call to engage the world on its own terms, knowing full well that life—in its joy, sorrow, pain, triumph, and tragedy—is infused with the transformative power of God's Spirit. Ultimately, it is in this grace and hope that the possibilities of discipleship for the common good are set before us.

Acknowledgments

HEARTFELT THANKS TO THE many family, friends, professors, and colleagues who have helped make this project a reality and bring it to completion. This book took original form as my doctoral dissertation in the joint PhD in Theology program between Fuller Theological Seminary in Pasadena, California and the Vrije Universiteit Amsterdam, Netherlands. My mentors—Grayson Carter, Glen Stassen, Richard Mouw, George Harinck, and Cornelis Van der Kooi—provided invaluable support, guidance, and encouragement as I worked through the many stages and iterations of this project.

The Theologische Universiteit Gereformeerde Kerken in Kampen (TUK) provided generous support for me as an Associated Guest Researcher for the Neo-Calvinism Project during the 2013–14 academic year. Their generosity allowed my family to live with me in the Netherlands while conducting much of the research and writing that was central to this project. I am also thankful for the financial support of the Stichting De Honderd Gulden Reis in providing resources to conduct a study trip into Germany while I was in the Netherlands.

Many thanks to Richard Mouw from Fuller Seminary for writing the forward to this book. Chris Spinks, my editor, and the Pickwick Publications team at Wipf and Stock have also been wonderful to work with during this revision and publication process. And thank you, reader, for taking the time to engage with the ideas and implications that are introduced here.

Finally, thank you to my family. Madelyn and Geoffrey—thank you for your contagious love and joy. You mean the world to me, and the overwhelming hope that I see in you is what keeps me pressing into God's call every day. Jackie—this journey is worth it because of you. I thank God every day that he saw fit to allow me by your side.

This book represents a revision of my 2015 doctoral dissertation, versions of which were submitted to Fuller Theological Seminary and the

Vrije Universiteit Amsterdam as "For a Better Worldliness: The Theological Discipleship of Abraham Kuyper and Dietrich Bonhoeffer." In addition, parts of this book have appeared in publication in various forms. A 2011 article entitled "Discipleship as Theological Praxis: Dietrich Bonhoeffer as a Resource for Educational Ministry" is the first iteration of the concept of the four movements of discipleship that are developed throughout this book. The article is in *Christian Education Journal* series 3, vol. 8, no. 2 (Fall 2011): 263–77. In addition, an article entitled "Distinct Discipleship: Abraham Kuyper, Dietrich Bonhoeffer, and Christian Engagement in Public Life" appeared in *The Kuyper Center Review, Volume 4: Calvinism and Democracy*, edited by John Bowlin (Grand Rapids: Eerdmans, 2014), 147–70. Revised and expanded aspects of this article appear here in Chapter 5. Lastly, parts of an article entitled "A Better Worldliness: Discipleship for the Common Good" appear here in Chapters 2 and 5; the original article appears in *Verbum Incarnatum, Volume 6: Peace and Social Justice* (University of the Incarnate Word, 2014): 38–61.

Introduction

There is nothing in the whole creation that is not the expression, the embodiment, the revelation of a thought of God.

—Abraham Kuyper, *Common Grace in Science*

The Question of Discipleship

DISCIPLESHIP IS THEOLOGY IN action. It is the intersection of belief and practice that permeates all aspects of life. To separate the two is to deny the holistic call to follow-after Jesus Christ in and through every endeavor. Therefore, this study is about the theological, ethical, and historical interaction between both the *concept* and *practice* of discipleship. It seeks a *definition* of discipleship that is theologically grounded in Christian orthodoxy, just as it searches for a tenable *practice* of discipleship that can faithfully yield to the simple, profound call of Jesus Christ. To do so, this study reaches out into notably diverse Christian traditions of the twentieth century in order to discern the potential for theological convergence, refinement, and application for today. The result is a re-examination of the relationship between discipleship and the common good, asking, what good is Christian discipleship if it neglects the world around it? Finally, at its culmination, this study is about possibility and potential, wondering at the profound opportunities for joyous participation in God's work in and for the world. This project is fundamentally about the question of discipleship—in history, in theology, and in ethics. But discipleship is not a singular journey; because of Jesus Christ, it is not a description of one set path with one set of guidelines. History shows us that a disciple can be a prime minister who unabashedly and successfully campaigned on his Calvinistic principles, just as a disciple can be a participant in a *coup d'état* launched against a tyrant, leading to the disciple's own imprisonment and death. Jesus Christ calls—whether to the height of political office, or to the dank prison cell, or (more likely for us) to somewhere in between.

Discipleship is a concept of action, of *doing* something. But it also must *mean* something—something theologically rich and profound—in order to find its affect and purpose. Discipleship cannot simply be reduced to a set of tasks—read your Bible, pray, and, if you are really serious, fast. It certainly includes these things; but the issue of spiritual disciplines is not to be equated with the concept of discipleship. Discipleship must be a *theological* concept in order to sustain the transformative call of Jesus Christ. Apart from its theological foundations, discipleship is nothing more than feel-good self-help; and in such a deflated form, "discipleship" cannot truly exist.

Abraham Kuyper understood this. Discipleship was a way of life that encompassed all aspects of his thought and work. In the language of his famous Stone Lectures in 1898, discipleship was a comprehensive "world and life view."[1] Kuyper found the clearest expression of the unity of Christian theology and practice in Calvinism—and the Stone Lectures make this explicit. But when Kuyper speaks of "Calvinism" in this all-encompassing manner, he is, at its base, describing a dedicated life of following-after Jesus Christ—of discipleship. "Calvinism" was Kuyper's frame of reference to live out his calling to discipleship in all aspects of his life, because this calling was ultimately to the sovereign Lord Jesus Christ. We can see how Kuyper expressed this full-life commitment in a speech he gave on April 1, 1897. He was being honored for his role as editor-in-chief at the twenty-fifth anniversary celebration of the founding of his newspaper, *De Standaard*. To a crowd of 5,000 in the large concert hall at the Palace of the People's Industry, he declared:

> All that I am . . . what is it finally but His talent and His work? He who created me, He who predestined me, He who led me since my youth, He who without my presuming it in the least, brought me to this position without my knowing it, to defend His holy name, it was He alone who also gave me access to your hearts. And even if you ask me whether behind all the gifts and talent there is not also an "I" to be found in my person, and whether that "I" is not the person who makes all gifts to glow and be inspired, then still my answer is: "even that 'I,' even that person does not come from me, but is only given by God to me."[2]

1. See Kuyper, *Lectures on Calvinism*.
2. As quoted in de Bruijn, *Abraham Kuyper*, 225.

In this speech, Kuyper was describing his life of discipleship. For twenty-five years now, he had been at the helm of a periodical whose mission it was to inform and shape public opinion on matters of religious, political, and national interest. True, *De Standaard* was just one aspect of his life, but Kuyper had a remarkable ability strategically to weave together all of his professional and personal responsibilities—which included matters of the church, family, education, journalism, and politics. For Kuyper, "All that I am" was "only given by God to me." This was his statement of discipleship.

Kuyper's life of discipleship is notable also for its world-directed trajectory. Like we will see in Bonhoeffer, Kuyper was driven by the desire to see God's work in his own life translate to a sense of hope in and for the common good of society. At the end of his *De Standaard* twenty-fifth anniversary speech, Kuyper recited a poem to sum up his life's aim:

> For me, one desire rules my life
> One urge drives soul and will . . .
> It is to re-establish God's holy ordinances
> In church and home, in state and school,
> Regardless of the world's protestations,
> For the benefit of the nation.
> It is to engrave those divine ordinances,
> To which Word and Creation witness,
> So clearly on the nation
> That once again it bows its knee to God.[3]

In advancing such an over-arching vision for society, Kuyper faced countless challenges and formidable opponents. Indeed, his brash and bullish personality left a steady stream of opponents and adversaries trailing in his wake. The disciple was certainly not without his flaws. But Kuyper was committed, and he was capable—and this earned the on-going respect of his colleagues. In the memorial book that was published to mark the anniversary of his editorship, journalists from all sides wrote tributes to Kuyper. Even his opponents respected and valued his work, including Herman Schaepman, a Catholic priest and member of parliament: "As a journalist Dr. Kuyper is the opponent of the great principles which I am privileged to serve. In a world in which one does not live without opponents I am grateful for such an opponent."[4] Kuyper lived a very public life, contributing extensively to journalism, politics, the church, and education. But throughout the course of his career, Kuyper's public actions were driven by his single, foundational

---

3. As quoted in Heslam, *Creating a Christian Worldview*, 54–55.

4. As quoted in Heslam, *Creating a Christian Worldview*, 55. See also Heemskerk, *Gedenkboek*, 109.

commitment to the will of God, for and in all aspects of his faith and life. Simply put, Kuyper lived thoroughly the life of discipleship, seeking out the newness of its meaning each and every day.

Dietrich Bonhoeffer, too, understood the necessity of constant wrestling with the question of discipleship. In April 1934, he was seven months into his pastorate with the German speaking congregation in London. He had left Germany in protest and frustration (if not confusion) over the weak response of the German Evangelical Church to the new Aryan laws, and the growing influence of the Nazi-backed German Christians. From his new post in London, Bonhoeffer gained much-needed distance and began to concentrate on the development and promotion of the Confessing Church movement; he also came to value the very practical experience of regular preaching and pastoral care that now fell to him. Even while in London, some five years before the outbreak of the Second World War, he had a sense of the chaos that was beginning to overtake Germany, and he was diligently seeking a way forward.

Erwin Sutz was one of Bonhoeffer's trusted conversation partners. He was a Swiss Reformed pastor and theologian whom Bonhoeffer had met during his year at Union Seminary in New York. On April 24, 1934 Bonhoeffer wrote to him from London. Near the end of the letter, revealed the extent of his present confusion:

> I cannot yet see clearly, only shadowy outlines of what is happening and what should happen, but your constant, ongoing questioning has not been the least of that which has brought me to where I am. . . . Please write and tell me sometime how you preach the Sermon on the Mount. I'm currently trying to do so, to keep it infinitely plain and simple, but it always comes back to *keeping* the commandments and not trying to evade them. *Following* [*Nachfolge*] Christ—what that really is, I'd like to know—it is not exhausted by our concept of faith.[5]

Bonhoeffer's reflection on—and study of—the Sermon on the Mount led to the writing of his most famous book, *Discipleship* (*Nachfolge*), in 1937. Based largely on his experience and lectures as director of the Confessing Church's underground seminary at Finkenwalde, the book is a focused and poignant exploration of the question he had put to Sutz: what does it really mean to follow Christ?

Ten years later, Bonhoeffer occupied cell 92 at Tegel Military Prison in Berlin. July 20, 1944 marked the day of the failed *Valkyrie* assassination attempt on Hitler. Bonhoeffer's role in this plot was as yet undiscovered by

---

5. Bonhoeffer, *DBWE* 13:136.

the Nazis, and the next day, on July 21, he wrote to his closest friend and future biographer Eberhard Bethge:

> I thought I myself could learn to have faith by trying to live something like a saintly life. I suppose I wrote *Discipleship* at the end of this path. Today I clearly see the dangers of that book, though I still stand by it. Later on I discovered, and am still discovering to this day, that one only learns to have faith by living in the full this-worldliness of life.[6]

In this letter, Bonhoeffer reassessed the nature of his question of what it meant to follow Christ. He now began to articulate a perspective and commitment that embraced a Christian life lived fully in the world, as opposed to an isolated pursuit of sanctification. The question now was basically the same as it had been ten years earlier, though the process and conclusions had developed during the intervening period. Foundationally, though, Bonhoeffer continued to pursue the question of what it really meant to follow-after Jesus Christ. His personal circumstances, as well as his developing theology related to the Sermon on the Mount, allowed him to form different—and highly nuanced—perspectives on the question, but his concern to live a life of discipleship remained steadfast. Indeed, as it was for Kuyper, Christian discipleship was the central question of Bonhoeffer's entire life and theology.

Surely Kuyper and Bonhoeffer are not unique in the Christian tradition for wanting to follow Jesus Christ with all their hearts. With two thousand years of church history to cull from, opportunities for historical and theological investigations around the concept of discipleship are many. Even in twentieth-century theology—the purview of this study—there are powerful stories of tragedy and triumph needing to be further explored and synthesized.[7] In a book that puts forth the effort of comparative theology, it might seem unfortunate that the two figures are not more diverse: despite differences in their respective vocations—one a Dutch Calvinist prime minister and the other a German Lutheran theologian executed by the Nazis—they both emerged from privileged, highly-educated, and well-connected backgrounds, and (although not exact contemporaries) they nevertheless shared a number of social and political assumptions held by European males of similar upbringings. But it would be a significant loss to dismiss the value of comparing Kuyper and Bonhoeffer on the basis of their external similarities. Historical figures of all cultures, times, and beliefs are

---

6. Bonhoeffer, *DBWE* 8:486.

7. See, for example, Marsh, *Beloved Community*; and Jenkins and McBride, *Bonhoeffer and King*.

worth studying in their own right—because history, in all its diversity and mystery, has a story to tell about where we came from and how that has influenced where we are headed. Kuyper and Bonhoeffer (among countless others) form an important part of the political and religious landscape of the twentieth century. And how we understand and interpret the details and implications of their stories will impact our story in the twenty-first century and beyond—particularly, in how Christians understand and live out the distinct call to discipleship.

For All Their Differences . . .

Kuyper and Bonhoeffer were indeed two very different historical and theological figures. Kuyper (1837–1920), the son of a Dutch Reformed minister, spent his life building and advocating a Calvinistic worldview in the Netherlands. Bonhoeffer (1906–1945), born into the old Prussian aristocracy, chose the life of a Lutheran pastor, theologian, and resistance fighter against the Nazi regime. Kuyper died after a long and successful career; he founded several institutions, including the Free University, the Antirevolutionary Party (the first modern, organized popular political party in the Netherlands), and two newspapers, and at the height of his career he became the prime minister of the Netherlands. Bonhoeffer died at the young age of 39; he was killed in a Nazi concentration camp for his role in the *Valkyrie* assassination attempt on Hitler. His short life was incredibly productive, though, and some of his theological writings on discipleship, ethics, and the nature of the church have become spiritual classics. Kuyper would not have known of Bonhoeffer, and Bonhoeffer's interactions with Reformed writings seem to lack any direct connection to (or engagement with) Kuyper.[8]

For all their differences, however, the outlook of both men were markedly similar, especially in their commitment to Christian engagement with the world. While they employed different methods, emphasized different dogmas, and advocated for different outcomes, Kuyper and Bonhoeffer were really after the same thing. Both were convinced that the nature of the Christian faith demanded clear and direct action in the public arena. As a result, they both sought to build a theology that could make sense of—and meaningfully engage with—the pressing issues in their respective historical circumstances. Kuyper looked to the roots of the Reformed faith in Calvin

---

8. De Gruchy gives an example of Reformed influence on Bonhoeffer by making the case that Bonhoeffer found himself outside his Lutheran heritage and embracing notions of the Reformed tradition in the decision to participate in the conspiracy against Hitler. See *Bonhoeffer and South Africa*, 98–100.

and worked to construct a theology that was both faithful to its foundations and relevant for the time. Bonhoeffer, on the other hand, sought to refine and re-imagine the Lutheran theological tradition in order to articulate a biblical way forward in the context of the rise of National Socialism and the outbreak of war. Their different historical contexts nevertheless led them to a strikingly similar conviction: Christian disciples are called to bear essential witness to the reality of Jesus Christ in the world. Kuyper and Bonhoeffer are therefore excellent resources for exploring the very public nature of Christian discipleship.

Personal discipleship demands public engagement because the reality of life in Christ is public, in that it infuses all aspects of life.[9] Kuyper and Bonhoeffer constructed theologies of discipleship that spoke to the mandate of Christian involvement in and for the world. Their conclusions were both general and specific; they interacted with the world from a set of theological convictions, and yet they allowed their unique situation to inform the outworking of that theology. As such, this study explores the specific historical context and theological implications of concepts from a selection of writings from Kuyper and Bonhoeffer. Methodologically, all explorations of Kuyper and Bonhoeffer have been limited by focusing research on a particular time period in each of their lives. Specifically, the investigation into Kuyper's life and work is confined to the years 1894 to 1905—the height of his political career, culminating in his service as prime minister from 1901 to 1905. The investigation of Bonhoeffer is similarly limited to about a decade (1935–1945), in order to bring focus to the culmination of his life and writings while in prison. Of course, at times it is necessary to utilize primary source material drawn from outside of this tight chronological framework. On the other hand, restricting our study to (in each case) a ten to eleven year period allows for the consideration of a more historically nuanced concept of discipleship.

This is all not to say that the concept of discipleship holds any sort of agreed upon status in the scholarship surrounding either Kuyper or Bonhoeffer. Historically, questions of Kuyper's theology of discipleship remain largely unexplored. While the neo-Calvinist tradition offers robust and growing contributions to questions of public theology and cultural discipleship, these studies are for the most part aimed at contemporary philosophy, ethics, and constructive theology.[10] And while the question and concept of Kuyper's own theological understanding and historical practice of disciple-

---

9. Note that the use of "public" throughout the book is not limited to "politics," but rather signifies a theological orientation to all aspects of our interconnected society and life, including occupations, societies, economics, family, etc.

10. See, for example, Mouw, *Challenges of Cultural Discipleship*.

ship can in part be deduced from previous studies—indeed, much is often made of the connection between Kuyper's private and public life—his explicit notion of "discipleship" remains underdeveloped. This study, on the other hand, is primarily a work of historical theology which aims to examine how Kuyper developed a concept of personal discipleship that applied directly to his dealings in politics and global society. In doing so, it shows how Kuyper's key political actions between 1894 and 1905 were directly influenced by his personal theology and practice of discipleship.

Consideration of this subject is important because it offers a direct connection between the development of Kuyper's personal faith and its expression in the public realm. While Kuyper scholarship has often explored the notion of his "public theology," this study aims to focus on the importance of *discipleship* for understanding how that public theology emerged and was practiced. It is clear that Kuyper himself wrestled with the implications and calling of his faith—and this calling for him was always in and to the public realm. For example, in 1903 he wrote to his daughter, "My calling is high, my task is wonderful, and above my bed hangs a painting of the crucifixion, and when I look upon it, it seems as if the Lord asks me every night: 'What is your struggle at my drinking cup?' His service is so uplifting and wonderful."[11] "What is your struggle at my drinking cup?" This was the question of discipleship for Kuyper. His journey was a daily following-after of Jesus Christ. So, while Kuyper's writings may not contain a notable amount of instances of the Dutch word *discipelschap*, this is not to say that the concept and practice of discipleship was not real and pressing for him. Struggling at the drinking cup of Christ is a powerful image of discipleship. This was a question Kuyper faced daily, a calling he thoroughly embraced.

Admittedly, this focus on discipleship in Kuyper may seem unusual, particularly to readers in the Dutch context. As a former prime minister, Kuyper's national reputation is strongest in the realm of politics—and his perception is not likely to be wholly favorable. Kuyper was often a bullish force that had to be reckoned with, and his strong personality coupled with his distinct Calvinistic vision for the nation earned him admirers and adversaries alike. While Kuyper is certainly remembered and respected historically, the on-going significance of his life and work is not a pressing question in the Netherlands today, outside of the niche academy. As a progressive, liberal society, many people in the Netherlands see Kuyper as a relic from the past. In the North American context, on the other hand, the Dutch Reformed tradition continues to embrace and press Kuyper's significance in society. He does not retain the narrow political associations

---

11. Kuyper and Kuyper, *De levensavond van dr. A. Kuyper*, 83.

in North America that he does in the Netherlands. Consequently, Kuyper scholarship outside the Netherlands is now moving beyond its rather narrow origins within the Dutch Reformed tradition, and examining such themes as Kuyper's contributions to scholarship, journalism, social and political theory, international relations, peace studies, and comparative theology, among others. Many of those now interested in Kuyper are drawn from beyond the Dutch Reformed tradition, having located in Kuyper a plethora of significant contributions to a vast range of areas. The author of the present study, for example, who comes from outside the Dutch Reformed tradition, was attracted to Kuyper's theories in historical theology and the life of the contemporary church. The question of discipleship addressed herein represents a distinct—and not fully obvious—approach to understanding Kuyper—albeit a historically and theologically significant approach that has consequence for readers in the Netherlands, North America, and beyond.

The direct question of discipleship in Bonhoeffer scholarship is much more present than in Kuyper studies, but that is because there has already been considerable debate in how to interpret Bonhoeffer's own theological development. To be sure, Bonhoeffer scholarship is not in agreement on how to reconcile the tensions that emerge between his theology in 1934 and his emerging "new" theology of 1944—and this requires an explanation. Broadly speaking, two main lines of interpretation identify the continuity between Bonhoeffer's early and late theology.[12] First, the teleological view interprets the later works, which contain Bonhoeffer's thoughts on worldliness and religionless Christianity as expressed in his *Letters and Papers from Prison*, over and against his earlier works, such as *Discipleship*. Scholars such as Hanfried Müller and John A. Phillips claim that a distinct break exists between these two periods, and they aim to show how the later theology superseded the earlier theology. The second approach interprets Bonhoeffer from the perspective of historical-contextual analysis and understanding. Eberhard Bethge and Clifford Green, for example, are advocates for the consistent development of Bonhoeffer's thought, and take into account the shifts and changes from a strongly biographical perspective. The results of these two approaches differ significantly. Within the teleological perspective, Bonhoeffer has been placed in the service of Marxist secular humanism and the so-called "death of God" theologians. The historical-contextual approach, on the other hand, is committed to understanding the unique

12. Bonhoeffer scholars often identify additional models of interpretation in addition to the main teleological and historical streams addressed in this study. For example, Clifford Green adds the thematic and comparative approaches and Stephen Haynes describes five main perspectives of interpretation: Bonhoeffer as seer, prophet, apostle, bridge, and saint. See Green, *Bonhoeffer*, 8–9; and Haynes, *Bonhoeffer Phenomenon*.

interplay between Bonhoeffer's life and writings, and would be remiss if it interprets one element while neglecting the other.

These two methodological approaches have offered starkly different interpretations of Bonhoeffer's quest to discover what it really means to follow Christ. The teleological interpreters have focused on Bonhoeffer's *Ethics* and *Letters and Papers from Prison*, and work from this limited perspective in hopes of shaping the next wave of contemporary theological inquiry. In the past, this has given way to the embrace of the concept of "religionless Christianity" as a kind of atheism and humanism; following Christ meant following the historical example of the human (or non-incarnate) Jesus. On the other hand, a historical-contextual approach relies on an explicit assessment of the circumstances that surround his writings. This view is more apt to recognize the frequent—and nuanced—shifts in Bonhoeffer's development, which it often explains as occurring in three connected but distinct stages: the early, middle, and late periods. These shifts in Bonhoeffer's thought are identified in terms of the contextual differences that occur between the various periods. Themes such as Christology, ecclesiology, pacifism, and theological ethics have been proposed as important concepts to interpret accurately and appropriately Bonhoeffer's theological development. While such rich concepts are vital to developing a balanced historical understanding of Bonhoeffer's life and thought, they fall short presenting a comprehensive answer to the question plaguing Bonhoeffer: what does it really mean to follow Jesus Christ?

This project identifies with the historical-contextual tradition in Bonhoeffer studies and proposes that the concept of discipleship, or following-after Jesus Christ, is a unifying theological hermeneutic in Bonhoeffer's life and thought. During the final years of his life, Bonhoeffer developed a penetrating theology and practice of discipleship, and this provides a uniquely comprehensive lens through which he—and his theological thought—can be considered. Discipleship is not a phase that Bonhoeffer slips in and out of casually. It is a profound and transformative concept with deep personal implications, and he wrestles with its meaning consistently and passionately for many years. As such, discipleship is one of the most significant theological approaches to understanding Bonhoeffer, and a helpful way of interacting with some of the most pressing theological and cultural issues of our own day.

Introduction

The Path Ahead: History, Theology, and Discipleship

Up to this point, the academic scholarship on both Kuyper and Bonhoeffer lacks comprehensive investigations of each of their respective theological and contextual understandings of discipleship. Kuyper's specific concept of discipleship remains largely unexplored, while Bonhoeffer's understanding has mainly been investigated in terms of its relation to Christology, its psychological and practical dimension, and its connection to theological ethics. These previous studies in Kuyper and Bonhoeffer are of considerable importance, and some of their findings certainly impact the nature and progress of this present study. However, no study has yet adequately demonstrated the depth of either Kuyper's or Bonhoeffer's theological and personal encounter with the notion of discipleship.[13] Furthermore, no investigation has specifically compared both Kuyper *and* Bonhoeffer on the question of discipleship itself.

This project, then, seeks to offer a historically-based constructive theology of discipleship within Kuyper and Bonhoeffer. It asks: *how does a historical and theological comparison of Abraham Kuyper, as a Dutch theologian and politician from 1894–1905, and Dietrich Bonhoeffer, as a German pastor then prisoner from 1935–1945, contribute to a concept of discipleship that is for the common good?* Obviously, there are several dynamics at play here. First, this is a work of historical theology. Kuyper and Bonhoeffer are investigated within specific historical contexts and circumstances, and these situations drive the theological analysis. Admittedly, more can and should be done to explore the notion of discipleship across the entirety of Kuyper's and Bonhoeffer's life and thought, but the scope of this project simply does not allow for such a large undertaking. The respective decades and texts, however, were chosen carefully. Kuyper reached the height of his political career at the turn of the twentieth century, and also penned some of his most significant theological and political writings during this time. Similarly, Bonhoeffer's life came to its culmination during the tumultuous decade leading into and through the Second World War. His famous writings on the theme of discipleship emerged during this time, right before he was forced to reconcile the personal question of his ethical responsibility to Jesus Christ, the church, and his country. The chosen time periods and texts, then, become critical factors in this historical and theological analysis because they represent a culmination of life and thought in each figure.

---

13. It is not uncommon for writers to look to Bonhoeffer for theological insights into the practice of ministry. See, for example, Anderson, *Shape of Practical Theology*; and Osmer, *Teaching Ministry of Congregations*. Still, these studies do not seek to identify Bonhoeffer's own theology of discipleship.

Both Kuyper and Bonhoeffer wrote extensively throughout their lives, and these respective "culminating" time periods were no different. By nature, this study cannot give due attention to each text that an author produced during these times. So, there is less focus, for example, on Kuyper's *Lectures on Calvinism* and Bonhoeffer's *Ethics* in order to concentrate on some of the less familiar—but similarly significant—texts. Rather than maintaining strict concentration on the seminal works, this study analyzes previously under-researched texts like Kuyper's *Dienst des Woords* and Bonhoeffer's correspondence related to theological education underground. The result is an argument for a more holistic concept of discipleship, while also contributing something new to the field of research. It is also the case that not all of the relevant texts on discipleship by these authors can be explored in this study. The texts and time periods were chosen carefully and with the intention of further illuminating the proposed four-movement framework of discipleship. Certainly, further research in this field will reveal additional important texts from Kuyper and Bonhoeffer as they relate to a holistic, theologically grounded concept of discipleship.

But there is also a third factor: "culmination" meant very different things for Kuyper and Bonhoeffer. The height of Kuyper's career was *het Torentje*—the "little tower" in The Hague that traditionally holds the prime minister's office. Bonhoeffer's culminating life experience was a cell at the Tegel Military Prison in Berlin, a few miles from his home. Indeed, the differences in their circumstances are stark. More so, these are two very different people from two very different times and places, who even heralded from two very different theological traditions. Yet, it will be argued that there is a striking convergence in their life and theology—one that comes together around their lived-out concept of discipleship—which finds its ultimate potential in being for the common good of the world. This fourth and final aspect of this study leads to the transition from strict historical theology to constructive theology and ethical application. The question of discipleship was dynamic and moving for both Kuyper and Bonhoeffer, as it should be for us today.

Finally, there is the issue of the definition of "discipleship" itself. In the church and academy today, it is common to address the concept of discipleship as a set of personal spiritual practices, with a particular focus on congregational or small group ministry. This book argues for a definition of discipleship that includes *but is not limited to* understanding discipleship as a set of spiritual practices or disciplines. Indeed, the concept of "theological discipleship" is employed throughout the study in order to affirm a broader and more holistic understanding of discipleship itself. In this way, the study affirms recent scholarship which describes discipleship in a wide array of theological concepts and historical perspectives. For example, Daniel Patte argues that concepts of discipleship often fall into two broad understandings, "whose central feature is either (1) doing God's will, as taught by Jesus, or (2) imitating Christ."[14] He explains:

> Theologians, churches, denominations, and individual Christians usually display a preference for one of these ways of understanding and practicing discipleship. Yet each choice is grounded in biblical texts and traditions, intertwined with choices regarding other theological concepts, and needs to be weighted in terms of its contextual implications.[15]

The strategy here, then, is to discern if and how a more holistic understanding of discipleship could move beyond the concepts of *either* doing God's will, *or* imitating Christ. Were Kuyper and Bonhoeffer the kind of theologians and Christians who could move beyond a preference for one of these ways of understanding and practicing discipleship? Did they instead embody a theology of discipleship that allowed them to both discern and follow God's will *and* imitate Christ?[16]

In order to discern a holistic theology of discipleship, the book is divided into three parts and is organized chronologically. Part 1 (chapters 1 and 2) focuses on Kuyper, part 2 (chapters 3 and 4) investigates Bonhoeffer, and part 3 (chapter 5 and the conclusion) offers a comparison, synthesis, and a way forward for engaging the question of discipleship. As a way to bring structure to this analysis, this study employs a four-movement framework (or hermeneutic) of discipleship:

- The *foundation* of discipleship is the *revelation* of God.
- The *reality* of discipleship is the sovereignty of *Jesus Christ*.
- The *action* of discipleship is the necessity of *belief-obedience*.
- The *possibility* of discipleship is participating in the ultimate promise of God's redemptive work for the *common good* of the world.

Both Kuyper's and Bonhoeffer's concept of discipleship can best be understood with this new interpretive framework—and its application can be especially relevant today. Note that it is not being argued here that Kuyper and/or Bonhoeffer consciously developed and intentionally created or used

14. Patte, "Discipleship," 326.
15. Patte, "Discipleship," 327.
16. Other recent definitions of discipleship similarly refer to a broad, holistic understanding. See Hastings, "Discipleship," 169; Strecker and Starke, "Discipleship," 851–53; and Augsburger, "Discipleship," 235–37.

this (or any similar) framework of discipleship in their own writings and understanding. At the same time, this particular understanding would not be entirely foreign to their historical or theological contexts. The goal in employing this particular lens of discipleship in this investigation is not to force Kuyper and Bonhoeffer into a single, limited framework; rather it is to provide an opportunity for their similarities and differences to be brought to light. So, the four-movement concept of discipleship that permeates this study is admittedly an interpretive tool, but one that is intended to be both useful for historical and theological understanding *and* for comparison and contemporary application. As such, the goal throughout this work is to keep a single guiding question at the forefront: what does it really mean to follow-after Jesus Christ?

Part 1

Abraham Kuyper's Theology of Discipleship

1894–1905

Chapter 1

Locating a Framework for Discipleship, 1894–1898

Alas, people read the Sermon on the Mount and find it beautiful, but they do not believe Jesus really meant it that way. They find it to be delightful poetry but spiritually too high for the prose of our lives. Even the best Christian always retains a small chapel for Mammon.

—Abraham Kuyper, *Christ and the Needy*

The Politics of Forgiveness

ON OCTOBER 13, 1895, Charles Boissevain, liberal editor of the Amsterdam daily newspaper *Algemeen Handelsblad*, published a scathing critique of Abraham Kuyper. The *Handelsblad* mocked Kuyper's disingenuous attempt at forgiving his one-time friend and close colleague Alexander F. de Savornin Lohman, calling his efforts at reconciliation "laughable" and his methods of reasoning as "wicked."[1] If Kuyper's readers embraced the sincerity and nuance of his plea for forgiveness, the *Handelsblad* reasoned, they could only do so with a qualified and collective sigh at their talented but pompous Antirevolutionary Party (ARP) leader. Kuyper, for his part, clearly took issue with the *Handelsblad's* poignant remarks. In a letter to the editor dated

---

1. Editorial, "Van dag tot dag."

eleven days later, Kuyper took some pains to explain the nature of Christian forgiveness, noting that it was demanded not only upon a father to his child, but also towards those who assailed and slandered one's character. "Such forgiveness," explained Kuyper, "demands self-control, hard struggle, and the strength of faith as that of saints and martyrs."[2] Christian forgiveness, in other words, was no glib act. In fact, it was in the sincerity of action more so than the weaving of words that forgiveness was most genuinely expressed. The *Handelsblad* may have had its doubts of Kuyper's motivation and method of seeking forgiveness from Lohman, but certainly the rival newspaper had more to gain from Kuyper's downfall than from his party's reconciliation. It would be up to Kuyper's actions to try and demonstrate the genuine nature of his feelings towards Lohman. But after all that the two had been through, reconciliation was hardly guaranteed.

Kuyper and Lohman had a long history, having worked closely together on numerous occasions in church, university, and political affairs. When Kuyper suffered from exhaustion in 1876 and 1877, it was Lohman who took over Kuyper's editorial duties at *De Standaard*. In 1879, Lohman helped Kuyper establish the Free University, and he served on its law faculty from 1883 to 1896. By 1886 the two were collaborating in the Doleantie church conflict by breaking into Amsterdam's Nieuwe Kerk and wresting control of the building from the national Dutch Reformed Church. Lohman's aristocratic background certainly contrasted with Kuyper's upbringing as the son of a common preacher, but the two had similar anti-revolutionary sentiments—in the vein of Guillaume Groen van Prinsterer (1801–1876)—and so could naturally coalesce around Kuyper's new political party and his emerging church denomination. Lohman also was a landowner and served on the provincial bench in North Brabant. He thus brought valuable credentials and important practical experience to the wide array of Kuyper's initiatives. In 1894, Kuyper and Lohman were serving in the Dutch parliament together, but a tense political situation arose that would soon—and literally—tear them apart.[3]

The year 1894 brought with it the urgency of the franchise question. For many years the Dutch parliament had debated if and how to extend voting rights, and now J. P. R. Tak van Poortvliet of the liberal government set forth a definitive plan aimed at resolving the issue. But Kuyper and Lohman found themselves on opposing sides of this conflict. Tak's bill laid the groundwork for eventual universal suffrage, a democratic right that

---

2. Kuyper, "Aan den schrijver van Van dag tot dag."

3. See Bratt, *Abraham Kuyper*, 97, 121, and 149–50. See also Kossmann, *Low Countries*, 359–61, 494; and Van Dyke, "Abraham Kuyper," 641.

Kuyper supported, in part, because it gave voice to the *kleine luyden*—the "little people," or commoners who were the core of Kuyper's constituency. While Kuyper's preference was that the franchise would be extended only to all heads of households, he found Tak's bill sufficiently compatible with his own view because it expanded democracy. However, the bill exposed a rift among Kuyper's ARP, and among the Dutch parliament as a whole. Lohman was aligned with the anti-Takkians in maintaining that the right to vote had to be earned, through traditional means such as education and economic independence. Expanding the franchise too much and too quickly, they felt, would only lead to unrest as the lower classes clamored for more material goods. Unable to resolve the differences in parliament, the government leader resigned and the House was dissolved. New elections were called as a referendum on Tak's bill, and Kuyper and Lohman were soon campaigning against each other's views.[4]

In preparation for a pre-election party meeting, Lohman issued a rallying memorandum to convince the Antirevolutionary voting clubs that they had a moral responsibility to vote against Tak's bill. Not to be outdone, Kuyper called Lohman's memo a "fatal manifesto" and pulled together more than enough support from delegates in the ARP to pass a resolution in favor of Tak's bill. In the midst of the heated debate, Kuyper fumed that perhaps it was time for the right and left wings of the party to go their separate ways. Lohman obliged, and broke off from Kuyper to form the Free Antirevolutionaries.[5]

While Kuyper and Lohman had often found themselves partners against a pressing liberalism, their fundamentally different social locations ultimately led to their split. Kuyper was the son of a preacher and remained committed to bringing the voice of the commoners to the halls of parliament. Lohman, on the other hand, came from a "double name" tradition of gentry, barons, and squires.[6] He countered Kuyper's more liberal social leanings with a stark conservatism, and their differences soon became too glaring to share the same political platform. In the midst of the franchise debate, Kuyper wrote that it was clear that Christ aligned himself with the oppressed and against the powerful. Such a pointed claim left Lohman—himself a wealthy nobleman—feeling personally attacked, irritated, and deeply aggrieved.[7] Their differing views on the Tak bill were now hitting at core character traits, and Lohman could not help but take Kuyper's harsh

---

4. See Van Dyke, "Abraham Kuyper," 641–42; and Bratt, *Abraham Kuyper*, 229–38.
5. See Van Dyke, "Abraham Kuyper," 643.
6. See Bratt, *Abraham Kuyper*, 233.
7. See Kuyper, *Christ and the Needy*, 647; and Van Dyke, "Abraham Kuyper," 641.

words against the wealthy personally. The disagreement led to the Antirevolutionary Party splitting into conservative and liberal wings, each led respectively by Lohman and Kuyper. After working so closely together in the past, the two would hardly be on speaking terms for the next twenty years.

But as the split was unfolding, Kuyper took the time to write an article for the *Handelsblad* addressing a key aspect of Christian discipleship—forgiveness. It is interesting that such a fundamental Christian concept would bubble to the surface during this political debate, especially because once forgiveness was offered, the party split continued and Lohman and Kuyper's relationship remained seemingly irreparable. Yet the theme of forgiveness is an apt starting place to investigate this developmental era of Kuyper's theology of discipleship because it provides a focused test case of the interaction between theological thought and real-life practice. Indeed, a seeming disparity between Kuyper's words and actions of forgiveness was not lost on his opponents. So, we are faced with two pressing questions: what was the nature of Christian forgiveness for Kuyper, and what was the relationship between personal exchanges of forgiveness and subsequent political decisions and actions?

Kuyper realized that he had offended Lohman on the campaign trail in 1894, and soon after he addressed this issue in a series of articles published both in *De Standaard* and as a separate pamphlet in 1895 as *Christ and the Needy*. Kuyper wrote:

> On several occasions during the last election campaign the relationship between the rich and the poor was referred to, also by us apparently, without proper care. We have to accept that this is so, now that one of our warmest friends [Lohman], who is also from a prominent family, has told us that our words had offended him on more than one occasion. There is, of course, always the possibility that the offense was in part taken rather than given, but when a loyal brother tells us that he was "irritated and aggrieved," then we are inclined for our part to seek the responsibility for this in the thoughtlessness of our words, and to entreat the aggrieved and irritated brother not to hold this terminological bumbling against us.
>
> Happily, forgiveness is always easy among us Christians, and when issues arise there is always one authority to which we are prepared to surrender unconditionally from the outset: *the authority of our Lord and Savior*.[8]

---

8. Kuyper, *Christ and the Needy*, 647.

Kuyper was concerned with the offering and accepting of forgiveness here, but he did not lose the chance to continue pressing his point—submitting to the authority of Jesus Christ should naturally lead fellow Christians to his same conclusions regarding the relationship between the rich and the poor. In the rest of the article, Kuyper spent his time not pining for forgiveness, but instead returning to the underlying franchise question by providing a detailed explanation of how the rich and poor were portrayed in the Bible. Kuyper was willing to admit that "some ill-considered words may have escaped my pen," yet he asked his detractors—and fellow Christians—to consider that his understanding of Jesus' views from Scripture may be right. In other words, Kuyper was sorry if Lohman and others were offended by his words, but those words still may be true; ultimately it would be up to God to judge.[9]

As seen earlier, the editors at the *Algemeen Handelsblad* newspaper were not impressed by Kuyper's apology.[10] It was only three years ago, they reminded Kuyper, that Lohman was honored in a speech at the Free University, and was hailed as the hope and political future of the Calvinist nation. Now, the Tak bill had split the party, and Lohman was being forced out of the faculty of the Free University. The friendship and alliance of the two heads of the anti-revolutionary movement, which had been shown in force on the steps of the Nieuwe Kerk, was now shipwrecked. What was more, Kuyper's attempt at an apology in his pamphlet on *Christ and the Needy* was not only insincere but opportunistic. Asking for forgiveness from one's enemy was shown by humble deeds, not by apologizing for "ill-considered" words and then subsequently publishing a ten-series segment undermining the other's position. True forgiveness demanded self-control, they wrote, and this Kuyper did not possess.[11]

Kuyper wasted little time in penning a response to the writers in the *Handelsblad*. In this article—unlike in *Christ and the Needy*—Kuyper stayed focused solely on the issue of forgiveness. In addressing their critique, Kuyper took a softer tone and wrote about the daily necessity of quieting one's heart before God, and—not in public slogan but in personal silence—asking God for forgiveness of one's own debts and for help in forgiving others. Kuyper highlighted that this was a daily task, even a Christian duty, and so he understood his actions of forgiveness towards Lohman first as only

---

9. See Kuyper, *Christ and the Needy*, 648.

10. The *Algemeen Handelsblad* was a daily newspaper published in Amsterdam. It was not uncommon for Kuyper and the liberal editor Charles Boissevain to spar back and forth with editorials and articles published in their respective papers (Kuyper, in his *De Standaard*).

11. See Editorial, "Van dag tot dag."

possible through God's own forgiveness of himself and second as a shared and routine act between fellow Christians. From the foundation of God's own forgiveness, Kuyper wrote that he held no ill-will against those at the *Handelsblad* or against his political opponents. Yet Kuyper also recognized that his temperament often posed a challenge for others, and so he reiterated the need for a gracious and humble heart from him who forgives.[12] Kuyper knew his limits, he knew his faults, and he counted on the reality and power of God's own forgiveness for peace and reconciliation.

Still, the puzzle remains that if Kuyper offered a genuine word of apology and forgiveness to Lohman—a loyal brother with whom forgiveness should come easily—why did their professional and personal relationship breakdown? Does not reconciliation accompany forgiveness? For now, the question stands.

Theological Movements of Discipleship

Kuyper's seminal theological work of the 1890s was his *Encyclopedia of Sacred Theology: Its Principles*. Published in Dutch in three large volumes between 1893–95, the first 53 pages of Volume 1 and the entirety of Volume 2—totaling almost 700 pages—were translated into English and published as one volume in time for Kuyper's visit to America in the Fall of 1898. This text was unique in its time due to its commitment to a scientific explanation of theological and (by extension) Calvinistic concepts. By "scientific," Kuyper meant to place theology alongside the other academic disciplines in giving it a thorough and systematic treatment; but Kuyper also recognized that—like the other sciences—theology must be approached on its own terms, namely, from the starting point of revelation. For our purposes, the *Encyclopedia* offers a deep theological well from which foundational principles for Kuyper's understanding of Christian discipleship can be drawn. Indeed, if the concept of discipleship has theological underpinnings in Kuyper's thought, surely they can be discerned in a theological work as definitive as the *Encyclopedia*.

Throughout this book, discipleship is described as *the response to the call to follow-after Jesus Christ in all aspects of human life and endeavor, from the cultivation of inner spiritual disciplines to the deliberate shaping of culture—in the very midst of the world.* To work out this definition, a theology of discipleship is investigated through a framework of four movements: *the foundation of discipleship is the revelation of God; the reality of discipleship is the sovereignty of Jesus Christ, in and through the church; the action of*

---

12. See Kuyper, "Aan de schrijver van Van dag tot dag."

discipleship is belief-obedience; and the possibility of discipleship, grounded in the ultimate promise of redemption, is turning towards the world for the common good. Thus, this investigation of Kuyper's understanding of discipleship looks for how these four movements inform and interact with each other. The thesis is *not* that, historically, Kuyper systematically developed this particular four-movement theology of discipleship. Rather, this study argues that a distinct theology of discipleship within Kuyper's life and thought can indeed be discerned, and, in essence, these four movements help us to see how Kuyper approached the concept of discipleship—even if his official writings on the subject are tertiary. So, a selection of works from the 1894–1905 crescendo of Kuyper's career are analyzed, and the key concepts of revelation, reality, action, and possibility are connected in order to formulate a historical and theological understanding of Kuyper's concept of discipleship. Even though the hermeneutical key is an original construction, this study strives to present a contextually accurate picture of Kuyper and his thought.

Theological Foundations: The *Encyclopedia*

An encyclopedia may seem an odd place to begin an investigation of discipleship. Would not it be better to comb through devotionals, sermons, and catechesis to discover how Kuyper wrote and talked about the life of following Jesus Christ? Surely some of that appears in this study, but the *Encyclopedia of Sacred Theology* is an important and even essential starting point for the very reason that it provides an intricate treatment of foundational theological concepts. An understanding of discipleship needs to be anchored to *theology*, lest it drift about on waves of personal emotion or relativistic cultural currents. Kuyper's *Encyclopedia* provides just the sort of deliberate, scripturally-based, and historically aware theological explanation that is needed to introduce the four movements of discipleship. It is also telling that, while Kuyper certainly wrote about many aspects of theology in the *Encyclopedia*, all four movements of discipleship—revelation, reality, action, and possibility—are addressed here. Thus, this work provides a certain level of comprehensiveness in introducing a holistic understanding of discipleship.

The *Encyclopedia* opened with a linguistic investigation of the term "encyclopedia" itself. In the first of five etymological sections, Kuyper described the ancient Greek usage of the word. Right away, it is evident that Kuyper thought that an encyclopedia of knowledge was directly connected to *practical* matters of life and living. In analyzing the linguistic roots of "encyclopedia," Kuyper explained: "*παιδεία* means instruction, training, education"; "*ἐγκύκλιος* is all that presents itself as being included in a *κύκλος*, i.e., a ring or a circle." He continued: "Thus unconsciously the idea of that which was of *a daily* occurrence, and in a certain sense *ordinary* and *normal*, was included under *ἐγκύκλιος*; and it was in this process of thought that *ἐγκύκλιος* was added to *παιδεία* by which to indicate that kind and that measure of instruction or knowledge which was deemed indispensable for a normally developed Athenian citizen."[13] The purpose of an encyclopedia, in this sense, was in the gathering together and encircling of all the necessary instruction and knowledge needed to develop strong civil citizenship. The parallel to Christian discipleship could not be stronger: an encyclopedia of sacred theology gathered the foundational—even indispensable—knowledge Christians needed for faithful growth and service. Kuyper's *Encyclopedia*, while theologically technical, was concerned in the end with the training and equipping of everyday citizens for the kingdom of God. That is, the *Encyclopedia* was about discipleship.

Revelation: The Foundation of Discipleship

Turning to the beginning point—the foundation—of discipleship then requires an understanding of the beginning point of theology. Kuyper indulged in a lengthy and technical investigation of the nature of science and its relation to theology in the second division of his *Encyclopedia*. He started by acknowledging that, in writing an encyclopedia, science itself was the object of investigation.[14] But science had to be understood for what it was—ultimately as a means and a tool for comprehensive study of a subject. While an encyclopedia was "scientific" in its approach to knowledge, Kuyper also recognized that, as a science, "Theology has to deal with an object that is not susceptible to an abstract intellectual treatment."[15] Because the object of theology always ultimately remained unknown, by its nature, theology as a science could never be completely developed. However, what could be known was discerned in connection with the historical development in life.[16] This meant that an encyclopedia of theology—which had its eye on understanding the object—investigated what could be known in matters of exegesis, church history, and theology.[17] These disciplines were then

13. Kuyper, *Encyclopedia*, 2–3.
14. Kuyper, *Encyclopedia*, 14.
15. Kuyper, *Encyclopedia*, 49.
16. Kuyper, *Encyclopedia*, 49.
17. Kuyper, *Encyclopedia*, 58.

viewed as an organic part of general science; theology moved, grew, and developed—that was its nature as a science.

Kuyper further understood "science" as the deliberate process of seeking-finding-knowing.[18] The course of discovery was the same whether engaging in natural or theological science. However, Kuyper explained, there was a distinguishing factor: theology, over and against the other sciences, was engaged in seeking-finding-knowing *via* the revelation of the object itself. Kuyper marked a crucial distinction here in explaining the methodological differences between natural science and theological science. Natural science—whereby the subject mastered the object through observation, demonstration, and argumentation—was indeed a suitable way to study the cosmos, but, Kuyper argued, "observation or demonstration can never produce one single milligramme of religious gold." He continued: "The entire gold-mine of religion lies in the self-revelation of this central power to the subject, and the subject has no other means than *faith* by which to appropriate to itself the gold from this mine. He who has no certainty in himself on the ground of this *faith*, about some point or other in religion, can never be made certain by demonstration or argument. In this way you may produce outward religiousness, but never religion in the heart."[19]

Religion *in* the heart was both the method and result of theological science, and this only came by faith in the one who opened the mine and began to shine light on its inner treasures. Further, this understanding of revelation did nothing to damage the scientific nature of theology. Indeed, with a firm faith, the theologian "will no longer try, as in his naturalistic period, to denounce that Revelation as a vexatious hindrance, but will feel the need of it, will live in it, and profit by it."[20] This tethering of oneself to revelation would destroy the scientific character of theological knowledge "only if this Revelation consisted of nothing but a list of conclusions, and if he were not allowed subjectively to assimilate these conclusions."[21] But Kuyper described here a *living* faith, a life of discipleship; and as the revealed Word of God uncovered gold in the mine, it also, as Kuyper said, imposed upon us the obligation of mining it. What was mined was of such a nature that the subject was changed by it, and indeed "assimilates it in his own way, and brings it in relation to the deepest impulse and entire inner

---

18. Kuyper, *Encyclopedia*, 59. While "seeking-finding-knowing" is certainly an apt perspective for the task of theology, it is also particularly insightful when conceiving a concept of discipleship.

19. Kuyper, *Encyclopedia*, 149.

20. Kuyper, *Encyclopedia*, 171.

21. Kuyper, *Encyclopedia*, 171.

disposition of his being."²² Theology, then—as a revealed science—was also a character-forming science; because what was discovered from the revealer transformed one from the inside-out.

Kuyper thus embraced two critical factors: the pursuit of theology took place from a posture of discipleship, and theology (as the knowledge of God) was dependent upon God, the object, being situated over and above humankind, the subject. For theology, these two factors were closely related. In all other investigations of science, Kuyper explained, the subject was placed above the object—observing it, poking and prodding, and making judgments and conclusions. But in theology, "man stands no longer *above*, but *beneath* the object of his investigation, and over against this object he finds himself in a position of entire *dependence*."²³ Kuyper called this dependent knowledge "ectypal," because humanity stood as ectype over against God, the archetype. Ectypal knowledge was only the result of God's action toward humankind; that is, theological knowledge was God's action of self-revelation.²⁴ Yet Kuyper was adamant that ectypal theological knowledge did not imply a disposition of indifference between object and subject. "On the contrary," he wrote, "all revelation assumes (1) one who reveals Himself; (2) one to whom he reveals Himself; and (3) the possibility of the required relation between these two."²⁵ Relationship was thus the foundational connection between theology and discipleship, and it was the fulcrum of Kuyper's scientific theology.

However, there was an important caveat here. Since revelation took into account humankind—it reckoned with sinful humankind. What, then, was the relationship between revelation and soteriology (salvation)? Was revelation inherently soteriological? Kuyper argued that as a result of original sin humans can never attain a true knowledge of God unless the form of revelation was soteriological. But the soteriological was a means and not the end. Kuyper explained: "It is nevertheless necessary that in our representation of revelation also the fact be emphasized that the soteriological element is ever accidental, bears merely an intervenient character, and remains dependent upon the fundamental conception of revelation which is given in creation itself, and which teleologically looks forward to a state of things in which there shall be no more sin, so that every soteriological act shall belong to a never-returning past."²⁶

22. Kuyper, *Encyclopedia*, 171.
23. Kuyper, *Encyclopedia*, 248.
24. Kuyper, *Encyclopedia*, 256.
25. Kuyper, *Encyclopedia*, 257.
26. Kuyper, *Encyclopedia*, 258.

Revelation, then, functioned *interveniently* in the soteriological. First and foremost, Kuyper emphasized that God revealed himself for *God's own sake*. To make the salvific function of revelation primary was to place humankind at the center, and not God. On the other hand, to understand the creation as the foundation of revelation was to affirm the final end of revelation in God, and not humankind. The great confession—*I believe in God the Father Almighty, Creator of heaven and earth*—established that the motive for creation and revelation was in God alone. "Not," as Kuyper said, "in an eternal law (*lex aeterna*), a fate (μοῖρα) or necessity (ἀνάγκή), nor in some need of God nature, nor in the creature that was not yet created. He who does not worship God as self-sufficient and sovereign, misconceives and profanes His Being."[27] Creation was thus viewed as a sovereign act of the almighty God—and all further revelation, as given in creation, then found its end in the pleasure of God.

In the next instance, though, the pleasure of God was realized in transposing revelation into subjective knowledge. Revelation had as its aim the very knowledge of God in humankind. At the base, God revealed in order to be known—not by God's self, but by humankind. God already knew himself completely, and so humankind—as reasonable, responsible, and spiritual creature—was "indispensable in order that revelation can be *revelation*."[28] Kuyper explained that God was not a light which unconsciously radiated and illuminated. God's self-knowledge was absolute, and so God revealed not for greater self-knowledge, but in order to be known by the creature. As the object became known through revelation, "theology"—the knowledge of God—was the result. The implication here, wrote Kuyper, was that humankind must then by nature be adapted to receive and interpret God's revelation into subjective and relational knowledge.

Ectypal theology thus constituted three mutually relatable elements: revelation, faith, and logical action.[29] "Without *revelation*," Kuyper explained, "nothing is known; without *faith* there is no apprehension nor appropriation of that revelation; and without the logical action, that which has been perceived cannot be transmuted into subjective knowledge of God."[30] This underscored, again, the relational character of theological revelation, as distinct from an intellectualistic religion. Faith became the catalyst to the reception of revelation, and logical action placed knowledge of God into the throes of deliberate, responsive action. Kuyper was clear: "Neither knowl-

27. Kuyper, *Encyclopedia*, 259.
28. Kuyper, *Encyclopedia*, 262.
29. An interesting correlation to this study's fourfold movements of discipleship.
30. Kuyper, *Encyclopedia*, 274.

edge nor pious feeling by themselves can ever be called religion. Only when your God and you have met each other and associate and walk together, does religion *live* in your heart."[31]

Further, this faith-filled action was an inherently *human* characteristic; faith only became unfaith with the advent of sin. Kuyper argued that faith was an attitude (*habitus*) of our human nature; "consequently, it must have been present in the first man; and it must still be discernible in the sinner."[32] Kuyper pointed out that after the fall, revelation, faith, and logical action continued to develop and discover theological knowledge. The world was distorted, Kuyper explained, and so "we understand what darkness is only from the antithesis of light."[33] While theology recognized the reality of sin, it acknowledged that God's revelation—and humanity's inherent faith—existed before sin, and continued to exist after sin.

Indeed, after the fall God's revelation was discerned only through the particular fruit of *common grace*. Without God's sustaining grace beating back the effects of sin, "nothing would have remained but spiritual darkness, and all 'knowledge of God' would have turned into its opposite."[34] But there was knowledge of God on this side of humanity's fall. So, Kuyper asked, what then was the effect of sin on the three factors of God—revelation, faith, and logical action? Kuyper addressed each factor in turn. First, God's *revelation* did not cease with sin; God continued to reveal, and the human soul continued to be receptive. What was more, there was no escape from God's revelation: "If I make my bed in hell, behold, Thou art there."[35] Kuyper claimed the same was true for the second factor, *faith* (πίστις). Since faith belonged also to human nature (as in *habitus*, discussed above), even sin could not destroy it. What could happen, though, was a distorted quest for faith—which then became unfaith (ἀπιστία). "After he has become a sinner, man still continues to seek after a *something* to which to cleave with his faith."[36] Even when the quest was for unbelief, humanity still sought an outlet for inherent faith. Thirdly, Kuyper argued that *logical action* remained operative after sin as well. It was still the case that humanity strove to reflect and apply the perceptions of faith, whether directed for or against God.

To be clear, in a sin-filled world, revelation, faith, and logical action could not maintain a sustained vision toward God without the deliberate

31. Kuyper, *Encyclopedia*, 268.
32. Kuyper, *Encyclopedia*, 266.
33. Kuyper, *Encyclopedia*, 274.
34. Kuyper, *Encyclopedia*, 275.
35. Kuyper, *Encyclopedia*, 276. See also Ps 139:8.
36. Kuyper, *Encyclopedia*, 277.

action of God on behalf of humankind. In a world of sin, "there would have been no Theology; and nothing could have been done on the part of the sinner to create light in this darkness. This light could only come from the side of God."[37] Kuyper further explained that the "special" revelation of God's redemptive grace must first postulate *common grace*, "i.e., that act of God by which *negatively* He curbs the operations of Satan, death, and sin, and by which *positively* He creates an intermediate state for this cosmos, as well as for our human race, which is and continues to be deeply and radically sinful, but in which sin cannot work out its end ($\tau \acute{\epsilon} \lambda o \varsigma$)."[38] The wheels of sin continued to churn, but, by common grace, *the brakes were on*. Sin did not have the last word. To be sure, the sinner who stood in common grace remained a sinner, "dead in trespasses and sin."[39] Yet, in common grace, the special revelation of God's redemptive and particular grace could be worked out in the life of a sinner. In Kuyper's thinking, particular grace assumed common grace. The three factors of the knowledge of God—revelation, faith, and logical action—operated in and through common grace, so that salvific particular grace could take root and shape in the life of an emerging disciple.

Jesus Christ: The Reality of Discipleship

The *reality* of life in common grace, then, hinged on the sovereignty of God in the person and work of *Jesus Christ*. The second movement in this proposed framework of discipleship received an insightful introductory treatment in Kuyper's closing remarks on the concept of revelation. But Kuyper was careful (as was Bonhoeffer[40]) not to limit the incarnation only to the soteriological impact on the individual: "Surely whosoever believes on Christ shall be saved; this is possible first and only because God has sent His Son, but the aim, and therefore also the end, of all this is, to make us see how God has loved *His* world, and that therefore the creation of this cosmos, even in the face of sin, has been no *failure*."[41] The incarnation defined the state of reality by pointing us both to God's revelation at the creation, and also to his

---

37. Kuyper, *Encyclopedia*, 278.
38. Kuyper, *Encyclopedia*, 279.
39. Kuyper, *Encyclopedia*, 279.
40. "Hasn't the individualistic question of saving our personal souls almost faded away for most of us? Isn't our impression that there are really more important things than this question (—perhaps not more important than this *matter*, but certainly more important than the *question*!?)?" Bonhoeffer, *DBWE* 8:372.
41. Kuyper, *Encyclopedia*, 283.

promise of re-creation. Thus, believing humanity finds its life in Jesus Christ and forms "the body of Christ."[42] To live was to return from unbelief to faith; it was to affirm the *habitus* of faith inherent in humanity's creation.

This reality was not an abstraction. Restored humanity, as the body of Christ, demanded real, tangible, and logical action. As the *Logos*, Christ was the truth and the light, and so supported both the being and thought that was revealed to humanity. As flesh and blood, Jesus Christ was grounded in the reality of existence. But as the Word—what Kuyper called inscripturation[43]—the *Logos* also shaped our consciousness and thought. If the incarnation was only physical, it could not have shaped consciousness; if it was not physical it remained only a mental abstraction. Kuyper explained: "Since, however, the subject of the incarnation is one with the subject of the revealed word, there is not merely harmony between the two, but organic relation"—and this organic relation operated in the reality of the present body of Christ, descending from the head to individual believers.[44] In this sense, Kuyper argued that revelation to the sinner was an accommodation that worked outward from God to humankind. Mediated through the reality of Jesus Christ, the knowledge of God that came to the sinner as unbelief was changed to faith, which was only possible through God's work of re-creation.[45]

Kuyper used the metaphor of a tree trunk to further describe this reality of life in Jesus Christ.[46] Taking the Psalmist's declaration seriously—only "in thy light shall we see light"—Kuyper affirmed Jesus Christ as "the absolute ground of explanation for *all* human knowledge."[47] He elaborated on the nature of this reality by imagining the world as a tree trunk. Life in Jesus Christ did not consist in the growing of a new branch; instead, Jesus Christ was the new root, and the trunk was transformed and grown anew. While new branches sprouted, and leaves and flowers bloomed, they represented the effects of a sustaining common grace in the world. The trunk, however, was tapped deeply into the earth, and "this body of Christ *is the real trunk of our human race.*"[48] It is the community of saints—of saved sinners—which

---

42. Kuyper, *Encyclopedia*, 284.

43. Kuyper does not limit "inscripturation" to the scriptural part of conscious revelation. Kuyper, *Encyclopedia*, 285.

44. Kuyper, *Encyclopedia*, 286.

45. Kuyper, *Encyclopedia*, 291.

46. Bonhoeffer also offers a christological interpretation of a famous biblical tree. See *DBWE* 3:141–44.

47. Kuyper, *Encyclopedia*, 389.

48. Kuyper, *Encyclopedia*, 395.

bear witness to this reality of the world. The Dutch theologian A. van Egmond explains:

> It is not that in the end the trunk dies and the elect are saved from the dead tree as a wreath of still living twigs and leaves. It is rather the opposite: under the tree of this world condemned to death, temporarily preserved by common grace, a new root has been placed: Christ. And slowly but surely the new trunk replaces the old. And finally, the trunk stands: the new world of God's elect and what does not belong to it are the withered and dead branches of the old: the reprobate. This is a positive view of the world, but only because the new world is formed by the elect. They will never be powerful . . . but *they are the world*.[49]

The body of Jesus Christ was the reality of the world, and it participated in the nurture, sustainment, and even hope for the world. The world was not abandoned; it was renewed in the election of Jesus Christ.

Indeed, it was the church as living organism, as the communion of saints, that proclaimed the message of Christ to those clinging to dead and withered branches. It was precisely as a community that the church preached the gospel, and helped the seeds of faith to germinate into full-fledged belief. That the church was an organic communion was critical to the nature of faith. For Kuyper, "it remains a question whether anyone but Christ Himself, in that absolute sense, has stood alone in his faith. This is the very profound meaning of Gethsemane. Sin, and hence unbelief, scatters, individualizes, and pulverizes; but grace, and hence faith, restores life in organic connection, viz. the life of each member in the body."[50] This *communis fides* proclaimed the gospel by shining Christ's light into the world, all the while building up the faith of the believers.[51] But Kuyper did not neglect the other key factor in shaping the body of Christ as the reality of the world: the Holy Spirit.

Through the Holy Spirit, the *communis fides* gained the eyesight to see and understand the world. It was the Holy Spirit who opened our eyes to the Holy Scripture, for example, so "we may see a representation of our *ego*, of the world and of the eternal things."[52] But here a struggle ensued, as believers wrestled with the knowledge of "ourselves as sinners, the unreality of the

---

49. Van Egmond, "Kuyper's Dogmatic Theology," 94.

50. Kuyper, *Encyclopedia*, 556.

51. James Bratt notes that Kuyper's ecclesiology "marked the crossroads where his twin passions of divine sovereignty and social formation intersected." See Bratt, *Abraham Kuyper*, 173.

52. Kuyper, *Encyclopedia*, 557.

world, and the reality of the Divine."[53] In this struggle, Kuyper described the work of the Holy Spirit in lifting the veil so that believers' eyes could turn towards the divine light radiating from Scripture: "We see it as one born blind, who being healed, sees the beauty of colors, or as one deaf, whose hearing being restored, catches the melodies from the world of sounds, and with his whole soul delights himself in them."[54] For Kuyper, the reality of the world in Jesus Christ was fused with the work of the Holy Spirit in forming and shaping the church as organism—an organism that uniquely anchored its life to the Holy Scriptures.

Belief and Obedience: The Action of Discipleship

The Holy Spirit was not limited to illuminating the meaning of Scripture in the life of the church; the Holy Spirit was also central in empowering the faith-response of belief and obedience. As was mentioned above, Kuyper believed that the purpose of an "encyclopedia" was so that one would learn how to live. Knowledge and teaching were for the purposes of living and application. Even Kuyper's three-fold conception of "theology" as the knowledge of God—revelation, faith, and logical action—had a clear component of tangible practicality. In this sense, Kuyper argued that theology had to include an investigation into the life of the church, i.e., church history, and it had to address the life-consequences of reading and living with the Holy Scriptures. As such, inherent in the very conception of theology was the notion of action through the relationship of belief and obedience. For Kuyper, explaining the Holy Spirit's work both in church history and the Holy Scriptures provided a compelling framework for an inherent understanding of the necessity of action in the life of the disciple.

Kuyper argued that in order to gain full knowledge of an object, it needed to be studied in its states both of rest and action. The action of the church was studied, for example, in history, but the Word of God also had its own action: "It is 'quick and powerful and sharper than any two-edged sword,' 'a hammer that breaketh the rock into pieces.' It also works as a living seed that is sown, and which, according to the nature of the soil, germinates and brings forth fruit."[55] The Holy Scriptures, explained Kuyper, was not hidden "in some sacred grotto" to await tantalizing scientific investigation; "no, it was carried into the world, by reading and recitation, by teaching and

---

53. Kuyper, *Encyclopedia*, 558.
54. Kuyper, *Encyclopedia*, 558.
55. Kuyper, *Encyclopedia*, 571.

preaching, in apologetic and in polemic writings."[56] And once in the world, the Holy Scriptures have exerted influence; they have changed and shaped the world, both through ecclesiastical confessions, structures, and institutions, and also through the transformation and witness of countless individuals. The action of discipleship, therefore, took into account the binding relationship between the Holy Scriptures and the catholic-universal church. "Not that the Word by itself was able to found a Church or a church life," but rather it is understood that "the domain of the Church can be described as the domain in which the Holy Scripture prevails and operates."[57] Theology thus remained incomplete, even incomprehensible, outside of its action in the world; and this occurred, namely, through the historical development—and present participation—in the life of the church.

Discipleship was then understood as theology in action—and, as Kuyper explained, theology was incomplete without broad, robust participation in the life of the historical church. Theology disconnected from the church was no longer theology. What is more, the church kept theology from being an abstraction; "it springs of necessity from the life of the Church, upon which it exerts an influence in all the stages of its development."[58] However, theology did not exist "merely" for the sake of rendering an auxiliary service to the church. The purpose of theology was knowledge of God; and the church played a vital (but not exclusive) role in rendering this knowledge. Theological knowledge remained the prerogative of God's own self-revelation, made real in the unfolding possibilities of history.

The Possibilities of Discipleship

In the concluding chapters of the *Encyclopedia*, Kuyper summarized the historical development of theology in the church. A final section was titled "*The Period of Resurrection*," and it served as an apt reminder as to the possibilities of discipleship.[59] This section was a historical and at times technical accounting of changes in theology during the eighteenth and nineteenth centuries. The conclusions drawn here are admittedly broader than Kuyper's narrow historical argument—but not unrelated. As Kuyper recounted the nineteenth century, he made a keen observation: the revivals in Europe and America, the significant movements in philosophy, and the shifts in scientific inquiry during this time, in essence, opened-up theology to the

56. Kuyper, *Encyclopedia*, 572.
57. Kuyper, *Encyclopedia*, 572.
58. Kuyper, *Encyclopedia*, 329.
59. See Kuyper, *Encyclopedia*, 672–79.

world. However, Kuyper insisted that this same theology remain tightly anchored to the historic church and its Holy Scriptures. To do otherwise—to capitulate to the latest philosophical or theological trends—was to abandon confessional faith. So the lessons were clear: Kuyper's account of theology viewed historical development and cultural engagement as a positive necessity; however, theology needed to maintain its confessional roots. The possibility of theological discipleship for Kuyper, then, faltered only when confession and worldview were compromised.

For its part, Kuyper's theological worldview demanded clear and coherent interaction in society, as we will see in his political writings. He understood that discipleship was a daily task, taking place in the surroundings of an ever changing and adapting world. As such, the possibilities for discipleship were contextually unique and culturally challenging. Kuyper's life in Dutch politics thus certainly provides tangible grounds for further investigating his understanding of the possibilities of discipleship. First, however, it is instructive to investigate how Kuyper's commitment to theological training affirmed and informed his commitment to discipleship.

"Dienst des Woords:" Discipleship in the Making

By the early 1890s, Kuyper had succeeded in forming a new church denomination, the Gereformeerde Kerken in Nederland (GKN)—made up of a merger between churches who split off from the national Hervormde Kerk during the Doleantie and almost all those from the Secession churches from 1834. Meanwhile, in September of 1894, the Gereformeerde mannenvereeniging "Voetius" (Reformed men's society, "Voetius") was founded in Rotterdam for the purpose of promoting and supporting the new Reformed church movement. Since Kuyper lived in Amsterdam, he was not a member of this society. However, the "Voetius" group approached Kuyper about the possibility of publishing a series of articles as part of a new monthly publication, *Gereformeerde Stemmen uit vroeger en later tijd* (Reformed voices from earlier and later times). Kuyper took the opportunity to gather previous articles he had written for *De Heraut* in 1890 and 1891 for reprint in *Gereformeerde Stemmen*. He wanted to address all the members of the newly formed GKN with a fresh voice, and the Rotterdam publisher would distribute his texts nationwide.[60]

60. George Harinck, e-mail message to author, January 15, 2014: "Since Voetius was a Rotterdam association and Kuyper lived in Amsterdam, he was not a Voetius-member. The answer to me seems to be that Kuyper was asked by the Rotterdam association to write on this topic—maybe after he gave a lecture on the topic or wrote an article on

As originally planned, *Gereformeerde Stemmen* would be published in twelve monthly installments, beginning in July 1895. However, one of the central components would be Kuyper's series "Dienst des Woords" ("Service of the Word"). Because the subscribers wanted all of the articles of this series to be published together, the installments were increased to seventeen, with the final issue published in December 1896.[61] Kuyper often contributed articles in addition to "Dienst des Woords," and other *Gereformeerde Stemmen* contributors included Dr. Mr. W. van den Bergh, J. P. Tazelaar, Dr. F. L. Rutgers, and G. Voetius. The articles covered a wide range of topics, including "The union of all Reformed," "The relationship of Scripture and Confession," "When should Holy Baptism be administered," "Ethicism," "World conformity," and "Church and Society." In addition to Kuyper's monthly series on "Service of the Word," he contributed articles (usually reprints from *De Heraut*) with titles such as "Grudge not against one another," "Orthodox," "Your neck is an iron sinew," "Confirmation of members," "Church and State," and "Of the Christmas tree." After initial monthly distribution, the issues were bound together, and the printer, A. ter Weeme in Rotterdam, provided a title page and table of contents.[62]

The focus here is on Kuyper's central series "Dienst des Woords." These articles served, to some extent, as a training manual for pastors, describing what did and did not comprise service of the Word.[63] The articles addressed key themes such as evangelism, gospel, witness, calling, service, the Holy Spirit, revelation, and the importance of exegetical and church history training for the pastor. While Kuyper's immediate audience was pastors, it readily becomes clear that Kuyper was concerned with the make-up and spiritual formation of church congregations themselves. Kuyper wanted congregations with clear convictions and deeply grounded theological understanding. So, his entreaty to pastors was, in essence, a call to discipleship. "Dienst des Woords" served as a program for building and continuing a culture of discipleship among the *kleine luyden*; and such a program began with the ministers themselves.

---

it. Kuyper certainly did not accept every request, so I think he thought it instructive for the recently organized Gereformeerde Kerken in Nederland to write about this topic. Maybe he already had had the idea of writing on this topic. By doing this for Voetius he could address all the members of this denomination, especially when a Rotterdam publisher would distribute his text, as happened."

61. See Kuipers, *Abraham Kuyper*, 250.
62. See Kuipers, *Abraham Kuyper*, 250.
63. See Kuipers, *Abraham Kuyper*, 250.

Setting the Boundaries

Kuyper opened the series of articles on the "Service of the Word" by marking a clear boundary between holistic preaching and a narrower understanding of evangelism: "*Dienst des Woords* is not, in the proper sense, evangelism."[64] Kuyper explained that it had become more and more common over the previous century to equate "gospel" with the particular stories and passages of the New Testament church. The minister of the Word became the minister of the gospel to such an extent that "nine-tenths of Scripture in the pulpit remained a closed book, and a certain number of texts (like John 3:16) were ever again chosen as a motto or theme for the sermon."[65] But, Kuyper argued, there was a further error—based on a perverse reading of the holy apostles. "Woe to me if I do not preach the gospel" became a rallying cry in inaugural sermons, but Kuyper recognized this vital error, pointing out that the New Testament apostles had a particular calling that was much different than the calling of a Dutch pastor to minister and serve the Word in the context of a localized congregation. Certainly a connection existed to the holy apostles; but a connection did not signal an identical calling. The difference was important to Kuyper. The apostolic ministry was missions oriented, and was to adults who did not yet know Christ, for the purpose of baptism and the founding of churches. Conversely, the ministry of the Word was preaching to adults and children who had already been baptized and confessed, to the extent of their years, that Jesus was the Christ.

This was a significant point for Kuyper. The missionary and the minister had completely different contexts and callings: "The whole consignment, the whole operation, and the whole action is entirely distinct. It is another vocation, and a different context; they are completely different hearers."[66] It was the missionary that went out to those not baptized, to strangers in new places. The minister of the Word had a particular church, Kuyper explained, while the missionary had a universal mission—that was not associated with just one particular church—to plant new churches and then to care for them. In a meeting of believers, the evangelist took on a role of service, and the congregation was treated as if they knew and affirmed the foundations of the faith. On the other hand, the minister of the Word served the congregation by preparing a nutritious meal of bread and solid food, with "occasionally some milk for the children."[67] In Kuyper's mind, the

---

64. Kuyper, "Dienst des Woords," 6.
65. Kuyper, "Dienst des Woords," 7.
66. Kuyper, "Dienst des Woords," 7.
67. Kuyper, "Dienst des Woords," 8.

apostle and missionary certainly took part in establishing the foundation of churches, but the duty of building up the congregation fell deliberately to the minister of the Word. And the minister had a clear task: "'The meetings of the faithful,'" Kuyper wrote, "should not be a convent of small theologies, but a meeting of men and women full of strength and of the Holy Ghost."[68]

For his part, Kuyper was careful not to sever the preaching of the gospel from the ministry of the Word. In his second installment of "Dienst des Woords," Kuyper cited examples from the Gospels, Hebrews, and Timothy to show that "the word Gospel can be understood as *the Word* equivalent."[69] Indeed, the service of the Word required the gospel message; but the gospel message could not neglect the entirety of the biblical witness. Therefore a clear demarcation of office was necessary, as was a distinct understanding that the service of the Word was for the building up of a strong and growing community of disciples.

Discipleship as Witness

After delineating the differences between evangelism and the service of the Word, Kuyper addressed the meaning of *witness* in the third and fourth installments of "Dienst des Woords." Kuyper began his discussion by describing a dangerous tendency in some quarters of the contemporary church: the temptation to place the personal convictions of the minister at the center of church life. The problem, Kuyper explained, was that the personal and subjective convictions of one person created a sandy and unstable foundation; only the solid ground of the Holy Scriptures could sustain the construction of a faithful church community. A witness who was under the terms of Scripture, therefore, struggled at the intersection of what was right or wrong, and worked to discern what was truth or a lie. In making the connection to bearing the witness of God's revealed truth to the world, Kuyper recognized the origins of "witness" in the Greek word "martyr." "So often," recounted Kuyper, "it comes down to standing up against the lie of the world. For God's truth must be witnessed, and this testimony sustained, even though it amounts to reproach, and yes, it even costs us death."[70] Therefore, a disciple of the Lord—whether a teacher or farmer, a man or a woman—was always called to the vocation of standing as witness for the King in the midst of the world. This servant, whoever it may be, had the responsibility to stand as a witness against the creeping heresies of the day and to call the church back

---

68. Kuyper, "Dienst des Woords," 8.
69. Kuyper, "Dienst des Woords," 16.
70. Kuyper, "Dienst des Woords," 23.

to its original confession and to the authority of God's Word. Discipleship was then something more than personally acting as a witness—it was the church of God in its entirety, giving faithful testimony to the world.

For Kuyper, however, the witness of the pulpit did not discount the personal testimony of the minister. While guarding against the modern tendency of unbelief and superstition, the minister acted as a witness to the personal impact of the Holy Spirit, "in the spirit of the famous saying: 'I will tell you what God has done for my soul,' or what John says, 'We know that we have passed from death into life.'"[71] This remained a challenge for some. Students in sacred theology, preparing for tenures in the pulpit, may have mastered languages, facts, and figures, but if they remained foreign to the work and teaching of the Holy Spirit, they forfeited the possibility of a clean conscience before the congregation. For it took a heart filled with the Spirit to animate the lips of a preacher and prevent the freezing of the house of worship. Kuyper did not advocate fanaticism (which too often resulted in heresy and "spiritual madness"), but demanded that the Word of God remained the only solid rock on which to stand. And there was more: Kuyper warned that a minister, even and especially one filled with the Holy Spirit, contained unique talents and gifts—gifts that very well may not contain the fireworks of some of the great heroes of the faith. The twelve disciples, for example, were not all equally heralded. Peter, James, and John remained at the forefront, even though God, in his sovereignty, could simply have given all the disciples similar impact. The same was true in church history, with the likes of Calvin and Luther gaining prominence. While the church was not without its strong personalities, overall, it was ordinary people that God's Spirit filled. So, Kuyper pleaded, let the minister be cherished by the congregation's love and carried in their prayers, for that is how he, as one among a community of disciples, gained the strength to bring faithful witness to God's Word.

Holy Scripture

Kuyper's next four installments of "Dienst des Woords" served as a central, solid core for the entire series. His commitment to the centrality and infallibility of the Holy Scriptures was on display here: it was to the Scriptures that Kuyper pressed both the minister and congregation, and from the Scriptures that he proposed new ideas and practical applications. That Kuyper's thoughts on the Holy Scriptures fell in the middle of the series was probably no accident, because in Kuyper's theology Scripture provided both the

---

71. Kuyper, "Dienst des Woords," 30.

foundation for Christian belief and the catalyst for Christian action. This dual-purpose of Scripture was an important element in Kuyper's teaching in "Dienst des Woords."

Kuyper protected the authority of Scripture by insisting that a clear line separated the experiences of the minister from the ultimate truths of Scripture. The Word, by itself, was to be preached—not the subjective experience of the minister. To place experience above the Word was akin to the minister becoming a second mediator between God and the congregation. Kuyper criticized this as "[Roman] Catholic and not Scriptural," and said that "there is only one mediator between God and men, the man Christ Jesus."[72] The servant of the Word, then, was called to bring the richness of God's truth out of the text, and to drive the congregation into the text themselves. Kuyper argued that the minister should never declare: "Believe this and that because my soul has experienced it."[73] Kuyper insisted that the authority of God's Word should not rest on the subjective experience of another. Rather, God's Word had its own authority, beckoning one to faith and to belief because it is *God* who says. To be sure, there were times and places for ministers to share the inner workings of their souls, but not in the ministering of the Word. "On the pulpit," Kuyper instructed, "and so in the congregation of believers, the Word of God is to be preached—not what God is in your soul, but what he says in the Holy Scriptures to the church."[74] The preacher, in a very real sense, was then the *Verbi Divini Minister*—the Minister of the Divine Word.

The minister of God's Word was, more accurately, the *servant* of God's Word. Kuyper explained: "He's a servant, he holds a subordinate position, and he is in the service of the One greater than he."[75] Further, the servant was not in a position as one who came in their own right. He was not a knight or a hero of old, who relied on his own shield and sword. Instead, he was conscripted, and owed an oath of allegiance to the general. The servant of the Word, then, was only recognized by his armor—the sword of the Word. As the spiritual battle raged, the servant stood firm in the pulpit and brought the Word of God to the congregation. But if the servant were to stray from the battle and sheath his sword, it would be the congregation's right to admonish and remove him, an unfaithful servant. The leaders of the church would make sure that a true servant came to take charge of the Lord's house.

72. Kuyper, "Dienst des Woords," 39.
73. Kuyper, "Dienst des Woords," 40.
74. Kuyper, "Dienst des Woords," 40.
75. Kuyper, "Dienst des Woords," 47.

What were the marks of a true and dedicated servant of the Word? Significantly, the Word of God must be taken as a whole. The Word did not reside "in a definite text, or in a particular chapter, or in a single book, but in all the books, chapters, and verses together. In short, the Word of God resides throughout all the Scriptures."[76] The task and art of the minister of the Word was then to place these different pieces together, and to understand that those pieces of revelation must be put in context in a very distinguished manner. "Each of these pieces speaks another something to our hearts, our senses, in our conscience, or in our consciousness," Kuyper wrote. And only now, when all these pieces come together, "does the melody of the one Word of God come to us, and our souls understand the eternal."[77] The servant of the Word thus brought unity to the Scriptures through preaching and understanding the entirety of God's Word.

But God's Word was as deep as it was broad and wide. And it would not do to look at God's Word as a book "of so many hundred pages, with so many thousand verses, and where you can take out each verse and say: 'Here I am, God's Word.' That is a dead and mechanical view of the Holy Scriptures, actually aligning it with our own Civil Code."[78] The Scriptures were not a code of articles which commanded or forbade, threatening punishment. The Scriptures were an all-encompassing, living word, and the preacher must then discern each day what Word God was speaking to the church. Kuyper explained: "Now this whole world of thought, as God has deposited in his Holy Scripture, is very large, and runs on about everything: not only about God, but also about humanity; not only about our souls, but also our bodies; not only about the church, but also about society; not only about our piety, but also about our profession; not only about the spiritual, but also the natural. Over all, we have in one Word what human existence and human life is in its origin, that now and forever, belongs in God."[79]

A fruit of good preaching, Kuyper continued to argue, must therefore consistently combat the idea that the Word was reduced, and did not or cannot speak to the entirety of human existence. On the contrary, the revelation of the Word of God in the Scriptures spoke in unity about the gracious acts of God in overcoming a world of sin. The preacher, therefore, in clinging to the Word of God, served and bore witness to the power of God in the world. In this sense, the pastor played a vital role in the formation of disciples. As discipleship was about hearing and responding to the call of Jesus Christ in

---

76. Kuyper, "Dienst des Woords," 55.
77. Kuyper, "Dienst des Woords," 55.
78. Kuyper, "Dienst des Woords," 63.
79. Kuyper, "Dienst des Woords," 64.

all aspects of human life—"not only about our souls, but also our bodies; not only about the church, but also about society; not only about our piety, but also about our profession"—individuals were charged with receiving this call from the very Word of God. It was the pastor's responsibility, explained Kuyper, to issue such a faithful call to discipleship among the congregation, for a true invitation to follow Christ could only come from the entirety of God's Word.

The Ministry of Preparation

In the next several installments of "Dienst des Woords," Kuyper wrote about numerous aspects of how ministers prepared for their vocation. First he addressed the relationship between the universal mission of God and the individual calling of the minister. The mission of God was a crucial ingredient for the ministry of the Word; without this mission, Kuyper explained, the ministry of the Word was not possible or conceivable. Inner calling, too, was an indispensable aspect of the mission of God, but it was not the mission itself, and could exist even outside the mission of God and ministry of the Word.[80] Since inner vocational calling could take on any number of forms—even in the service of the church—Kuyper emphasized the necessity for the minister of the Word to understand that the inner call of God and the external mission of the church must go together. Kuyper explained that it should go without saying that the inner calling was indispensable for the minister. Without this, another word—that of a church, or of a philosophy, or of doctors A or B—could replace the Word of God. It must be remembered that this was the office of the divine Word.[81]

In a sense, as Kuyper explained, the relationship between internal and external calling served as a litmus test for the minister. Someone could have a very strong urge to act as a servant of the Word, but the road may be blocked; there may not be a church that calls; the time may not yet have come. "God calls in two parts, both by the outward call of the church, and by the internal call of the Holy Spirit, and only where both are present is the call of God to the ministry of the Word complete."[82] The inner call was nothing but an inner urge of the Spirit to serve God in the proclamation of the gospel, "but it does not fix the manner in which this will be done."[83] But the outward call of the church was to a particular place and context, and binds

---

80. Kuyper, "Dienst des Woords," 71.
81. Kuyper, "Dienst des Woords," 78:
82. Kuyper, "Dienst des Woords," 79.
83. Kuyper, "Dienst des Woords," 79.

the minister to the service of the Word and to the confessions of the church. Therefore there must be a balanced agreement between the inner and outer callings. This guarded against the minister taking undue charge based on an inner feeling, and it called the church to accountability in choosing someone who may have logic of the mind but not a Spirit-filled heart.

Kuyper knew that as churches and potential ministers set out to discern their respective callings to the ministry of the Word, they faced the present reality of a great shortage of pastors. In installment eleven of "Dienst des Woords," Kuyper explained the numbers: "the rule should be that a Servant cares for at most a thousand souls, that is, plus or minus two hundred families. Then and only then is quiet and conscientious labor soul care possible."[84] There was, then, a need for five- or perhaps ten thousand ministers for the spiritual care of the nation. "The staff, however," Kuyper lamented, "is lacking."[85] But even in the case of an emergency, Kuyper warned against taking shortcuts. Thorough preparation was still needed to ensure that it was the Word of God and not the word of humans that was preached in the churches. So, to fulfill both the inner and outer callings upon the minister, Kuyper advocated a specific course in sacred theology, which included a thorough understanding of Greek and Hebrew, exegetical understanding of the content and context of Scripture, and studies in church history and dogmatics.

Both exegesis and dogmatics must ultimately be for the service of the church, Kuyper argued. Academic study in these areas trained pastors to discern the biblical message and mission of Christ, even as they were faced with ever emerging and competing worldviews. It was the Word of God that must be served in the church, demanded Kuyper. Not philosophical spells, but biblical texts must be preached for the cultivation of disciples. Exegesis, church history, biblical languages, and dogmatics were for the purpose of serving the Word. Academics were for the formation—for the discipleship—of the pastor and for the congregation, and responsible formation could not take place outside of a clear knowledge of the biblical, historical, and theological development of the church.

Discipleship in Action

Kuyper concluded the final few installments of "Dienst des Woords" with reflections on congregational application. It was not sufficient, Kuyper wrote, for a minister of the Word to claim mere "understanding"—for the

84. Kuyper, "Dienst des Woords," 86.
85. Kuyper, "Dienst des Woords," 86.

real task was in the application. In addition, application was impossible unless the congregation manifested through and through a deep-seated conviction of what the Lord God was saying in his Word to his congregation, in that particular time and place.[86] This occurred when someone came out of the church and felt that God had actually done something in his or her soul. In these cases, it was evident that the sermon had lived up to its purpose—to *act*. "Every sermon must act," proclaimed Kuyper. "It must act not only to make the still unconverted repent with sincerity to God, but also to those who have repented still discover more about themselves," bringing them further into relationship with God and with one another.[87] Further, sermons had the most potential for action when they were delivered to a familiar congregation. A good doctor did not write the same prescription to different series of beds in the hospital; a good doctor knew his patients, and acted accordingly.

Knowledge of the congregation was thus an indispensable aspect of how the minister served the Word of God. This was a very practical matter for Kuyper. Ministers needed to know their congregation, through visits of spiritual care and moments of social engagement. Unless pastors knew the faces, names, and circumstances of the congregation, they could not provide adequate teaching for knowledge and formation—and the Word would then not be fully served. As life was rich in grace and diversity, so pastors needed to know and experience the diversity of their congregation and surroundings. "This makes the preaching rich and fascinating, full of discovery and comfort," explained Kuyper. And such commitment to the gracious diversity of God's creation "is also the best means for the Servant to learn and understand his congregation."[88]

Kuyper then concluded that as the minister applied knowledge of the Bible and knowledge of the congregation into the service of the Word, a three-fold action occurred. First, God spoke to the congregation, bringing truth, comfort, grace, repentance, and peace. Next, the believers responded to God, through singing, prayer, and service. Finally, the believers spoke and acted among each other, for the service of the congregation and the ministry toward the world.[89] The ministry of the Word thus served God, the congregation, and the world. It was true that all of the minister's training, education, and preparation aimed towards faithful worship and service to the Lord God. But Kuyper understood that spiritual formation—disciple-

---

86. See Kuyper, "Dienst des Woords," 101.
87. Kuyper, "Dienst des Woords," 102.
88. Kuyper, "Dienst des Woords," 104.
89. Kuyper, "Dienst des Woords," 126.

ship—was the congregational response of faithful service, and he expected that service to extend out beyond the borders of the church and to permeate into the world.

As an *ad-hoc* course on the practical matters of pastoral training, "Dienst des Woords" does not hold the same measure of theological exploration as the *Encyclopedia*. Hence, the focus of this section centered on demonstrating and summarizing some of the technical practicalities that Kuyper was concerned with in relation to the formation of thriving church congregations and their pastors. So, while the theology of discipleship might be more limited in this section, it is the content and practice of discipleship that takes the forefront here. Indeed, it is clear from the *Encyclopedia* that Kuyper possesses no shortage of theological reasoning; "Dienst des Woords," then, can be viewed as an outworking of that theological development and creativity.

In terms of discipleship, therefore, a few important conclusions can be drawn from "Dienst des Woords." First, practically speaking, Kuyper shows us that discipleship formation takes on a deliberate course of study and action. Pastors require training in biblical languages, exegesis, church history, and dogmatics; the message of the evangelist need not be the same as the message of the minister; and the congregation members receive the Word not only for responsive worship in the church, but for empowerment and vocational direction in their daily lives. Moreover, a central purpose of the minister is for the building up of disciples in the community. Kuyper wrote quite specifically about how many members one minister could reasonably serve, and he emphasized the need to visit the congregation and know about their lives. Discipleship requires time and investment. It is not only directed by the minister, but the minister has the responsibility to create a culture of discipleship within the church and its members. Finally, discipleship is ultimately a response to God's glory. The end of a worship service is not a room full of warmed souls; rather, Kuyper knew that a thriving church will naturally spill out into the streets and fields of the town—helping, supporting, and demonstrating the love of Christ in the midst of the world. This going-out into the world is the "possibility" of discipleship. The concept will be more fully developed throughout the book, but it is worth noting that it is seen now, in the parting words of encouragement in "Dienst des Woords:" the ministry of the Word ultimately serves God, the congregation, and the *world*.

Questions of Belief and Obedience: *Christ and the Needy*

While "Dienst des Woords" was written to mobilize and inform emerging cohorts of GKN ministers, Kuyper was also readily involved in issues that impacted the societal needs of the country as a whole. *Christ and the Needy* (*De Christus en de Sociale nooden*) was first published as a series of ten articles in *De Standaard* during June and July of 1894. The articles proved to be so popular that they were compiled and published in book form the next year. The immediate context of *Christ and the Needy* was the introduction and subsequently heated parliamentary debate over the Tak bill on extending the franchise. As was recounted at the beginning of the chapter, Kuyper took a much different position than his ARP colleague Alexander F. de Savornin Lohman—and the result of their differences was a bitter fight and the eventual party split. Yet, it is instructive to return to this document and its underlying political context for a few key reasons. First, *Christ and the Needy* is an important example of how Kuyper worked furiously to connect the spiritual with the social in his own understanding of discipleship; and now equipped with a framework of discipleship, the document nicely demonstrates the relationship between belief and obedience. Second, the document gives further insight into how Kuyper approached the demand of forgiveness, especially toward his own friend and Christian brother, Lohman. Finally, periodically returning to the issue of forgiveness throughout the book affords the opportunity for a multi-faceted reflection on a very concrete aspect of discipleship. In a work that runs the risk of remaining too abstract, forgiveness is one area where the rubber meets the road.

To be sure, *Christ and the Needy* was not a treatise on forgiveness. It was Kuyper's argument for a biblical perspective on Christians' posture towards the poor. But the catalyst for the series of articles was the political tension with Lohman, and Kuyper clearly made efforts at seeking forgiveness both within the articles and through other means (for example, in the *Handelsblad* correspondence mentioned above). The disagreement with Lohman clearly bothered Kuyper. *Christ and the Needy* was an opportunity for the two to get on similar exegetical ground—which could hopefully lead to reconciliation within the fracturing Antirevolutionary Party. Kuyper made an impassioned case.

The crux of Kuyper's argument revolved around Jesus' attitude toward the poor in the Sermon on the Mount. However, before coming to Jesus and the New Testament, Kuyper described the great Jewish tradition of social justice in the Old Testament and he even praised ancient Roman society as possessing a well-developed program of care for the poor. Kuyper was working to debunk the claim that Jesus' words needed to be softened for the contemporary context. He argued that, on the contrary and in many ways—particularly concerning care for the poor—the situation was more dire today.[90] Kuyper also pondered the lowly foundations of Jesus' own birth and upbringing: "This must, of course, have been for a *reason*. There must have been something that moved him to avoid the palaces and houses of the mighty in order to seek the quiet dwellings of the little folk in the land."[91] Indeed, Kuyper felt, "that the importance of this fact *for our social relationships* has not been sufficiently felt. People called attention to it in order to honor Jesus' humility. They spiritualized his earthly smallness and used it to exhort to heavenly mindedness."[92] But in so spiritualizing Jesus and his ministry, people blatantly ignored Jesus' own words and deeds. Kuyper reminded his readers that Jesus began his own ministry with a telling quotation from Isaiah 61: "The Spirit of the Lord is upon me, because he has anointed me to proclaim good news to the poor. He has sent me to proclaim liberty to the captives and recovering of sight to the blind, to set at liberty those who are oppressed, to proclaim the year of the Lord's favor."[93] The Sermon on the Mount repeated these themes, and Kuyper carefully described Jesus' central spiritual and social concern for the poor.

Kuyper recognized the differing textual accounts of the beatitudes in Matthew and in Luke: Matthew 5:3 said, "Blessed are the poor in spirit, for theirs is the kingdom of heaven," while Luke 6:20 read, "Blessed are you who are poor, for yours is the kingdom of heaven." How did one account for these semantic differences? Was Luke just a shortened version of Matthew, and thus meant to be spiritualized? "Or," asked Kuyper, "should Luke and Matthew be brought into harmony such that *both* social poverty and spiritual poverty, the latter as connected with the former, are done equal justice?"[94] For an answer, Kuyper turned to the Calvinist authority figures of John Calvin and F. L. Godet (so as, he wrote, his own explanation would not be considered suspect). To start, Kuyper quoted Calvin: "While the words of Luke and Matthew must mean the same thing, there can be no doubt that Jesus speaks of the blessed as those who are oppressed by adversity and who suffer affliction, with this difference only, that Matthew, by his addi-

90. See Kuyper, *Christ and the Needy*, 652–54.
91. Kuyper, *Christ and the Needy*, 660.
92. Kuyper, *Christ and the Needy*, 660.
93. Luke 4:18–19 (ESV).
94. Kuyper, *Christ and the Needy*, 662.

tion, restricts the blessedness for the oppressed to those who have learned to be humble under the discipline of the cross."[95] Kuyper then concluded that this beatitude was not in reference to the spiritual but to the socially poor and repressed, noting that Calvin "restricts this pronouncement of blessedness, with a view to Matthew 5:3, quite correctly to the poor and oppressed who are quiet before God."[96] The social aspect of the beatitude was affirmed in both Luke and Matthew, with Matthew narrowing the interpretation to those who were also humble before God. Kuyper's investigation of Godet's "well-known commentary on the Gospel of Luke"[97] yielded the same conclusion. Here, Godet explained the difference in the Evangelists' wording on Matthew's transfer of Luke's original rendering from the second to the third person. While Luke wrote, "blessed are *you* who are poor," he was referring to the circle of disciples and believing poor who were surrounding him. When Matthew transferred the beatitudes to the third person, "the saying 'blessed are *the* poor' would have become baseless. Or how could all of the poor, including the most mischievous among them, be blessed?"[98] Godet claimed that Matthew added a spiritual element in order to affirm and clarify Luke's rendering of the social nature of the beatitudes.

Kuyper took much care to clarify this point because he viewed the separation of the spiritual from the social as an acute danger in modern preaching. Given that Jesus' words clearly conveyed his blessing on the poor in the social sense—for the purpose of cultivating faith and a fear of God—Kuyper railed against taking the easy way out: "One can hardly approve of the constant *spiritualization* of all these statements [i.e., the beatitudes] in today's preaching such that every connection with life is eliminated from them by ignoring the social meaning implicit in them."[99] And the problem, he continued, had to do with one's theology: "Yet it all comes down to one's point of departure. Once one imagines that all such statements by Jesus apply only to the condition of the soul, one breaks the connection between *soul* and *body*, between our inner and outer life situation—a connection to which both Scripture and Jesus hold fast; and so one slides unnoticed onto the wrong track."[100]

That wrong track was the view that Jesus first came to the rich, and then engaged in a bit of "inner-city mission"—Jesus came, and fortunately

95. As quoted in Kuyper, *Christ and the Needy*, 662.
96. Kuyper, *Christ and the Needy*, 662.
97. Kuyper, *Christ and the Needy*, 662.
98. Kuyper, *Christ and the Needy*, 662.
99. Kuyper, *Christ and the Needy*, 663.
100. Kuyper, *Christ and the Needy*, 663.

happened not to forget the poor. But no, Kuyper's careful reading of Scripture affirmed that the messiah came in the first place to the lower classes, "not to the powerful of Jerusalem but to the poor people of Galilee."[101] To be sure, the rich are not forgotten or cast aside, but what hailed Jesus as the messiah was his coming first to and among the poor. Equipped with this perspective, Kuyper aimed to shield the interpretation and teaching of the Bible from a diminished message: "O, how different things would be in Christendom if Jesus' preaching on this point were also our preaching and if the basic principles of his Kingdom were not cut off and alienated from our society by over-spiritualization."[102] Kuyper was clamoring to return the social concerns of Jesus to the central message of the gospel—to keep concerns for the soul and body, and the inner and outer life together. To further his point, he next turned to four key themes from the larger context of the Sermon on the Mount.

Kuyper claimed that there were four basic ideas in the Sermon on the Mount that were important for distilling the social differences in society. These concepts reveal Kuyper's foundational concerns with the integration of *belief* and *obedience* in his understanding of discipleship. It was the calling of all followers of Jesus—rich and poor—to strive for the balance of social and spiritual well-being described in the Sermon, for the physical dangers that Jesus described have a clear bearing on spiritual matters. First, Kuyper summarized Jesus' teachings on money. He recognized that money had become a ruthless idol on earth, diametrically opposed to the power and rule of God. Quite literally, in the times of ancient Israel, the idol of mammon "was served, incensed, and worshipped as a means to make a fortune, to become rich and, even if by less than honest means, to make one's purse overflow."[103] Jesus himself recognized that this idol—even if just as an "idea"—still held captive the imaginations of the people, and so a choice had to be made: "No one can serve two masters, for either he will hate the one and love the other, or he will be devoted to the one and despise the other. You cannot serve God and money [mammon]."[104] The choice was clear: serve the Lord God, or serve a love of money.

This led naturally to the next main idea that Kuyper drew from the Sermon on the Mount, namely, the goal toward which disciples lives were directed. "Do not lay up for yourselves treasure on earth," Kuyper reiterated from Matthew 6:19–21, "where moth and rust destroy and where thieves

---

101. Kuyper, *Christ and the Needy*, 663.
102. Kuyper, *Christ and the Needy*, 665.
103. Kuyper, *Christ and the Needy*, 665.
104. Kuyper, *Christ and the Needy*, 665. See Matt 6:24.

break in and steal, but lay up for yourselves treasures in heaven, where neither moth nor rust destroys and where thieves do not break in and steal. For where your treasure is, there your heart will be also." The present danger, Kuyper declared, was that "everything stalks money. Everything thirsts for money."[105] He diagnosed the goal of his fellow countrymen with unabashed precision: "Financial power, climbing higher, collecting treasures in stocks and precious metals, purchasing houses and landed properties, becoming the master of earthly goods—this, it may be safely said, is the main thought that exercises the heads and hearts and senses nowadays at the stock exchange and in the world of our young people."[106]

But, Kuyper wrote, this is precisely what Jesus did not want. The thirst for money annexed one's heart away from God. It even stole away all that was human and noble, debasing the human being, a precious creature of God. People who clamored after this kind of physical wealth only corrupted themselves in the process. The social was inextricably linked with the spiritual. So, Kuyper explained, Jesus "does not want and will not tolerate the laying up of such treasures. The soul's longing and the heart's desire must be focused on something entirely different—on spiritual goods, on heavenly goods" which cannot disintegrate or be stolen.[107] The love of money had to be overcome with the love of what was truly necessary—the love of God. A spiritual commitment to God was incomplete without a physical ordering of disciples' lives away from the goal of earthly treasures, and toward the eternal.

The love of God was further cultivated with a third lesson from the Sermon on the Mount. "Give us this day our daily bread"[108] was a prayer of sustenance, and a rejection of life in perpetual worship of mammon. Kuyper recounted Jesus' words in Matthew 6:25-34: "Therefore I tell you, do not be anxious about your life, what you will eat or what you will drink, nor about your body, what you will put on. . . . But seek first the kingdom of God and his righteousness, and all these things will be added to you." The driving force that Kuyper identified here was that of desire. And desire led to domination. "Money and goods are a temptation because physically and socially we have all sorts of needs and all sorts of wants."[109] There are clothes to buy and food to find; "we need a place to live; and ever so much more."[110] But

---

105. Kuyper, *Christ and the Needy*, 666.
106. Kuyper, *Christ and the Needy*, 666.
107. Kuyper, *Christ and the Needy*, 666.
108. Matt 6:11.
109. Kuyper, *Christ and the Needy*, 667.
110. Kuyper, *Christ and the Needy*, 667.

Jesus not only provided hope for the better way, he provided—in Kuyper's words—a threefold weapon. As a start, Jesus instructed his disciples to moderate their desires. Then, he asked for a change in perspective—that disciples place their hope not in themselves, the creature, but in God, the creator. Finally, Kuyper explained, Jesus beckoned his followers to place the needs of the soul higher than bodily needs and comforts.[111] Such a call was not, in the end, merely for sacrifice; it was for freedom. "Free yourselves by limiting your desires. Become spiritually strong by hardening yourself in material respects."[112] Even though such a call ran directly against the cultural clamoring for further goods, luxury, and power, Jesus maintained his insistence—for this was the better way. "Alas," lamented Kuyper, "people read the Sermon on the Mount and find it beautiful, but they do not believe Jesus really meant it that way. They find it to be delightful poetry but spiritually too high for the prose of our lives." And then he cut straight to the matter: "Even the best Christian always retains a small chapel for Mammon."[113] However in doing so, the disciple severed obedience from the unity of true faith.

The fourth and final theme that Kuyper extracted from the Sermon on the Mount concerned possessions. The reality of the matter was that people simply had possessions, and even if the idol of money was vanquished, the soul stored grace and not greed, and desires were rightly moderated, disciples still had to decide how to manage what possessions they did carry. Kuyper distilled Jesus' instruction about possessions to three key statements: "First, do not insist too strictly on your property rights. Second, lend to the one who appeals to you for help. Third, give alms."[114] Kuyper first explained that Jesus did not demand a community of goods, but rather assumed that unequal distribution of property would persist. Equality of possessions was an eschatological reality, but not a present one. What Jesus did want in the matter of possessions, "is that not *envy* but *love* should reign, and that this love should level the inequality as much as possible."[115] Jesus did not call for the rich to give away everything except for their daily morsel of bread. He did not insist at the wedding at Cana that the wine should be replaced with water and the money saved given to the poor; he did not admonish Mary for pouring out the costly vile of perfume on his feet. Instead, Jesus called for a loosening of property rights: "If anyone would sue and take your tunic,

---

111. See Kuyper, *Christ and the Needy*, 667.
112. Kuyper, *Christ and the Needy*, 668.
113. Kuyper, *Christ and the Needy*, 669.
114. Kuyper, *Christ and the Needy*, 669.
115. Kuyper, *Christ and the Needy*, 670.

let him have your cloak as well."[116] It was not greed that overcame greed, Kuyper explained, "but forbearance and quiet sufferance that must triumph over injustice."[117] Lending, on the other hand, served as a temporary evening-out of "excessive inequality of possessions." When two people stood side by side, one of whom had two beds, two tunics, and a double portion of food, and the other had nothing—"this cries out to heaven."[118] Lending was distinguished from alms in that it addressed a temporary need, where the recipient paid back what was given. Alms, on the other hand, expected no repayment, and further, it was not a means to be rid of some annoyance, to gain honor, or to earn salvation. "The giving of alms should be the fruit of a stirring compassion in your heart. You see a need, a want, a pain, and the very sight should stir you as a human being."[119] But all outward show of giving alms must be redressed—"for everything that smacks of show is fatal to mercy."[120] So, while Jesus did not call for an equality of possessions, he did expect certain equalization around the basic requirements of life. "*Shelter, bed, clothing,* and the *daily morsel* must not be scanty and inefficient but such that these needs are met for all alike, and then for all alike not through coercion but through the power of charity and mercy."[121] Meeting physical needs in a very real sense was connected to the spiritual needs of both the giver and the receiver. As Jesus said in Matthew 25: "For I was hungry and you gave me no food, I was thirsty and you gave me no drink." And those who did not do to the least of these, did not do to me, and so "will go the way of eternal punishment."

What Kuyper effectively described here was Jesus' vision of the kingdom of heaven. Kuyper distinguished himself politically on this point by making a sharp distinction between making social reform for its own sake, and recognizing that Jesus' ministry was always in connection to the kingdom of heaven: "For what shall it profit a man, if he shall gain the whole world, and lose his own soul?"[122] Christians, he explained, carried a distinct platform, different from the Social Democrats or the Socialists of the day. Kuyper certainly advocated for social reform and for effective social programs, but he always wanted to keep focused on Jesus' own social

---

116. Kuyper, *Christ and the Needy*, 670. See Matt 5:40 and Luke 6:29.
117. Kuyper, *Christ and the Needy*, 671.
118. Kuyper, *Christ and the Needy*, 671.
119. Kuyper, *Christ and the Needy*, 672.
120. Kuyper, *Christ and the Needy*, 672.
121. Kuyper, *Christ and the Needy*, 672.
122. Mark 8:36.

program—the kingdom of heaven.[123] Here is where Kuyper sought to appeal to his Christian brothers and sisters, who were fast splitting away from his party.[124] In a call for unity—and even a call for reconciliation—Kuyper recognized that all Christians had a unique responsibility to heed Jesus' words and actively advocate for both the social and spiritual needs of the poor. He was adamant: "We *may* not, we *can* not, we *will* not fail, in the name of Jesus to raise this testimony in this generation."[125] And in what could be perceived as a final olive branch to his friend Lohman, a man of the noble class, Kuyper wrote:

> We respect the notables among Christians; we thank God that even among those of high social rank he has plucked a few out of the fire; we value highly the blessing they can bring us. Thus precisely for this reason the voice may not be stifled that tries to persuade them to follow in Jesus' footsteps also in the social field. Even in the midst of social unrest they can be a credit to their Savior, but only if, like Jesus, they stretch their hands toward the multitude and say with undivided heart, "These are my mother, and my brothers, and my sisters," and so keep them from greed and iniquity.[126]

Even with flattery and the pointed words of Jesus, Kuyper's efforts at seeking forgiveness, explaining his convictions, and offering a hand of unity were of no avail in healing the split with Lohman. Yet, in penning this treatise on Christ and the social question, Kuyper effectively articulated a much-needed biblical explication of his position. The connection between the spiritual and the social was indeed vital.

Forgiveness often has a way of working itself out over time. But for the next twenty years, Lohman and Kuyper would barely speak to each other. Discipleship is never easy, and disciples still live in the midst of a world constantly battling against itself. That Kuyper and Lohman did not reunite at this point amidst tears of joy and forgiveness is hardly the point. The two pressed forward, in their convictions and in their belief. Kuyper sought forgiveness from his old friend and even reigned in his tone and rhetoric. But even with the casualty of a friendship, Kuyper stayed his resolve to live—and even legislate—with the goal of remaining true to Jesus' call of faithful obedience.

---

123. Kuyper, *Christ and the Needy*, 674.
124. Kuyper, *Christ and the Needy*, 681.
125. Kuyper, *Christ and the Needy*, 682.
126. Kuyper, *Christ and the Needy*, 682–83.

The key factor for understanding our framework of discipleship from Kuyper's work in *Christ and the Needy* is related to the *action* of discipleship. Discipleship cannot be understood outside of the relationship between *faith* and *obedience*. This was the underlying theme that Kuyper kept pushing at throughout the document. The Sermon on the Mount was not only a spiritual reality; it also described a commitment to physical action. Jesus called his disciples—both then and now—to approach money, possessions, the poor, and social conditions from the reality of God's kingdom and Jesus' own values. This meant admitting that money can maintain its powerful grip even upon the best intentioned disciples, and then making a commitment to throw off this stranglehold—by both spiritually and physically acting different. Discipleship is not a spiritual exercise of thinking about how to approach money and treating the poor—it requires *action*. Belief without obedience is not belief at all.

Possibilities: America, the Stone Lectures, and Beyond

On August 31, 1898—while suffering through a blistering heat wave in New York City—Kuyper sent a telegram to his new queen, Wilhelmina:

> To her Majesty the Queen of the Netherlands. On the day of Her Majesty's enthronement I beg most respectfully to tender My Most Gracious Queen my allegiance as a loyal subject and my entire concurrence with the forthcoming swearing in of the States General. May Her Majesty's reign be long and prosperous, and may God bless it to Her Majesty's happiness, to the welfare of the Netherland commonwealth and to the glory of His name. Dr. A. Kuyper, Member of the States General.[127]

Kuyper was noticeably absent from the monumental events of the Queen's assumption of her office on August 31—her eighteenth birthday—and he would similarly be missing from the September 6 inauguration ceremony, held by a joint session of the States General in the Nieuwe Kerk in Amsterdam. As if to further highlight the perception of Kuyper's ambivalence towards the Royal House of Orange by being out of the continent for the celebrations, he had to put off a particularly important role he had assumed as a member of Parliament: the chairman of the committee that would host the approximately 160 foreign journalists attending the inauguration ceremony on behalf of the Dutch Association of Journalists.[128] Although Kuyper had

---

127. Kuyper, *Kuyper in America*, 13.
128. See Kuyper, *Kuyper in America*, iv, 7.

indicated far in advance that he would be away from the celebrations due to "pressing business" in the United States, this certainly was not the most flattering expression of loyalty that a member of parliament (and a future prime minister) could show his new monarch. So, what was it that pressed upon Kuyper so urgently as to keep him away from his home country during this important time? Why take what amounted to an almost five-month trip across the ocean in the late summer and autumn of 1898?

The presenting occasion of Kuyper's trip to America in 1898 was the awarding of an honorary doctorate from Princeton University and an invitation to deliver the prestigious Stone Lectures in Miller Chapel at Princeton Seminary.[129] Initially, Kuyper had received this invitation from the Princeton faculty to come in 1896, at the 150th anniversary of the University's founding, and had postponed the trip twice—so that, as a matter of professional gratitude, the commitment to come in the fall of 1898 had to be honored. The Stone Lectures formed the axis of Kuyper's trip in America. He delivered six *Lectures on Calvinism* in October, and this treatise quickly became famous as the most influential and precise presentation of his neo-Calvinist program. Kuyper's initial two or three month planned trip soon cascaded into an absolutely packed four month speaking and lecture tour. His itinerary grew to include meetings, receptions, lectures, and visits in a long list of Dutch and Reformed-influenced localities: New York, Boston, Hartford, Princeton, Detroit, Grand Rapids, Holland, Chicago, Pella, Des Moines, Orange City, Cleveland, Rochester, Paterson, New Brunswick, Baltimore, Washington D.C. (for a meeting with President McKinley and members of his cabinet), Philadelphia, and back again through New York.[130]

While Kuyper addressed a range of theological and political issues with his various audiences, the themes from *Lectures on Calvinism* permeated throughout. As such, it is appropriate to focus on the *Lectures* to gain insight into Kuyper's theological understanding and practice of discipleship. At this, the height of his intellectual career, it is also instructive to view particular aspects of the *Lectures* with an eye towards examining the *possibilities* of discipleship. Since much has been written on Kuyper's *Lectures*—including the comprehensive study by Peter Heslam[131]—this section forgoes providing a thorough summary of each lecture. Instead, Kuyper's theological concept of discipleship is explored with the coming possibilities of his tenure as Dutch prime minister in mind. In particular, the possibility

---

129. See Kuyper, *Kuyper in America*, iii–vi; and Bratt, *Abraham Kuyper*, 261–64.
130. See Kuyper, *Kuyper in America*, ix–x.
131. Heslam, *Creating a Christian Worldview*.

of discipleship is viewed through the themes of two particular lectures: "Calvinism and Politics," and "Calvinism and the Future."[132]

Kuyper's Calvinist "world and life-system" was steeped in theology. The foundational principles so thoroughly described in the *Encyclopedia* made another appearance here in the *Lectures*, only this time those principles were in dialogue with the competing historical, philosophical, and political ideas of the day. "Calvinism and Politics," Kuyper's third lecture, built off the theoretical formulations of the first two. Kuyper was always careful to set out a clear theological starting point—and describing the life-system of Calvinism and its relation to religion in the opening lectures established the key theme of sovereignty that would now be explored politically.[133] Politics was a possibility of discipleship because of the very nature of God's sovereignty in the world. Kuyper explained that Calvinism could have an influence in political development because of its very cosmological root principle: "This dominating principle was not, soteriologically, justification by faith, but in the widest sense cosmologically, the *Sovereignty of the Triune God over the whole Cosmos*, in all its spheres and kingdoms, visible and invisible."[134] Kuyper understood this sovereignty as taking a three-fold shape in the world: sovereignty in the state, in society, and in the church. In the sphere of the state, Kuyper described the necessity of politics and rulers to manage a human race divided by land, language, and tradition. While Calvinism affirmed that each ruler was instituted by God, it also took into account the thorough permeation of sin. "By the grace of God" kings reign, and by the grace of God, sin was restrained and held back—even as it rebelled against God's ultimate rule.[135] Against philosophies of popular and pantheistic sovereignty, rising from France and Germany respectively, Calvinism's state sovereignty placed ultimate authority in God—not the people and not in a mysterious "state-consciousness."[136] As God alone was sovereign, the spheres of society and church assumed a role alongside, and not under, the state. This was a crucial point for Kuyper, in that it enabled the differentiation and plurality that was the hallmark of successful nation-building. Certainly, government had the responsibility to protect the boundary lines of each of the spheres, to defend the weak ones within them, and to demand participation from all to bear the personal and

132. Kuyper delivered six lectures: Calvinism a Life-system, Calvinism and Religion, Calvinism and Politics, Calvinism and Science, Calvinism and Art, and Calvinism and the Future.

133. See Heslam, *Creating a Christian Worldview*, 142.

134. Kuyper, *Lectures on Calvinism*, 79.

135. See Kuyper, *Lectures on Calvinism*, 82–85.

136. Kuyper, *Lectures on Calvinism*, 88.

financial necessities in the maintenance and unity of the state.[137] But these were divine appointments of the state, and not actions of a state that was all-encompassing and dominated every aspect of society. Politics, then, was a means of pursuing and protecting the common good, in all spheres of life. It thus provided an ultimate opportunity for Calvinists to extend their faithful following of Jesus Christ into all areas of society and culture. Under the rule of an all-sovereign God, the possibilities for faithful discipleship were many.

Kuyper summarized this possibility in his last lecture, "Calvinism and the Future." He reiterated that "Calvinism *did* not stop at a church-order, but expanded in a *life-system*, and did not exhaust its energy in a dogmatical construction, but created a *life-* and *world-view*, and such a one as was, and still is, able to fit itself to the needs of every stage of human development in every department of life."[138] How, then, was Calvinism to "fit itself" to an ever-changing world society? In a world that "considers itself in ever-increasing measure as having *outgrown* Christianity,"[139] what did Kuyper have to offer? Again, he unearthed the root of the matter. Modern life, he explained, looked for the origin of things not in the sovereignty of God, but in the wisdom and knowledge of humankind. These were the ideas that clamored after the latest ideas in evolution, or embraced the *Übermensch*.[140] Kuyper, on the other hand, called for a return to a Calvinistic form of Christianity. He was not so ignorant, he explained, as to think all believing Protestants—and anyone else—would somehow subscribe to all the tenets of the Reformed faith: "I am far from cherishing so crude, so ignorant, so unhistorical a desire," he wrote.[141] However, Kuyper argued for the continuing influence of Calvinism, contending that there was much this strong faith still had to offer a modern world. To maintain this possibility of future influence, Kuyper identified four points: first, Calvinism needed to be strengthened, not ignored, where it was already showing an influence; second, Calvinism needed to be studied so that the outside world could know it; third, its principles needed to be developed and applied according to the needs and demands of the time; fourth, the churches which confessed Calvinism needed to cease from shying away from their heritage, and instead lay a clear confessional claim.[142]

---

137. See Kuyper, *Lectures on Calvinism*, 97.
138. Kuyper, *Lectures on Calvinism*, 171.
139. Kuyper, *Lectures on Calvinism*, 175.
140. See Kuyper, *Lectures on Calvinism*, 173.
141. Kuyper, *Lectures on Calvinism*, 191.
142. See Kuyper, *Lectures on Calvinism*, 192.

Locating a Framework for Discipleship, 1894-1898

Thus, there was much work to do for Kuyper and his Calvinist brothers and sisters. Here before them was a comprehensive theological worldview that, while embracing them in a nurturing spirituality, subsequently demanded action and engagement with the world around them. Confessionalism was claimed not as a form of retreat into the walls of an impenetrable church, but as a strategy for meeting the world on its terms. But not, to be sure, for the purpose of accommodating the fleeting passions of modernism, evolution, or even revolution. Rather, Calvinism presented a different narrative, of a sovereign God, sustaining the world with grace. And while the times seemed dire for such a religious worldview, Kuyper could hold out hope:

> Unless God send forth His Spirit, there will be no turn, and fearfully rapid will be the descent of the waters. But you remember the Aeolian Harp, which men were wont to place outside their casement, that the breeze might wake its music to life. Until the wind blew, the harp remained silent, while, again, even though the wind arose, if the harp did not lie in readiness, a rustling of the breeze might be heard, but not a single note of ethereal music delighted the ear. Now, let Calvinism be nothing but such an Aeolian Harp—absolutely powerless, as it is, without the quickening Spirit of God—still we feel it our God-given duty to keep our harp, its strings tuned aright in the window of God's Holy Zion, awaiting the breath of the Spirit.[143]

The *possibility* of discipleship was thus a driving force in Kuyper's *Lectures*. Calvinism—as a life-system, a religion, in relation to politics, art, and the future—moved into creative and vital possibilities for engagement with the world because it was fully sustained by God's mighty sovereignty. What's more, Calvinism's confessional claims offered something unique and of inherent value to the pressing issues of politics and culture. This was not a religion pulling its adherents into cloisters protected from the secularizing movements of the world. God's sovereignty not only empowered, but also offered grace, sustainment, and even culture-building forces for the world. Discipleship thus culminated not sequestered within the individual, but by engaging the complexities of politics and in believing and participating in the future development of culture and society—for the glory and truth of God.

---

143. Kuyper, *Lectures on Calvinism*, 199.

Conclusion: Kuyper's Discipleship

The documents discussed here, covering the years 1894–98, in no means provide a complete or even systematic picture of Kuyper. Instead, they are a lesson in how Kuyper taut the strings of a harp, awaiting the breath of the Holy Spirit. Discipleship, likewise, is never straightforward. Certainly, it has its beginnings, middle, and ends; but those ends can be endlessly pursued, while never being tied down. The goal of this chapter was to provide—not impose—a framework for understanding Kuyper's theological and practical understanding of discipleship. The *Encyclopedia* provided the foundational theological concepts for the fourfold movements of revelation, Jesus Christ, belief-obedience, and possibility. The additional documents provided opportunities for further exploration of how Kuyper worked in these various modes of discipleship. "Dienst des Woords" set out a minister's program for how to build strong disciples within a local church congregation. Issues of formation—both for the minister and for the worshipping congregation—ultimately led Kuyper to affirm that responding to God's glory entailed the threefold actions of loving and serving God, each other, and the world. *Christ and the Needy* revealed Kuyper's passionate concern that a disciple's belief bears a strong resemblance to his or her action in the world. Kuyper would not allow the spiritual calls to *belief* in the Sermon on the Mount be separated from the physical calls to *obedience* in how disciples handle money and treat the poor. Finally, the *Lectures on Calvinism* set the framework for Kuyper's political philosophy and provide a ground from which to launch this next chapter on his career as prime minister. As Kuyper espoused the *possibilities* of discipleship in these lectures, soon he would readily have the opportunity to test his theories of cultural engagement from the heights of political power and influence. So, throughout this period, we see that Kuyper is a human being—espousing grandiose ideas, creating theology and organizations, and even losing friends along the way. The standard for a disciple must not be perfection, but faithfulness. The immediate context of Kuyper's rising political career is just such an opportunity for testing that standard.

Chapter 2

Discipleship in Politics, 1899–1905

Close fellowship with God must become actual in the full and vigorous revelation of our life. It must permeate and give color to our feeling, perceptions, sensations, thoughts, imagination, purposes, acts, and words. It must not stand as a foreign factor by the side of our life, but be the glow that casts its sheen upon our whole existence.

—Abraham Kuyper, *To Be Near Unto God*

The View from *het Torentje*

IN THE NETHERLANDS, THE prime minister's office is known as *het Torentje*—the little tower. From here, at the center of political power and at the height of his professional career, Abraham Kuyper had an immense opportunity to implement ideas and policies that would serve the common good of the nation. His work in pastoral ministry, journalism, education, theology, social justice, and foreign affairs all culminated with the majority election of his party's coalition in 1901, and as the leader of the winning Antirevolutionary Party (ARP), Kuyper was invited by the Queen to form a cabinet. He would face a challenging agenda. Kuyper's involvement with the South African crisis from 1899 continued when he took the first minister's chair, and the implementation of his Ethical Policy in Dutch foreign affairs would mark an early victory for his rule. But his move to the center of power also rendered him susceptible to unforeseen crisis. In particular, the labor strikes in 1903 went a long way toward defining—and marring—Kuyper's political legacy. However, by the end of his first and only term as prime minister, Kuyper would be able to point proudly to the success of one of his central goals—education reform. Kuyper's term in office was often tumultuous, but he was also stubbornly productive—politically and theologically. The South African crisis, the labor strikes of 1903, and his efforts at education reform serve, then, as an opportunity for both a political and personal exploration of the connection between Kuyper's theological notion of discipleship and his efforts at governing with concern for the common good.

This chapter addresses three key events surrounding Kuyper's tenure in the prime minister's office, but it does so with a specific eye towards a developing concept of discipleship. Kuyper did not—more so, could not—address the political realities of foreign and domestic policy as isolated from his Reformed faith. He had argued throughout his career for the place of a distinctly Christian worldview among the other ideologies scrambling for space in the nation. And he continued to invoke the foundations of his faith as he maneuvered strategically through the political realities of war in South Africa, dangerous labor strikes, and domestic debates on education reform. Moreover, as Kuyper delved into parliamentary debates and law-making, he simultaneously produced and published some of the most theologically creative and spiritually compelling work of his entire life. In 1900, for example, his definitive book from 1888 on *The Work of the Holy Spirit* was published in English. At this time, he was heavily invested in finding a mediating solution for the war between Britain and South Africa, and the appearance of his writings on the Holy Spirit to an English speaking audience gave witness to renewed vigor and commitment for the Spirit's power for re-creation and love. Then, as the Dutch nation faced a dramatic crisis in the labor markets in 1903, Kuyper published some of his most reflective and even spiritually mystic meditations on the knowledge of God, love, and forgiveness. Finally, as he pushed through some of the most significant reforms in the history of the Dutch education system, Kuyper's final volumes of the creative theological work *Common Grace* were being published.

So, here we have before us, side by side, dramatic political situations—on both the international and domestic scale—and exquisite and innovative theological writings that explore the many facets of knowing and following the will of God. This unique convergence provides a fascinating opportunity to discover and test the relationship between Kuyper's bold actions at the height of his political power and his understanding and practice of discipleship. The result, for Kuyper, was the deliberate practice of political discipleship, grounded in the foundations of theology that are distinctively directed at the common good.

Discipleship and International Affairs

When Kuyper visited Washington, D.C. in November 1898 to meet President McKinley, he had a particular agenda in mind: the growing crisis in South Africa. Kuyper was hoping to garner American support for the Transvaal, which was edging towards the brink of war with Britain. More so, Kuyper expressed his wider concern against the forces of imperialism still raging in America. He wanted the McKinley administration to consider other means for engaging international affairs, such as his own developing "ethical" foreign policy. The president, however, had a decisive pro-business and pro-British foreign policy, with the goal of opening up international markets and goods.[1] This short meeting with McKinley, while a disappointment for Kuyper, served to solidify Kuyper's own emerging—and distinct—approach to international affairs. It was an approach that combined Dutch nationalism, small-power realism, and Christian morality with Kuyper's unique theological convictions and political talent. Thus, as will become clear, Kuyper's ethical foreign policy was part and parcel of his theological convictions and practice of discipleship. His political actions as they specifically (but not exclusively) related to the South African War of 1899–1902, when examined alongside key theological writings, provide insight into the connections between Kuyper's Christian discipleship and his actions while holding high political office.

The Emergence of Kuyper's Foreign Policy

Kuyper's direct involvement in South African affairs dated to 1883. The Transvaal had been in a struggle to reclaim its independence from British annexation, and when Transvaal President Paul Kruger traveled to London to negotiate a treaty, he specifically requested two Dutch delegates to advise him: Jhr. G. H. Th. Beelaerts van Blokland and Abraham Kuyper. Despite Dutch roots dating to the 17th century, most people in the Netherlands were not concerned with a far-away British colonial annexation. However, in the winter of 1880–81, news came that the Boers were trying to assert their independence from the British, and a deep sense of kinship arose between the Netherlanders and their long-removed compatriots. Soon, the desire to

---

1. See Bratt, *Abraham Kuyper*, 273–74.

support the Boers was being discussed across all stripes of national newspapers, petitions were signed asking King William III to mediate the dispute, and both houses of the States-General discussed if and how they could help restore peace. The Dutch government decided on a strict policy of neutrality, so as not to alienate their British neighbors. This was based on the conclusion that a position of neutrality could better gain their desired outcome in favor of the Boers; a direct offer of mediation, the Dutch concluded, would only produce an embarrassing rejection from Britain on grounds of impertinence. When the conflict subsided, President Kruger had recognized the implicit Dutch support of the Boer cause, and so requested the advice of Beelaerts van Blokland and Kuyper during the London treaty negotiations. Upon Kruger's return to the Transvaal, he retained Beelaerts van Blokland as his European diplomat. Though Kuyper's direct services were no longer needed, he remained connected with Kruger; in fact, his professional investment in the Boer cause for independence was just beginning.[2]

By 1895, as relations between Great Britain and the South African republics continued to deteriorate, Dutch sentiment turned more anti-British. Soon the Netherlands began to cast an adoring eye towards Germany for possible assistance, while the British began to consider that war in South Africa could destabilize the entire continent. As tensions continued to mount, the Czar of Russia, Nicholas II, called for the First Hague Peace Conference to be held in 1899, "with the object of seeking the most effective means of ensuring to all peoples the benefits of a real and lasting peace, and, above all, of limiting the progressive development of existing armaments."[3] The Dutch government was surprised at their nomination to host the conference, and, as a small nation, even doubted their own ability to pull it off. They agreed to serve as host, however, and the conference was held from May 18 through July 29, 1899 at The Hague.

Governments from twenty six nations were represented, but notably absent from the guest list—and a cause of concern for Kuyper—were the South African republics. Kuyper had kept in contact with Kruger after assisting him in the negotiations for Transvaal freedom with British Prime Minister William Gladstone in 1883. Thus, Kuyper's sentiments were clearly in support of the Boers, and he increasingly made use of his growing political influence to try and persuade the world powers to keep Britain from making another power grab in South Africa. As we have seen, Kuyper had called upon President McKinley in an effort to garner support for the Boers, and this effort now extended to the British statesman John Morley. As the

2. See Vandenbosch, *Dutch Foreign Policy*, 72–73.
3. International Committee of the Red Cross, "Final Act."

Peace Conference was being organized, however, Kuyper heard rumors that the South African republics had not been invited. He made an inquiry with the Dutch Foreign Minister W. H. de Beaufort and learned that a South African presence would not be allowed. The formal explanation was that this conference had a specifically European agenda—to discuss the grave questions of armaments on the continent—and as such not all of the nations of the world could be invited.[4] Kuyper sensed that behind the scenes the British had threatened to pull out of the conference if the South Africans attended. But when Brazil informed Russia that they did not want to be invited, Beaufort had an out and could make the "European-only" argument. Privately, Beaufort chastised Kuyper for a recent speech in support of the Boers. While he admitted that the Netherlands and the South African republics had a national sympathy towards each other due to their historic ethnic and linguistic ties, such points must now be set aside. As he remarked, "it must not be forgotten that between national sympathy and international relations there is a great difference. These are two entirely different matters."[5] Kuyper was not sure the matters were so separate.

"The South African Crisis"

Despite the adoption of three conventions and the provision for the convening of a second conference, the First Hague Peace Conference of 1899 failed to reach an agreement on its primary objective: the limitation or reduction of armaments. By October of 1899, the Second Boer War broke out between Britain and the South African republics. In February of 1900, Kuyper publically entered into the fray by publishing a scathing critique of the now full-fledged war. "The South African Crisis" first appeared in French in the distinguished *Revue des Deux Mondes* before being translated into Dutch, Swedish, and then English by the "Stop the War Committee" in London.[6] Indeed, the article captured the attention of the European public and proved to be one of the most compelling descriptions of the Boer cause. Rather than focusing solely on the religious aspect of the conflict, Kuyper incorporated arguments from history, international law, and even contemporary social theory. Kuyper's foray into social theory—and race relations in particular—have produced some of the most damaging critiques and questions of Kuyper that ever appeared, and challenge the nature of his legacy. While racial issues remain of considerable historical and contemporary importance,

---

4. See Kuitenbrouwer, *War of Words*, 205.
5. As quoted in Vandenbosch, *Dutch Foreign Policy*, 77. See also 75–77.
6. See Bratt, *Abraham Kuyper*, 291.

this study will instead focus on aspects of Kuyper's theology that influenced his views on international affairs more generally.[7]

The opening remarks of Kuyper's essay were aimed at exposing the hypocrisy contained in Britain's opposition to the Boer's quest for freedom. He lamented how the nineteenth century, which had "opened with splendid promise for liberty and demands for the restitution of violated rights," was now coming to a close, just as such promises were being "disgraced . . . by a war of aggression which nothing can justify."[8] Kuyper further highlighted the irony of British participation in the recent Peace Conference, where a permanent court of arbitration had been established to manage the disputes that might potentially devolve into war. He charged: "What magnificent hopes for the future had not the Conference at the Hague disclosed to the heart of the nations bowed under the ever increasing burden of military charges! Instead of appeal to arms, arbitration was henceforth to settle international disputes. Yet England today, England which was one of the most zealous participants in the Hague Conference, at the first menace of war gives it the kick and knows it no more!"[9] Kuyper then issued a direct challenge to British morality and religion. While, he pointed out, European missionaries in Africa were proclaiming the Christmas message of "peace on earth" to the native people, "these savages are standing by while a murderous struggle is going on between Christian and Christian to see whether the Christians of Europe or the Christians of Africa will finally get the upper hand."[10] As such, a "cry of distress" had gone up to the conscience of Europe, aroused against a country that was once the pride of love and justice. "Is it not a sad spectacle? Has progress been arrested? Can it be that in the century about to be born we are going to slip backward?"[11] With these words, Kuyper had clearly staked out his moral position against British military intervention toward the Boers, and in doing so had grabbed the attention of many nations.

Much interesting detail can be gleaned from a close reading of Kuyper's entire twelve-section article. He presented a brief history of the sour Dutch-British relations concerning colonialization, he described the character of

---

7. There are several important studies that analyze and evaluate the issue of Kuyper's influence on the question of race and apartheid in South Africa, including De Gruchy, *Church in South Africa*; Van Koppen, "Abraham Kuyper en Zuid-Afrika"; Du Toit, "No Chosen People"; Kuiper, "Theory and Practice"; Harinck, "Abraham Kuyper, South Africa"; and Kilcrease, "Protestant Paranoia."

8. Kuyper, "South African Crisis," 325.

9. Kuyper, "South African Crisis," 325.

10. Kuyper, "South African Crisis," 325.

11. Kuyper, "South African Crisis," 325.

the Boer people with their Dutch but also French, Scottish, German, and Scandinavian roots, and he proudly noted their thoroughly Calvinistic religion. Throughout, he made a convincing case in support of the Boers and, even though some of his reasoning contained elements of the racism and Euro-centrism common at the time, there was something more at stake than merely Dutch affinity for a suppressed people. Kuyper was making a bold statement about the nature and impact of European imperialism—and his reasoning was in large part motivated by his theological understanding of discipleship waged for the common good. To illustrate this particular connection, it is helpful to highlight key statements and passages from this essay. Following this, various statements contained in the essay are examined in light of Kuyper's own theological developments.

First, despite its idealism, Kuyper believed in the peace process as broadly outlined in the First Hague Peace Conference. Not only did he chide Britain for quickly turning its back on some of the key conventions established at the conference, he also labored diligently on his own accord to broker a peace treaty between the two nations. In addition to his earlier discussions with McKinley and Chamberlain, once Kuyper assumed the position of first minister in 1901, he took it upon himself to attempt to mediate between the warring parties. Although Kuyper remained supportive of the Boer cause, he was even more interested in achieving peace and in bringing the conflict to a peaceful conclusion. After pledging to preserve the Netherlands as a neutral party, soon after his ascension to the office of prime minister in January 1902, he quietly approached the British government with an offer to mediate an end to the war. Though this offer was rebuffed, it did serve as the catalyst for the establishment of secret talks between Britain and the Transvaal.[12]

Kuyper's secret efforts to negotiate a peace settlement soon reached the ears of the public. The response was mixed. Some praised his efforts at taking the initiative towards peace, recognizing Kuyper's humanitarian motives to end what had now descended into a brutal conflict. It was also acknowledged that Kuyper's initiation caused the British to abandon their demand for an unconditional surrender. But Kuyper also had his loyal critics. Charles Boissevain, for one, charged Kuyper with playing into British hands, providing them with the opportunity to negotiate directly with the Transvaal, and not through their Boer diplomats residing in Europe. Such a move, Boissevain claimed, eliminated the desire for South Africa to negotiate through diplomacy its independence from European imperialism.[13] In

12. See Kuitenbrouwer, *War of Words*, 246.
13. See Kuitenbrouwer, *War of Words*, 247.

defending himself, Kuyper claimed that through these diplomatic efforts he wanted to provide the Boers with a chance to establish a viable society in the future; the continuing war with Britain, however, confronted the Boers with the very real possibility of their own extinction. When the peace treaty at Vereeniging was signed, and Transvaal independence was forfeited in favor of British annexation, there was certainly some shock and disappointment throughout the Netherlands. But the surrender had not been unconditional. The Boers had retained certain rights and the foundations were now set for the building of a new society, in which they could continue to live and in which they—and not just Europeans—could exercise direct influence over their future.[14]

Maintaining the local hegemony of the unique Boer society became an important goal for Kuyper, for he recognized its uniqueness and inherent value. At the same time, Kuyper made one glaring oversight, perhaps more obvious today than it was then: the denial of the native black population's desire for self-determination—ironic given that his own advocacy for the Boer cause had in part been based on the need for greater diversity in the region. In "The South African Crisis," for example, he extolled the many virtues of the Boers. It would be a mistake, he explained, to compare the "Boers"—which means farmers—"with French peasants, English farmers, or even American settlers," because this was a "conquering race that has established itself among the Hottentots and Bantus, as the Normans in the eleventh century planted themselves amongst the Anglo-Saxons."[15] As such, these people raised horses and cattle, managed thousands of hectares, and loved the chase—even deer-stalking. Moreover,

> They are intrepid horsemen and exercise themselves unremittingly in the handling of arms. Without being cultured or refined, they display that natural sagacity which has always been the gift of pioneer nations at the beginning of their historical development. Hence their thirst for independence and their insatiable love of liberty, social and political. They have too tough a backbone to bow the head under anybody's yoke, whoever they may be. Nowhere is there a public life more developed or more widely scattered. The Boer is *par excellence* the politician and military man combined.[16]

Kuyper went on to describe the virtues of their democratic organization and their cooperative military discipline. In virtue and in deed, he

14. See Kuitenbrouwer, *War of Words*, 249.
15. Kuyper, "South African Crisis," 330.
16. Kuyper, "South African Crisis," 331.

argued, the Boers were worth saving. But there was more; the religious roots of the Boer society were exceedingly important to Kuyper and his supporters: "Their religion, thoroughly Calvinistic, is the very soul of their chivalrous existence and completely harmonizes with it," he wrote.[17] Their "fervent piety" consolidated their national strength and "explains why they open their councils of war with prayer and march to battle singing the Psalms of David, reviving thus the traditions of the armies of Gustavus Adolphus, of the Huguenots, and of Cromwell."[18] In addition, they held high standards of morality by maintaining a pure married life, raising as many as fifteen children, and avoiding alcoholism. This contributed to the steady rise in their population and cultivated a strong sense of kinship and nationalism, especially among their strong and courageous women. The British, on the other hand, painted the Boers as "exhibiting a most lamentable picture of laziness and stupidity," and described their women as "passing a lazy, dull, and inactive life."[19] Clearly, for Kuyper, this was the wrong picture. "The English," he explained, "comprehend only what has some likeness to themselves and for that reason they try to assimilate everybody to their type. But the Boers remain obstinate, refractory, resolutely and absolutely unassimilable."[20] Central to Kuyper's perspective on the Boer's was the concept of diversity. That is, his support of their cause was in some sense related to the affirmation of their unique characteristics—physical, social, religious, and political—while his criticism of the English (particularly their colonial policy) rested on their desire to bring everyone under their own system. Hence, in addition to desiring peace in southern Africa, Kuyper also valued a certain measure of social diversity; moreover, in advancing this claim for diversity, he was making a pointed argument against the forces of imperialism.

Throughout "The South African Crisis," Kuyper traced—and then systematically dismantled—the logic and morality of Britain's imperialistic philosophy. From a pragmatic perspective, Kuyper believed that colonial governments would do well to "make every effort to respect the susceptibilities and customs of its new subjects as far as possible. To this end," he added, "any reasonable government will avoid all sudden changes in political and social organization, will study to make its yoke scarcely felt, will strive to create the impression that everything is to go on as before."[21] A wise government, he continued, would look to address the people's grievances against

---

17. Kuyper, "South African Crisis," 331.
18. Kuyper, "South African Crisis," 331.
19. Kuyper, "South African Crisis," 332.
20. Kuyper, "South African Crisis," 332.
21. Kuyper, "South African Crisis," 333.

it, and strive to win the hearts of the people it was seeking to rule. Britain, above all other nations, should have understood this. Yet with arrogance and unbridled power, "she ruffled the Boers from the start, wounding them in their religion, in their sense of honor, and in their material interests, and all in the most mischievous manner."[22] But mismanagement and provocation—in the form of depriving the Boers the legal use of their mother tongue, in unfair compensation upon the abolition of slavery, and even in pursuing those Boers who undertook the Great Trek—only solidified the Boer nerve and their resolve to throw off what could only be seen as the oppressive yoke of British colonial rule.[23]

Of course the British did not see it that way. Kuyper acknowledged that the more "enlightened circles of public opinion in England turned round and pleaded *the civilizing mission of Great Britain*."[24] After all, did not Britain have a moral obligation to bring up to date the medieval-bound Boer civilization? Even if the cause was noble, did a civilization have the right to propagate itself by war? At the same time, comparisons of morality had their own pitfalls. High-life social customs and clothes of a superior cut may have characterized the British; indeed, as Kuyper explained, "they are more expert in the exact sciences," even though "their libraries are full of all sorts of bad novels."[25] It was the British roaming the streets of Johannesburg who filled the bars, called on prostitutes, and picked street fights.[26] Arguing in favor of British moral superiority simply did not play out in real life. No, the correct moral path in this conflict would not be that of military force or arguments based on the superiority of one culture over another, but arbitration founded on international standards. But that would require Britain to disavow the seductive charms of imperial power, even though the trappings of such power may be too overwhelming to abandon. To this argument, Kuyper appended a warning. Unless Britain renounced the dream of imperialism, she would eventually be destroyed—as Rome had been destroyed—for imperialism wormed its way into the heart of a nation and led to the obsession to rule, assimilate, and swallow up diversity for the sake of power and control. But morality and imperialism were incompatible—a claim (as Kuyper pointed out) that was shared by none other than Chamberlain himself. As Kuyper explained, "morality imposes before everything unalterable respect for the rights of another, and Imperialism cannot do its

---

22. Kuyper, "South African Crisis," 333.
23. Kuyper, "South African Crisis," 333–34.
24. Kuyper, "South African Crisis," 343.
25. Kuyper, "South African Crisis," 343.
26. See Kuyper, "South African Crisis," 343.

dismal work without disregarding such rights."[27] What, then, was the way forward for the British? Was there a moral solution to the various pitfalls that inevitably accompanied imperialism, especially taking into account the *realpolitik* of the world situation?

The Ethical Policy

Colonialization, in fact, did not have to be this way. Kuyper himself advocated what he described as the Ethical Policy of foreign affairs for the Netherlands. He looked to the Dutch interest and influence in the East Indies as his prime example. As early as 1878, in *Ons Program*, Kuyper detailed the Antirevolutionary Party's "Ethical Policy" as it related to colonialization. The Dutch incursion into Indonesia had devolved since the early 1870s, when economic policy had shifted from state-controlled to the free-market. By the 1880s, the flood of entrepreneurial activity had created an economic bubble that threatened to burst. In addition, the Aceh War, which began in 1873 (and would officially last until 1912), revealed the broken social system of the colony—where unfettered capitalism promoted an extensive opium trade, and slave labor revealed the vast neglect of political and educational structures for the native population.[28] Kuyper's colonial policy, on the other hand, placed cultural responsibility over and above economic gain. He believed that the colonizing nation had the duty to provide for the development—not exploitation—of the native population. In this sense, he took a more paternalistic posture towards the East Indies, replacing neglect with systematic oversight, cultural shaping, and direct involvement in the affairs of the native people. Whatever the cost to the Dutch economy, Kuyper argued, the opium and slave trades should be abolished and the native population should be provided with schools and opportunities for civic engagement—all with the aim of one day granting independence.[29] Further, while not trampling on the rights of the majority native Muslim religion, Christian missions should be established with the support of the Dutch government in order to promote civility and education. Equal rights should be given to people of all faiths, but as a nation with a Christian heritage, the Dutch should actively support both Christian and public schools.[30]

Upon becoming prime minister in 1901, Kuyper had the opportunity to implement his Ethical Policy as the official Dutch position on

---

27. Kuyper, "South African Crisis," 350.
28. See Bratt, *Abraham Kuyper*, 219.
29. See Bratt, *Abraham Kuyper*, 220.
30. See Bratt, *Abraham Kuyper*, 220.

colonialization. He received widespread parliamentary support for this endeavor, and soon the Dutch government was in a place directly to intervene where native rule was corrupt or when crop failure and cattle disease led to economic suffering.[31] Over time, more and more nationals were incorporated into the colonial government, and a People's Council was created in 1918 to have greater influence in national affairs. Before Kuyper's death in 1920, he saw the Dutch merchant fleet increase two-fold, and commerce with the East Indies multiply in quantity and become more stable.[32] While complicated to enact, the Dutch were learning through the Aceh War that the challenges of colonialization were best met not with greater subjugation, but with a clear goal of ethical economic, political, and social development. Kuyper articulated this vision as early as 1878 and ushered it into practice beginning in 1901, and this helps explain why he became so frustrated with the contemporary British colonial policy in South Africa. Yet Kuyper's concern with promoting international peace and cultural diversity, all the while rejecting greedy imperialistic rule, was more than just a political platform. It was closely connected to his theological understanding of Christian discipleship, and its implications for the common good of the global society.

The Work of the Holy Spirit in Discipleship and Foreign Affairs

Kuyper's theological treatise *The Work of the Holy Spirit*, published in 1888, admittedly falls outside the bounds of this study's self-imposed timeframe. Nevertheless, its use can be justified on several grounds. First, *The Work of the Holy Spirit* was an especially important theological project for Kuyper; treating the Holy Spirit as its own prominent theme was a unique contribution to theology (then as now), and here he began to develop concepts that would later rise to prominence, such as common grace. Second, the English translation of this book was released in 1900, at the height of the South African crisis. Thus, it can be argued that a "reception date" fits into the chapter's timing. Furthermore, this shows that Kuyper himself, in endorsing publication of the translation, desired to see that his ideas—from more than a decade earlier—continue to be disseminated, perhaps especially in Britain and America. Finally, it is highly appropriate to examine *The Work of the Holy Spirit* for clues to Kuyper's theology of discipleship as related to international affairs, because his theology from 1888 was largely still relevant and accurate to his views in 1900. Certainly Kuyper's theology did not remain stagnant during those twelve years, but his developments still

---

31. See McGoldrick, *God's Renaissance Man*, 185.
32. See McGoldrick, *God's Renaissance Man*, 186.

affirmed the work undertaken in 1888. Of course, one of Kuyper's most important developments during this time was his concept of common grace—a theme, as revealed in his important work *De Gemeene Gratie* (*Common Grace*), that is explored later in the chapter. For now, *The Work of the Holy Spirit* helps to provide a theological lens through which his political convictions for international peace, cultural diversity, and moral/ethical practices of colonialization can be viewed.

Creation, Re-creation, and Love

There were three principle themes revealed in *The Work of the Holy Spirit* that can serve as points of connection between Kuyper's theology of discipleship and his politics of international affairs: *creation, re-creation*, and *love*. To start, Kuyper upheld the Reformed principle that the final purpose—the destiny—of creation was the glory of God. God's glory was most reflected in the elect, but was not confined to the elect. As the shell to the kernel, Kuyper made clear that the entire cosmos was organically related to the universal church. He explained: "We neither may nor can separate their [the elects'] spiritual life from their national, social, and domestic life. And since all differences of national, social, and domestic life are caused by climate and atmosphere, meat and drink, rain and drought, plant and insect—in a word by the whole economy of this material world, including comet and meteor, it is evident that all these affect the outcome of things that are related to the glory of God."[33]

God's glory was not only interested in the salvation of the elect; instead, the whole economy of creation was invested in God's glory—indeed this principle of life was its destiny. God's Spirit, then, worked not only to dwell in the hearts of the elect, but also to animate every rational being and to sustain the principle of life in every creature.[34] Here the elements of Kuyper's later concept of common grace began to emerge. The Spirit helped to lead creation to its *telos* in the glory of God, and in so doing not only sustained creation but also spurred it towards creative development.[35] All of creation was involved in the growth and progress of the created order for God's glory. In this sense, Kuyper also understood the Spirit to be at work in re-creating, "because God's grace creates not something inherently new, but a new life in an old and degraded nature."[36] In sustaining creation, the

33. Kuyper, *Work of the Holy Spirit*, 23.
34. See Kuyper, *Work of the Holy Spirit*, 26.
35. See Bacote, *Spirit in Public Theology*, 112–16.
36. Kuyper, *Work of the Holy Spirit*, 48.

Spirit worked at re-creation—and breathed new life into what was destroyed by sin.

Because the benefits of God's grace extended to the farthest reaches of creation, Kuyper understood the diversity of the world to be a matter of God's glory. This is why he could refer to the modernist sense of uniformity as a "curse,"[37] and why—in the context of international (or colonial) affairs—he supported activities that promoted cultural diversity.[38] In other words, Kuyper's theology of the Spirit's work in creation—specifically his understanding of sustaining the creation for God's glory—directly contributed to his political understanding of international affairs. The theological principle of (what would become) common grace directly informed his political stance, so much so that his political arguments were based on moral grounds. For example, as we have seen a central moral argument underlying Kuyper's disdain of British actions in South Africa was their blatant disregard for the diversity of the Boer people.[39] By ignoring the Spirit's work to create and sustain that diversity, he concluded, the British, through their imperialism, labored against God's creational structure. Discipleship, then, was played out not just in the lives of Christian believers, but also on the world stage, because discipleship impacted the common relationships between people and nations. At a fundamental level, Kuyper's theological conviction of God's revelation in and through creation impacted how he approached complicated matters of international politics. Kuyper's argument in favor of cultural diversity on the international stage emerged out of his Reformed principle of common creation, and it highlighted his belief in the animating and sustaining work of the Holy Spirit in re-creation.

In this framework of discipleship, Kuyper's concept of creation can be connected to his theological understanding of *revelation*. Creation is a part of revelation, and so it is related to Kuyper's theology of discipleship on the foundational level. *The Work of the Holy Spirit* also presents another layer of Kuyper's theology of discipleship—as related to action. *Belief* and *obedience* as the action of discipleship connect to Kuyper's concept of love as revealed in his treatise on the Holy Spirit—with love as the action of discipleship. We see this specifically as it informed Kuyper's commitments

---

37. See Kuyper, "Uniformity," 19–44.

38. Of course, he believed that native culture should be sustained, while at the same time the Christian gospel should be introduced and indigenized.

39. Kuyper's quarrel was with the British oppression of the Boer people; unfortunately, he did not hold the same disdain for the Boer subjugation of the native African people. In many ways, he unquestionably subscribed to the prevailing European race theory of his time, which placed the "Aryan" race at the top of a hierarchy, and the "Negro" race at the bottom. See Bratt, *Abraham Kuyper*, 292–94.

both to international peace efforts and to the development and deployment of his "ethical" foreign policy.

In this theological conception of love, Kuyper distinguished between natural love and Holy Love. "Our subject is not love in general, but *Love*," he explained. "The difference is evident. Love signifies the only pure, true, *divine* Love; by love in general is understood every expression of kindness, attachment, mutual affection, and devotion wherein are seen reflections of the glory of Eternal Love."[40] The love that occurred between a husband and wife, parents and children, mutual friends, or even among animals was but a reflection of Love. Natural love could indeed grow beyond instinctive love to spiritual love, but the movement into divine love was reserved for the work of the Holy Spirit[41]—in the life of discipleship. But Kuyper continued to explain that even between natural love in its highest forms and Holy Love, there was a wide chasm.[42] The movement to the truest form of Love sprouted only from God, the "very liberal Fountain of all good."[43]

Kuyper then came to a crucial point: on earth, "Love adopts this higher character only when it becomes self-consecrating, self-denying, self-sacrificing; when the object of love does not attract, but only repels."[44] In other words—in the context of international affairs—when confronted with one's adversaries. How else can Kuyper's commitment to arbitration over war be explained? Or his insistence that the Dutch place the physical and cultural needs of the Javanese people above Dutch own economic interests? Certainly, it would be quite possible that international arbitration and "ethical" foreign policy—actions that very likely would require a high measure of national self-sacrifice—would in the end not just be more moral than war and unfettered imperialism, but also, eventually, more economically viable for the vested parties. But to take on a posture of self-sacrifice and self-denial on the international stage was not likely the kind of image power-hungry countries wanted to convey. This, however, was the paradox of divine Love. Kuyper recognized that true life, true power—and true Love—only came from the sacrificial action of the triune God. Consequently, in order to apply a theology of discipleship that embraced divine Love as a central attribute to the international political arena, Kuyper recognized the need to take a strong stand for peace among nations and to pay close attention to morality in colonial affairs.

---

40. Kuyper, *Work of the Holy Spirit*, 508.
41. See Kuyper, *Work of the Holy Spirit*, 512.
42. Kuyper, *Work of the Holy Spirit*, 513.
43. Kuyper, *Work of the Holy Spirit*, 513.
44. Kuyper, *Work of the Holy Spirit*, 513.

Kuyper further understood the Holy Spirit to be at work not only in sanctifying the individual hearts of the redeemed, but also in unifying the house of God. Such a work of multiform unity would produce a broad and powerful witness of Love to the entire world: "Love even foreign to us, which coming from God penetrates and refreshes the soul; not the mere ideal of enthusiasts, but a divine power that masters and overcomes us; not an abstract conception merely charming us, but the Holy Spirit whom we feel and discover in the soul as Love; a warm, full, blessed outpouring of Love that is stronger than death and that many waters cannot quench."[45] Love was not just an individual affair; the sanctifying work of the Holy Spirit worked in the universal church, and Kuyper saw the potential for the expression of a powerful witness. A uniting Love would be stronger than death—even stronger than war, and the mighty waters of dissent, doubt, and disbelief in the world would not hold back the rushing wind of the Spirit among God's people.

Such was Kuyper's theological conviction regarding the importance of Christian service in the public realm. Through these high conceptions of unifying divine love the world could witness God's glory, and even reap the gracious benefits. Kuyper's action as prime minister, as a member of the Calvinist ARP, was a testament to this belief. The ARP, in coalition with other parties, could offer a unifying voice to address issues of national and international importance. That voice could—and did—operate from a conviction of divine love, working to craft policies that displayed a measure of God's grace in the world. Affirming multi-national cultural diversity, advocating international peace, and inaugurating the Ethical Policy of Dutch colonialism were just three such manifestations of the unifying effect of God's grace in Dutch, and world, affairs.

Meditations and the Railroad Workers' Strike

After the victory of Kuyper's ARP and the religious coalition in the 1901 elections, Queen Wilhelmina reluctantly summoned Kuyper to the palace with the charge to form a cabinet. But she had a strict message for him regarding South Africa—the Netherlands would remain a neutral party, so as not to jeopardize British naval assistance in the East Indies.[46] Kuyper agreed to preserve the efforts of the previous government to reform the army and to achieve the pacification of the Aceh. Wilhelmina's instructions were just the beginning of his taxing transition to power. For example, while

45. Kuyper, *Work of the Holy Spirit*, 521.
46. See Bratt, *Abraham Kuyper*, 302.

Kuyper had campaigned on a platform of social reform, he found that such considerable reform had been made in the last decade under liberal rule that his practical options were more limited than he had imagined. Kuyper also had difficulty securing talented and willing colleagues to fill cabinet posts. Lohman declined to head the ministry of Domestic Affairs, as did the previous ARP prime minister, Aeneas Mackay. Theo Heemskerk, widely seen as Kuyper's eventual successor (and who served as prime minister from 1908–13), also refused to serve with him. Though Kuyper's brash personality diminished his ability to attract talented politicians to accept office in the new government, he remained determined to push forward with the ARP agenda of pluralistic, social reform.[47]

By the fall of 1902, a full year into his leadership, Kuyper was feeling the slow drag of the political process. While his introduction of a new ethical policy into the East Indies affairs had proved a marked success, there was little else to show for his efforts. Though he was heavily involved in policy making, he was in a sense unprepared for the slow and often ponderous realities of legislating, that is, of forming, debating, and enacting laws. His lack of formal training in law or the judiciary meant he had to rely on others to work out the legal technicalities of his ideas. It was during this time—in the midst of the heat and pressure of leading the government—that Kuyper began retreating to the mystical and pastoral side of life. He began a series of weekly meditations in *De Heraut* that were soon collected and published as *To Be Near Unto God*. Here, the governmental minister and the Christian mystic coalesced. As he pondered themes such as knowing and dwelling in God, love, confession, and forgiveness, Kuyper advanced a significant spiritual counterpoint to his more secular work in parliament. Perhaps surprisingly, some of his deepest spiritual reflections occurred during his years as prime minister, and they were recorded for his faithful readers in *To Be Near Unto God*. These words on the spiritual formation of the disciple provide an especially intriguing backdrop set against the most volatile and unexpected event of Kuyper's tenure in office—the wildcat railroad strike of 1903.

Strike!

For industrializing nations, the onset of the twentieth century was often characterized by labor strife and the competing ideological forces of socialism and capitalism. While certainly not a socialist, Kuyper nonetheless had cultivated a political reputation based on his concern for fairness and dignity among the working class; he was, in short, an advocate for worker's

---

47. See Bratt, *Abraham Kuyper*, 302–3.

rights. As such, he understood that a certain amount of unrest among the laborers could be regarded as a positive catalyst for change. What Kuyper—or the rest of the nation—could not anticipate, however, was how quickly that murmur of unrest would ignite into a major strike that would cripple the country's transportation infrastructure and merchant trade.

The unrest was building throughout 1902. In Amsterdam, a series of labor disputes had occurred among the diamond workers, building tradesmen, and textile workers, and their plight brought labor issues into the consciousness of the common workers.[48] By early January 1903, a series of spontaneous work stoppages began to sprout in the port of Amsterdam. Some shipping companies were trying to force a wage cut by hiring non-union laborers, but labor groups mobilized and soon more and more dockworkers joined together in striking. Then suddenly, on January 30, the railway workers in Amsterdam joined the strike in solidarity with the dockworkers. The railway strike spread quickly to other parts of the country and the major form of transportation throughout the Netherlands ground to a halt. Everyone from shunters and brakemen to engineers and crossing guards joined the strike. Goods could not be moved, the postal service had quickly to coordinate their deliveries using automobiles, and even the transportation of soldiers from Amersfoort to Amsterdam was delayed. The railroad strike was swift and effective. The Dutch government was unprepared for such an uprising, as were the various companies concerned. Such was the seriousness of the labor action that the workers' demands were quickly agreed to and, on January 31, the strike was called off.[49]

In the aftermath of the strike, everyone remained in a bit of a state of shock. The strike, although brief, had been (and remains to this day) the greatest example of social unrest that the Netherlands has ever experienced. And while some parties celebrated in jubilee, others quivered at the implications of what had occurred. Historian A. J. C. Rüter described the national mood at the time of the settlement: "The Socialists believe they are in heaven, conservatives of every hue at hell's gate. In the recent struggle, Domela Nieuwenhuis celebrates the first of a series of work strikes, Troelstra recommends the transport workers' strike as a means of forcing through universal suffrage. De Savornin Lohman speaks of anarchy, Kuyper of a coup d' etat. Nothing is lacking to fan the flame."[50] Kuyper's cabinet had elected to keep its distance during the work stoppages at the port, but with events having

---

48. Gerber, *Anton Pannekoek and the Socialism of Workers' Self Emancipation*, 36.
49. See de Bruijn, *Abraham Kuyper*, 282.
50. As quoted in de Bruijn, *Abraham Kuyper*, 283. See Rüter, *De Spoorwegstakingen van 1903*.

escalated so rapidly and forcefully with the addition of the railroad strike, it was clear that legislative matters were now in order. The country had been exposed to the possibility of anarchy, and its economic lifeblood—transportation and international trade—had been violently choked. Consequently, on February 25 Kuyper introduced three bills that aimed to address the workers' grievances, while at the same time protecting the nation from additional rogue work stoppages.

Parliament quickly took up Kuyper's proposals for debate. The first measure would create an independent commission to investigate the underlying causes of the strikes—which included long, irregular working hours and low wages—and then recommend reforms as needed to the railway directors. A second law would allow for the government to take over operation of public utilities (for example, railroads) in times of emergency and provide substitute workers. In this vein, even before the laws were proposed, Kuyper had called up the militia and began providing soldiers with the necessary training so that the government could continue to run the railroads in the event of another work stoppage. The final measure would classify strikes into two separate categories with different legal implications: strikes carried out for economic reasons (that is, wage disputes) would be considered legal, but those conducted for political purposes would be illegal and punishable by law.[51] The Socialists and Anarchists immediately seized on the proposals, especially the last measure; they declared class warfare and denounced Kuyper's proposals as "strangulation laws." Kuyper insisted the state had a responsibility to protect its citizens from the revolutionary efforts of a fringe faction.[52] As parliament debated the measures throughout March and into April, the Socialists and Anarchists set about organizing yet another strike—this one doggedly political in nature.

A second railway strike was scheduled for the night of April 5, 1903. Despite the perceived severity of Kuyper's proposals, the various strands of the labor movement were far from united. While the far-left wing delegates of the various parties and trade organizations were eager for a fight, the moderate-left Social-Democratic Workers Party advised against another strike. The SDAP was overruled, and a decisive "political" railway strike was set in direct response to Kuyper's "strangulation laws." This time, however, the government was ready. Abandoned stations and signal boxes were quickly confiscated and manned by soldiers, and police protected those railway employees who wanted to work. Additional emergency measures went

51. See Bratt, *Abraham Kuyper*, 309.
52. See Veenendaal, *Railways in the Netherlands*, 107-9; and Bratt, *Abraham Kuyper*, 309.

into effect, including modified train schedules and mail carried by automobile.[53] While rail traffic was disrupted, most notably in the busy Amsterdam sector, the trains never stopped completely—and after two days it became apparent that the strike was not going well. Calls for a national general strike across all sectors of the economy were largely ignored, and by April 10 the strike was called off.

This second strike proved an effective catalyst for the Second Chamber quickly and resolutely to enact Kuyper's proposals. But enactment came at a cost. Now that thousands of striking workers had been fired by the railway companies, the image of Kuyper as a heavy-handed authoritarian was cemented in the minds of many. Kuyper maintained he was acting in the best interest of the country, and he pointed to similar government measures that were taking place in other Western countries. In addition, the fact that Kuyper followed Lohman's advice of strong government intervention alienated him even more from the common workers—as Lohman was perceived as representing first and foremost the interest of the gentry. As such, Kuyper's response to the strikes of 1903 seriously damaged Kuyper's reputation—an impression that persists even to the present day. There was a sense that Kuyper—the politician of the *kleine luyden*—had abandoned his core principles when the going got tough. Subsequently, he had to face relentless criticism in the Chamber from foes like P. J. Troelstra and, despite his future success in education reform, he could not shake the damage done to his image by the railroad strike. Consequently, in the elections of 1905 his religious coalition lost the parliamentary majority and Kuyper stepped down as prime minister.[54]

Meditations in the Mayhem

In what ways did the life of discipleship influence Kuyper during these extraordinary political and social circumstances? A close examination of Kuyper's spiritual response to the political drama surrounding the railway strikes of 1903 can shed important light on this question. More specifically,

---

53. See Veenendaal, *Railways in the Netherlands*, 108.

54. De Bruijn quotes the Marxist historian Jan Romein on Kuyper's role in 1903: "To blame Kuyper on the basis of the 'strangulation laws' is not fair. After all—not only a Liberal, but also a Catholic and even a Social Democrat minister would have acted in much the same way, although he may have put things differently. History has borne that out sufficiently since then. However, there remains an unbridgeable gap between these laws and the expectations everyone had of Kuyper as a social politician when he came to office." See de Bruijn, *Abraham Kuyper*, 290. See also Bratt, *Abraham Kuyper*, 321–22.

by comparing Kuyper's contemporaneous writings in *To Be Near Unto God* with the events unfolding in 1903, it is possible to gauge his reflections on the inner life of the disciple in the midst of political turmoil. The result provides considerable insight into the relationship between the inner spirituality and the outer political action in the life of one of the Netherlands' most prominent political disciples.[55]

Kuyper's meditations in *To Be Near Unto God*, published in *De Heraut* during the tumultuous months of the strike and its political aftermath (January through November 1903), contains three themes of particular relevance to this examination: knowledge of God, love, and forgiveness. To start, it is telling that during the days and weeks immediately surrounding the dockworkers and railway strikes of January 1903, Kuyper's meditations in *De Heraut* seem to retreat dramatically into the deep mysteries of the knowledge of God. His meditation "Under the Shadow of the Almighty"—published January 15, at precisely the moment when the dockworkers strike was beginning to gain momentum—explained that the imagery of Matthew 23:37 ("Jerusalem, Jerusalem, how often would I have gathered thy children together as a hen gathereth her chickens under her wings and yet ye would not") and spoke of the protection and compassion of the Lord. Abiding in the shadow of the almighty (Ps 91:1), under the protection of God's wings (Ps 61:4), was the safe and secure place of our spiritual fellowship, for it was God alone who was our protection and our strength. In faith and belief, to be near unto God was to find rest and peace in the midst of turmoil: "The blessed peace, the hallowed rest, the childlike confidence which God's elect have always enjoyed, even in seasons of bitterest trial, is not the result of reasoning. It is not the effect of deliverance. It is solely and alone the sweet outcome of taking refuge in the secret place of the most High, of abiding under the shadow of the Almighty, of knowing what it means, "To Be Near Unto God," and of enjoying it."[56]

Kuyper's meditation was a serene reminder to his readers that in God's presence was protection from any and all of life's trials. As the dockworkers strike was growing and becoming more socially disruptive, Kuyper found a profound sense of peace in his knowledge and experience of God's protective presence. Yet his hiding in the shadow of the Spirit's wings was not to be regarded as a retreat from the political situation. Rather, it was a spiritual foundation upon which Kuyper could find reassurance and take decisive

---

55. Bratt makes a similar conclusion about the relationship between *To Be Near Unto God* and the railway strikes of 1903. In *Abraham Kuyper*, 314–19, Bratt specifically traces Kuyper's published meditations in *De Heraut* with the political (and at times personal) sparring in the Second Chamber between Kuyper and Troelstra of the SDAP.

56. Kuyper, *To Be Near Unto God*, 80.

political action. Over the next several weeks, as the political and social situation grew even more dire, Kuyper would delve deeper and deeper into the mysterious safety of God's embrace.

Revealingly, on February 1, the day after the initial resolution of the strikes, Kuyper published a meditation on the peace of Paradise. Entitled, "In the Wind of the Day," it reflects on the soft, warm breeze that announces the approach of God's Spirit. Kuyper described the biblical symbolism of the wind, and concluded that the goal of the disciple is to hear and be moved by the voice of God on the wind, each and every day. To miss this voice on the wind was to lose the day; "while blessed in turn is each day in which in 'the wind of the day' God comes so near to the soul that the approach turns into communion, in the intimacy and tenderness of which with fresh draughts we enjoy again the unfailing love of God."[57]

Kuyper continued to reflect on this intimacy of God in the following week's meditation, "Thou Settest a Print Upon the Roots of My Feet," which was published on February 8. Continuing his penchant for drawing on the Psalms, he wrote of the realities of life's dangers, anxieties, and disasters, "which overwhelm us, which we have no strength to face, which nothing can prevent, and in the midst of which we become suddenly aware of our utter helplessness."[58] In these frightful moments, even faithful disciples may no longer retain a grip on their faith; and God, too, may seem to have momentarily let go. Indeed, as in the case of David, who cried out against God's anger, "O my God, look away from me that I may recover strength before I die," in such moments God's grace is revealed. It was at those moments when God seems farthest away that "the Comforter comes to the soul, that the shield of Christ is placed again before us." It is even through God's anger that the Christian disciple—as a child—most experiences the love of the Father.[59]

Kuyper continued to expound on the knowledge of God as comforter, protector, father, and present peace all throughout *To Be Near Unto God*, and, strikingly, throughout the most heated moments around the labor events of early 1903. His February 15 meditation, for example, was titled "My Shield," followed by "Immanuel"—God with us. In subsequent meditations, Kuyper attempted to connect the knowledge of God with the will of God. As he reminded his readers, Christian living was not only a matter of knowing, it was about obedience to God's specific call. The June 7, 1903 meditation, "If Any Man Will Do His Will," was typical of his reflections

---

57. Kuyper, *To Be Near Unto God*, 87.
58. Kuyper, *To Be Near Unto God*, 89.
59. Kuyper, *To Be Near Unto God*, 92.

during this time: "God becomes known to us by studious thought, by play of the imagination, by inner experience and in other ways. But it cannot be denied that he also becomes known to us by the will."[60] In other words, discipleship was not just a matter of mystical retreat into a spiritual connection with God; knowing God required an action of the will, of obedience. And a central action of Christian obedience was love.

Indeed, for all the political upheaval of the times, Kuyper kept himself and his constituents firmly grounded in the mysteries of God through extensive reflections on the action of love. Even as Kuyper's labor laws proceeded quickly through Parliament during the spring of 1903, he faced increasing criticism, especially that his "strangulation laws" revealed a deep-seated hypocrisy. Some of his harshest critics (including Troelstra, the leader of the SDAP party in the Second Chamber) even began to attack Kuyper's character. As historian James Bratt explains, however, love became an important counter-measure to such attacks.[61] In this regard, Kuyper's meditation series on love, which ran during the summer months of 1903, offered a splendid opportunity to put Christian conviction into practice.

Kuyper's meditations on love ran in *De Heraut* from July 19 to September 6. The new parliamentary session would open on the third Tuesday of September, with a *Troonrede* speech prepared by Kuyper and read by the Queen. By this time, the labor issues had been addressed through legislative action, though social criticism remained, especially when, in the speech, the strikes were described as "criminal." Kuyper's plea focused on the importance of consistent and profound Christian obedience to the love of God with all one's heart, soul, mind, and strength. Faced with a profoundly difficult and complicated situation, where one was likely to make enemies on any (or every) side of the argument, Kuyper reflected on the nature of Christian love. This reflection focused on several aspects of love.

For example, Kuyper maintained that the order of love was important; unless God was loved first and foremost—as described in the greatest commandment—self-love and neighborly love were not possible. This mandate to love God, he added, was not the easiest, but the hardest thing to which faith called us—because loving God was not a philanthropic effort that could easily be given to the unfortunate.[62] No, loving God required disciples to die to themselves, "to abandon everything that separates us from God, and every moment of our life to live wholly for God."[63] Loving God pushed

60. Kuyper, *To Be Near Unto God*, 148.
61. See Bratt, *Abraham Kuyper*, 317.
62. See Kuyper, *To Be Near Unto God*, 189.
63. Kuyper, *To Be Near Unto God*, 190.

everything aside that drew us away from God, and only then were we free to hold communion with God. Loving God with all our heart, soul, mind, and strength (each a subsequent meditation entry) then enabled Christians to love their neighbors and themselves. But God must remain first; that is the source of the power to act in love towards others. Without the deep cultivation of this holistic, godly love, actions of sacrifice were reduced to mere charity.

The action of Christian love, therefore, carried a distinct and ultimately transforming characteristic—forgiveness. Kuyper had earlier written about forgiveness in a meditation entitled "Increasing in the Knowledge of God," published on June 14, 1903. Here, he exonerated his readers: Christian forgiveness "must be honest forgiveness without any reservation. Our greatest enemy must be forgiven. Those who curse us we must bless. We must love those who despitefully use us. Consider it carefully: we must love our enemy."[64] Kuyper illustrated the nature of discipleship in a most tangible way; Christian forgiveness was a mandate in order to come into knowledge of God. Forgiveness, as in love, first turned the disciples' eyes away from themselves and onto God. Then, and only then, forgiveness can be directed towards others—even and especially towards our enemies.

Such a test of forgiveness moved from the theoretical to the practical when Kuyper received a particularly vicious attack on his character. In the March 8, 1903 edition of *Het Volk*, the political cartoonist Albert Hahn published a dark caricature of a beady-eyed Kuyper strangling a chained-down laborer; the caption quoted Kuyper's famous social justice speech to the Christian-Social Congress in 1891: "This is how one tames animals, this is how one breaks the wild, but this is not how one rules a nation." The implications were clear: Kuyper was viewed as not only brutally violent and authoritarian, but also as aggressively hypocritical. Kuyper commented that "I felt insulted by that picture in the most grievous way"—so much so that legal proceedings were brought against the exhibition of the caricature.[65] However, whatever the damage that had been done to his political image and personal character, Kuyper knew that even legal proceedings could not absolve the pain. Only Christian forgiveness could bring restoration—and he knew he needed to ink this truth in permanence, for himself: "Our greatest enemy must be forgiven. Those who curse us we must bless. We must love those who despitefully use us."[66] Kuyper penned these words out of his

---

64. Kuyper, *To Be Near Unto God*, 155.
65. See de Bruijn, *Abraham Kuyper*, 285.
66. Kuyper, *To Be Near Unto God*, 155.

own personal experience. And he knew they required the continual action of Christian love.

As the summer of 1903 moved into fall, and the days of November darkened earlier each day, Kuyper continued to deal with the fallout from the recent labor disputes. He knew he had made the best decision for the country, but he was still grieved—both by the continued backlash of his critics, and also because he truly believed in the importance of workers' rights. His political decisions were not a reversal of earlier positions, but a practical outworking and the necessity of action in a dangerous social situation. He continued to wonder what he could have done differently and what missteps had been taken. In politics as in other aspects of life, Kuyper meditated on the nature of conflict, affliction, forgiveness, confession, and even prayer and fasting. On November 8, he published a meditation entitled "I Acknowledge My Sin Unto Thee." Here, he admitted that, "in the end even sin is compelled to become a means of leading us into deeper knowledge of God and of making the majesty of the Lord to shine upon us more brightly."[67] Sin, terrible sin—in one's own life or in the life of others—had as its greater end the realization of God's holiness. In love, forgiveness, confession, and reconciliation, God was made known. To be near unto God, then, was a matter of spiritual meditation for the purpose and ability of Christian action; and, in this dynamic of being with God and acting in obedience to God, the disciple treasured the intimate peace and presence of the knowledge of God. From this place of spiritual certainty, Kuyper could re-group and face the second half of his cabinet's term with greater resolve. Before long, he was fully enveloped in shaping a lasting legacy of education reform. And while his theological convictions were as firm and insightful as ever, the political turmoil was far from over.

Education Reform and the Theological Practice of Common Grace

Education reform was one of the central concerns of Kuyper's entire political and professional career.[68] Reform of both the primary and higher education systems was a driving force behind his initial involvement as a member of the Second Chamber in the Dutch parliament as early as 1874, and then the issue dominated his cabinet's agenda during his tenure as prime minister. In addition, Kuyper had a personal stake in this matter; he had founded the Free University in Amsterdam in 1880 as the first institution of higher

---

67. Kuyper, *To Be Near Unto God*, 270.
68. See Himes, "Better Worldliness," for a previous version of this section.

education in the Netherlands to exist apart from state control, but even in 1904 the university did not enjoy equal institutional status with other Dutch universities. Education in the Netherlands was a complicated and storied issue, and so it is worth taking some time to set the stage for the reform debate. Keep in mind that not only this issue in itself, but also Kuyper's method of engagement—as a disciple—to effect change, offers important insight into the relationship between a concern for the common good and a foundational understanding of one of Kuyper's most important and lasting theological developments: the notion of common grace.

Education Reform in the Netherlands: A Brief History

The catalyst for the debate over education reform dated back to the aftermath (or impact) of the French Revolution on Dutch society. Prior to 1795, Dutch state schools incorporated the values of the Reformed tradition by teaching the *Heidelberg Catechism*. In this way, the Reformed tradition survived as a central resource for the moral and spiritual development of Dutch citizens. As the Revolution spilled into the Netherlands, however, with its emphasis on secularism and individual *lassie-faire* liberty, Dutch schools began to teach a form of Christianity deprived of its confessional nature. While both public and private primary schools were allowed to exist during the era of Napoleonic rule, a law passed in 1806 prevented state funds from subsidizing private Christian schools and promoted a kind of civil religion in the public schools. Napoleon believed that civil religion was necessary for the moral formation of society, but his policies—and those of the Dutch government after Napoleon's defeat in 1813—favored the rise of secular ideology in education.[69]

When Kuyper commenced his political career, it was in large part to influence education reform. He had served in a pastorate in the small country village of Beesd after finishing his theological studies at the University of Leiden in 1863. In 1867, he took a pastorate in Utrecht and then found himself entering into the debate regarding the state school system. He published articles arguing that state schools, with their promotion of secularism, were not neutral due to the intrinsic aggressive secular value system they had inherited from the Revolution.[70] Accordingly, he felt that

---

69. See McGoldrick, *God's Renaissance Man*, 53–54. See also Bratt, *Abraham Kuyper*, 10–11.

70. Note that the 1848 Constitution addressed the issue of secularization in the schools with a provision that public schools train children in "Christian and social virtues" while making sure not to offend any pupil or parent. This watered-down attempt

Christians should be able to establish private, confessionally-based schools that were independent of the state system. To his disdain, the conservative clergy in Utrecht refused to support him; and so, when he received a call to serve a pastorate in Amsterdam in 1870, he quickly and gratefully accepted. Once in Amsterdam, Kuyper became chief editor of the weekly religious newspaper *De Heraut*. He soon founded the daily periodical *De Standaard* in order to provide additional voice and leadership to the emerging cultural battle that lay ahead. Within a few short years of his arrival in Amsterdam, Kuyper ran for election to the lower house of Parliament. He easily won a seat, and in 1874—by state law—he resigned his clerical orders to take up the life of politics. Kuyper, however, as we have seen, always regarded himself as a religious leader, even (and perhaps especially) in the political realm. Fittingly, he took up the school question in his first parliamentary address, losing none of the Calvinist vigor he had exuded previously in the pulpit.[71]

At a fundamental level, the education question was about worldview. Kuyper argued that while the national government had the responsibility to set the standards for primary school education, it should not hold a monopoly on administering education because, in doing so, the state was institutionalizing a secular worldview. Kuyper believed that education was foundationally the responsibility of the family, and so he felt that parents had a right to send their children to schools that accorded with their own worldviews—religious or otherwise. He wanted the state to provide funding for both public and private schools, so as not to penalize families financially for wanting to educate their children in a manner that was consistent with their values and worldview.

The debate escalated in 1878 when the liberal ruling party introduced a wide-ranging education reform bill. The bill stipulated that the federal government would pay the cost of the reforms for the public schools, but not for the independent schools. After the bill was passed by parliament, but before it came to King Willem III for his signature, Kuyper joined with Catholic leaders to organize a massive petition-signing campaign protesting the nature of the bill. In August, they presented their petition to the king with 469,000 signatures, urging him to reject the bill—quite a feat considering at the time that only 122,000 people were eligible to vote. Although the king did receive the petition, he signed the law in August 1878. Despite their defeat, the petition-signing campaign provided Kuyper and his followers with a great sense of enthusiasm and momentum. In April 1879, they

---

at neutrality only clouded the educational values at stake. See Bratt, *Abraham Kuyper*, 68–69.

71. See Wolterstorff, "Abraham Kuyper (1837–1920)," 289–94.

organized into the first mass political party in the Netherlands under the name the Antirevolutionary Party (making a clear distinction from the secular values inherent in the French Revolution). One of their uniting causes was the formation of a national organization to aid in the establishment of independent Christian schools.[72]

About this time Kuyper was also taking action in the area of university reform. The 1848 Constitution had stipulated the principle of educational freedom, and, in 1876, parliament had passed a bill providing for the possibility of the establishment of independent institutions of higher education. From 1878, Kuyper worked toward the goal of establishing the first university apart from state control in the Netherlands.[73] His efforts were realized in 1880 with the opening of the Free University in Amsterdam, an institution that would bear the Reformed worldview within all subject matters, including not just theology, but also law, medicine, and aesthetics. In his inaugural address, Kuyper proclaimed that the concept of "sphere sovereignty" was the hallmark of the Free University, and as such (given its Reformed character) it held a distinct place within the nation's ranks of higher education. The concept of "sphere sovereignty" affirmed the lordship of Jesus Christ over all areas of life, and in doing so freed and encouraged the pursuit of revealed truth in all aspects of life and all academic subjects. In Kuyper's famous words, "No single piece of our mental world is to be hermetically sealed off from the rest, and there is not a square inch in the whole domain of our human existence over which Christ, who is sovereign over *all*, does not cry: 'Mine!'"[74]

The founding of the Free University was certainly an important milestone in Kuyper's education reform efforts, but his work in this area was just beginning. It soon became apparent that Kuyper's minority ARP would have a difficult, if not impossible, time gaining sufficient influence in parliament to enact its platform. In 1880, however, the first Catholic clergyman, Herman Schaepman, was elected as a representative to the Second Chamber of Parliament. Over time, Kuyper and Schaepman became friends, eventually agreeing to form an Antirevolutionary-Catholic political coalition. While their parties maintained their own distinct platforms, they both endeavored to enact a pluralistic education system in the Netherlands that would allow for the support of independent religious schools. Their parties also shared a commitment to various other causes, such as workers' rights and suffrage. Some within Kuyper's ranks were furious that he would partner with the

---

72. See Wolterstorff, "Abraham Kuyper (1837–1920)," 294–95.
73. See Wolterstorff, "Abraham Kuyper (1837–1920)," 295.
74. Kuyper, "Sphere Sovereignty," 488.

"papists," but this coalition succeeded in bringing power to its first government in 1888. This same coalition enabled Kuyper's rise to prime minister in 1901, and continued to be major political force for a further generation.[75]

The Antirevolutionary-Catholic cabinet that was formed as a result of the 1888 elections quickly enacted two major legislative reforms. Under Prime Minister Baron Aeneas Mackay, the government focused immediately on school reform and labor laws. The School Law of 1889 provided up to 30% government funding for primary private schools and was easily passed in a Parliament with a confessional-coalition majority. It was not the full-funding of private schools desired by Kuyper, but it was a step in the right direction—as the principle of a plural education system was introduced. It is also worth noting that the Labor Law of 1889 made a modest beginning towards the protection of workers. It set a minimum requirement of twelve years of age for workers, and it prevented women and those under sixteen from working more than eleven hours a day and from working at night. This was an important labor law in Dutch legislative history, and it was a signature achievement of the Antirevolutionary Party and its confessional coalition.[76]

Kuyper became prime minister when the Antirevolutionary-Catholic coalition once again gained the majority in the parliamentary elections of 1901. Not surprisingly, the reform of primary and higher education was one of the new cabinet's legislative priorities. Through much turmoil—including the massive railroad strike in 1903—Kuyper's cabinet was finally able to mediate a debate on higher education in 1904.[77] Kuyper argued for the complete liberation of Christian higher education from the state monopoly in the granting of degrees. True, the present law allowed for the establishment of non-public universities, but students at those schools were still required to take state-administered exams in order to receive a degree. Thus, the students at the Free University—the only such private institution at the time—in effect had to earn passing marks not only from their own institution, but also from the state sponsored education program. Kuyper's bill set-out to provide degree-granting status to all universities which met a certain set of state requirements, making the case-in-point that doctors, lawyers, and educators who were trained in a Reformed educational system were as qualified as those who had graduated from the state system. Additionally,

---

75. See Langley, *Practice of Political Spirituality*, 32 and 137. Note that the Protestant-Catholic coalition party was in power until 1994. See also Wolterstorff, "Abraham Kuyper (1837–1920)," 296.

76. See Langley, *Practice of Political Spirituality*, 39–41. See also Wolterstorff, "Abraham Kuyper (1837–1920)," 296.

77. See Flipse, *Christelijke wetenschap*.

the bill provided financial subsidies for private universities, and also established the provision for a new technical university. Kuyper's bill argued in favor of a form of educational pluralism that would place all universities in the Netherlands on equal footing. In his arguments, he noted that important contributions were coming from private institutions throughout the world, like the Catholic University in Belgium, and Johns Hopkins and Harvard in the United States. As such, this was not just a particular concern for the Free University, but also would promote the creation of any number of religious or non-religious institutions of higher education. Of course, the Catholics became an important ally in support of the bill, even though they would not open a university of their own in the Netherlands until 1923.

The debate over the bill was bitter. In March 1904, the Second Chamber succeeded in passing the bill, but it was rejected by the opposition-controlled First Chamber. Prime Minister Kuyper then made the unusual move of asking Queen Wilhelmina to dissolve the First Chamber and call for new elections. She obliged and new elections were held that summer. When the newly elected First Chamber convened, the confessional coalition held a majority. Kuyper reintroduced the bill and it passed on May 20, 1905. When the Queen signed the bill two days later, Kuyper had secured one of the crowning achievements of his life. He had helped to bring equality and opportunity not only to Christian higher education, but also to all future private universities in the Netherlands.[78]

Kuyper's Antirevolutionary Party suffered a narrow defeat in the elections of 1905. His subsequent resignation as prime minister was a great disappointment, in that he had not yet fulfilled all of his aspirations to enact educational reform, to say nothing of his desire to expand social justice and cultural pluralism. The confessional coalition was voted back in office in 1909, however, with Heemskerk serving as prime minister, Kuyper was not offered a cabinet position. While he continued to be involved as an elder statesman in the Party, Kuyper would no longer hold government office.[79] In 1913, the ARP lost the general election and the new prime minister, P. W. A. Cort van der Linden, formed a Liberal coalition which ruled until 1918. Linden's government sought to end the years of political tension between the liberal and confessional-coalition parties, and so introduced bills providing constitutional support of educational pluralism, including full state funding of private institutions. Another bill introduced proportional

---

78. See Langley, *Practice of Political Spirituality*, 103–12.

79. Kuyper was a member of the Second Chamber from 1908–12 and served in the First Chamber from 1913–20.

representation, as well as universal suffrage for men.[80] By 1917, Kuyper had lived to see the victory of his fifty-year struggle for educational pluralism and social justice.[81] Although the work of equality and democracy would never be complete, Kuyper could take great satisfaction in seeing the tangible results of his hard-fought advocacy for Christian principles.

Common Grace: The Lynchpin

Kuyper's involvement in the debates over education reform emerged from his core theological beliefs and convictions. Central to Kuyper's legislative goals was his understanding of God's sovereignty and grace. He fought hard to advance pluralism in Dutch education, not merely in order to allow him to establish a Christian university, but also because his understanding of the lordship of Jesus Christ meant that each sphere of society had a divine right to exist in its own form. Accordingly, the state should not hold captive the realm of education. The state certainly had a responsibility to support education, for the good of its citizens and for the good of society as a whole, but it was not primarily responsible for enacting education. That should be left to the schools—and the schools should represent the pluralistic views of the population. Kuyper articulated a unique concept of Christian grace, which emerged from his Reformed perspective, in support of educational pluralism. It is here that Kuyper's notion of common grace speaks most clearly to the question of a discipleship intended for the common good.

Kuyper's advocacy for various forms of pluralism emerged from his Calvinist conviction that God's grace enabled the on-going cultivation of culture and society in order to advance justice and liberation. Never reticent about expressing publically his Christian beliefs, the emergence of Kuyper's notion of common grace can be documented in the pages of *De Heraut* between 1895 and 1901. Upon completion, these articles were collected and published in three volumes under the title *De Gemeene Gratia* (*Common Grace*), the first appearing simultaneously with his election as prime minister in 1901. Kuyper's concept of common grace did not emerge without controversy. Some of his conservative opponents accused him of inventing a new teaching. Kuyper countered by insisting that he was only developing what had come before in Calvin. The result was a nuanced understanding of the relationship between the "saving" grace for the elect and the "common" grace which fell over the rest of creation. His comprehensive theological reasoning on these grounds provided for (among other things) the

---

80. Women were granted universal suffrage in 1919.
81. See Langley, *Practice of Political Spirituality*, 154.

framework for the ARP legislative platform, it allowed for the cooperation with the Catholic and other confessional political parties, and it provided his own Calvinist constituency the means and encouragement to engage with the broader realms of society. As James Bratt has remarked, "Common grace was thus a theology of public responsibility, of Christians' shared humanity with the rest of the world. It was also, in the words of one historian, 'the valve through which Kuyper pumped fresh air into his people.'"[82] Common grace built a bridge between Calvinists and the non-Calvinists; it encouraged contributions from Calvinists in a number of areas, including politics and scholarship; and, it introduced Calvinists to the wonders and beauty of the arts and sciences that flourished in the wider culture. To attempt to explain the existence of this bridge between Christians and the larger society, Kuyper presented his argument for common grace in two categories: creation and history, and church and culture.

Kuyper looked first to the creation account in Genesis to deduce two manifestations of God's grace. On the occasion of the first sin, he noted, "Death, in its full effect, did not set in on that day, and Reformed theologians have consistently pointed out how in this non-arrival of what was prophesied for ill we see the emergence of a saving and long-suffering grace."[83] Both forms of grace worked to advance God's glory. The first, a *saving* grace, would work to overcome the effects of sin and its consequences of death and eternal separation from God. The second, a *common* grace, was a temporal restraining grace that held back the full effects of sin in the present world, and extended to the whole of human life.[84] Anticipating his detractors, whom he believed would argue in terms of the antithesis between the elect and non-elect, Kuyper explained that special grace must presuppose common grace if there was to be an appropriate focus on God's glory. Such a focus emphasized the work of Jesus Christ not only as savior, but also as creator of the world. The lordship of Jesus Christ thus demanded an inseparable connection between grace and nature. As Kuyper explained: "You cannot see grace in all its riches if you do not perceive how its tiny roots and fibers everywhere penetrate into the joints and cracks of the life of nature. And you cannot validate that connectedness if, with respect to grace, you first look at the salvation of your own soul and not primarily on the *Christ of God*."[85] In retaining the connection between the concepts of nature and grace, Kuyper maintained that grace did not function exclusively in the

---

82. Bratt, "Editor's Introduction," 165.
83. Kuyper, "Common Grace," 167.
84. See Kuyper, "Common Grace," 168.
85. See Kuyper, "Common Grace," 173.

realm of the elect. In fact, human history was a testimony to the sustaining work of grace enacted for God's glory, which even for the elect remained something of a mystery. As he wrote, the work of common grace

> encompasses the whole life of the world, the life of Kaffirs in Africa, of Mongols in China and Japan, and of the Indians south of the Himalayas. In all previous centuries there was nothing among Egyptians and Greeks, in Babylon and Rome, nor is there anything today among the peoples of whatever continent that was or is not necessary. All of it was an indispensable part of the great work that God is doing to consummate the world's development. And though a great deal in all this *we* cannot connect with the Kingdom or the content of our faith, nevertheless it all has meaning. None of it can be spared because it pleases God, despite Satan's devices and human sin, to actualize everything he had put into this world at the time of creation, to insist on its realization, to develop it so completely that the full sum of its vital energies may enter the light of day at the consummation of the world.[86]

Common grace thus bore witness to the glorious and mysterious work of God's sovereignty over all creation and throughout all of history. And while some would argue that the cross of Christ was "the center of world history," Kuyper instead advanced an understanding of the creation and redemption of the world together in Jesus Christ.[87] He sought to explain this tension by describing the church not as an institution, but as an organism.

Kuyper felt it was important to make a distinction between the church as institution and the church as organism. As an institution, he explained, the church was an apparatus, "grounded in human choices, decisions, and acts of the will, consisting of members, officers, and useful supplies."[88] However, the church in fact was an organism, "in its hidden unity as the mystical body of Christ existing partly in heaven, partly on earth, and partly unborn, having penetrated all peoples and nations, possessing Christ as its natural and glorious head, and living by the Holy Spirit who as a life-engendering and life-maintaining force animates both head and members."[89] This is important because Kuyper understood that the nature of the church was primarily social. As such, it gave witness both to special, saving grace and

---

86. Kuyper, "Common Grace," 176.

87. Kuyper, "Common Grace," 182–83. Kuyper particularly looked to the Gospel of John to support his argument: "John begins not with the Mediator of redemption but with the Mediator of creation."

88. Kuyper, "Common Grace," 187.

89. Kuyper, "Common Grace," 187.

to common grace. The church certainly worked directly for the well-being of the elect, but it also worked "*indirectly* for the well-being of the whole of civil society, constraining it to civic virtue."[90] The church thus stood as a light shining on a hill in the very midst of society and culture. Rather than fleeing from the world, the church must allow its light to shine ever brighter through its windows, illuminating all aspects of society and culture with the gracious reality of Jesus Christ, creator and savior of all.

At this juncture, two points related to how Kuyper's life and thought contribute to an understanding of a discipleship for the common good become clear. His confessional commitment to the lordship of Jesus Christ over both creation and salvation enabled an extremely robust engagement in the political structures of the Netherlands. His concept of common grace allowed him to forge political partnerships through coalitions with the Catholics. While careful to respect the differences of the two bodies, Kuyper recognized that the basis for their similar outlooks forged them into effective allies standing firm against the rise of secularism in Dutch society. Furthermore, Kuyper's concept of common grace was the principle motivation behind his efforts to enact pluralism in education reform. He saw God's grace permeating all aspects of society, and so felt it was the responsibility of Christians to aid in the formation of—and participation in—culture. Creating the space for Christian education was not about isolating Christians from the influence of secularism; it was about affirming the rights of parents to educate their children in a diversity of worldviews and not allow the state unquestionably to advocate for a single particular ideology. This, at its base, was an issue of justice for Kuyper—which is why, in addition to education reform, his legislative program included (among other things) furthering the rights of ordinary people through expanded labor laws and voting rights. In short, for Kuyper common grace was the catalyst for a political career that focused on the promotion of the common good for all people in the Netherlands. His policies were not for the exclusive benefit of Calvinists, who formed only one segment of society. Kuyper had a much broader view for his task as a disciple; he worked for the good of the nation as a whole, and he did so from a conviction based on the reality of God's grace as manifested in the lordship of Jesus Christ.

Conclusion: Discipleship for the Common Good

Kuyper was incapable of separating his politics from his theological convictions. This often frustrated his opponents to no end, and it fittingly

90. Kuyper, "Common Grace," 190.

endeared him to his constituents. But the relationship between Kuyper's political actions and his spirituality was anything but opportunistic. Here, as we have seen, was a Christian disciple with the most furious theological commitments—to God's sovereignty, grace, love, and power—commitments that directly shaped and motivated his concerns for how the Dutch people could interact with each other and with the world. Kuyper's faith was not limited to personal piety. On the contrary, his faith was a very public affair—not only out of a concern to motivate his fellow Calvinists, but also because of his theological belief in God's concern and sustaining grace for the rest of the world. Kuyper saw in God's providence a commitment to the common good of all creation; theologically, therefore, he had no choice but to live a life of discipleship that was equally committed to the public good of society as a whole. Even as he sought to apply the traditional tenets of Calvinism in new and creative ways—thus the neo-Calvinist label that accompanies his particular Dutch brand of Reformed theology—he never lost sight of God's holiness and God's sustaining grace. Holding these together in a form of creative tension enabled Kuyper to demonstrate, through his writings and his life, the Christian mandate to follow Jesus Christ into all aspects of society and culture. From international conflict and debates over imperialism, to furious labor disputes, and even to complicated matters of educational reform, Kuyper's understanding of discipleship infused each of his actions. Building on the foundation of divine revelation, to the reality of the sovereignty of Jesus Christ, through the actions of love in belief and obedience, Kuyper's discipleship erupted into a myriad of possibilities and potentialities. His faith equipped him to face the most difficult and magnanimous political affairs of his generation, for it drew from the deep well of God's intimate mysteries. His was a life of Christian discipleship in every sense.

Part 2

Dietrich Bonhoeffer's Theology of Discipleship

1935–1945

Chapter 3

A Discipleship of Simple Obedience, 1935–1939

From a human point of view there are countless possibilities of understanding and interpreting the Sermon on the Mount. Jesus knows only one possibility: simply go and obey.

—Dietrich Bonhoeffer, *Discipleship*

Confusion, Confession, and Forgiveness

IN THE SUMMER OF 1936, Dietrich Bonhoeffer was directing the Confessing Church preachers' seminary in the Pomeranian outpost of Finkenwalde, near the Baltic Sea. This was the third six-month session at Finkenwalde, and so a certain rhythm of communal life had already been established; each day was punctuated with regular worship, shared meals, lectures, ministry, time alone, time together, and recreation.[1] During this session, Bonhoeffer gave a lecture series on pastoral care, where he placed a particular emphasis on the nature of personal confession and forgiveness. Wolf-Dieter Zimmermann was a student in Finkenwalde at the time, and his copious notes on these lectures provide a glimpse into both the content of Bonhoeffer's ideas and the reception of those ideas by a young Confessing

---

1. See Bonhoeffer, *DBWE* 14:1031–32.

Church seminarian. From Zimmermann's notes, it is clear that personal confession played a critical role in the life of the seminary.

Bonhoeffer taught the seminarians that personal confession was an essential practice in the life of the pastor; he identified it as the "heart of pastoral care" and equated the exhortation to be a Christian with the appeal to go to personal confession.[2] But questions were raised: "Why is my personal confession before God not sufficient? Why must I confess to my brother?"[3] The answer, explained Bonhoeffer, was threefold. First, confession was needed to guard against God simply being a phantom who appeared when one forgave his or her own sins. In other words, confession to another brought objectivity to sin, and it allowed another person to offer objective absolution of sin. Second, sin would continue to poison the individual (and perhaps even the community) as long as it remained hidden; there was "material decomposition within the soul" when sin was not exposed.[4] Confession was like the swift strike of the blade that cut off a snake's head when it came out of a hole. It put an immediate stop to sin's encroachment. Third, Bonhoeffer argued, because the root of sin was *superbia* (pride)—I want to be for myself and I have a right to myself—confession was a most profound humiliation before one's brother; but this humiliation was actually a liberation from the self-centeredness of pride.[5]

Confession, Bonhoeffer went on to describe, was a central act of discipleship: "In personal confession, we surrender ourselves completely to the mercy, help, and justice of God."[6] Discipleship meant surrender, and "leaving everything that is dear to us."[7] Bonhoeffer described here not just a material surrender, but an internal surrender of pride—a surrender only fully realized in the act of confessing to another. Confession thus established a strong fellowship, first among two people, and then among the entire church-community. As absolution resonated in the hearts of the downcast,

---

2. See Bonhoeffer, *DBWE* 14:592.
3. Bonhoeffer, *DBWE* 14:593.
4. Bonhoeffer, *DBWE* 14:593.
5. See Bonhoeffer, *DBWE* 14:593–94. See also Bonhoeffer's discussion of pride in *Life Together, DBWE* 5:111, where he wrote, in part: "In confession there occurs a *breakthrough to the cross*. The root of all sin is pride, *superbia*. I want to be for myself; I have a right to myself, a right to my hatred and my desires, my life and my death. The spirit and flesh of human beings are inflamed by pride, for it is precisely in their wickedness that human beings want to be like God."
6. Bonhoeffer, *DBWE* 14:594.
7. Bonhoeffer, *DBWE* 14:594.

God's mercy, love, and grace were realized. There was a new love for Christ, a new obedience and service, and a profound joy in the gospel.[8]

But, as Bonhoeffer and the Finkenwalde seminarians discovered, confession was not easy—and it could even be tumultuous in the life of the community. For example, as the summer session was coming to a close in August of 1936, Bonhoeffer cancelled classes for a few days so the brothers could spend time at the beach in Misdroy, along the Baltic coast. But even in times of recreation and relaxation, Bonhoeffer expected the seminarians to maintain a measure of order and moderation. And that expectation was not always well-received. In an August 2, 1936 letter to his friend and colleague Eberhard Bethge, Bonhoeffer described a frustrating incident that occurred between himself and five other brothers while at Misdroy. The evening started as usual, with dinner at 7:00 pm and then free time until devotions were held at 9:45 pm:

> At devotions I mentioned how, regardless of where we might be, we never get away from being Christians and theologians (Ps 119: "Your commandment lasts forever"). Not much different than is otherwise usually the case. Then all hell broke loose after the devotions. Dieter Zimmermann came up first, insisting that he just could not stand it any longer, because the contradiction between the world and his present existence was just unbearable. Between evening [dinner] and devotions, five brothers had gone out together and were overwhelmed by temptation at the sight of the "world," indeed by an unbearable desire for pleasure, dancing, girls, etc. Two went off with girls with whom they had spoken. Nothing else happened. But a terrible onslaught of nature against the world emerged. Then we had devotions, and that was just too much.[9]

Bonhoeffer went on to describe an "almost threatening" confrontation when the other four caught up with him and Zimmermann at about 11:00 pm: "We have to speak with you *now*."[10] They sat facing each other on the beach, with no one else around. As Bonhoeffer let them speak, one after the other, "there were wild outbursts of sexual desire against the word of God. They spoke in completely frank language."[11] Then there was silence. "After each had finished speaking, he seemed to be completely depleted. The five stood against me and against themselves. . . . All I could do was pray to myself and

8. See Bonhoeffer, *DBWE* 14:594.
9. Bonhoeffer, *DBWE* 14:229.
10. Bonhoeffer, *DBWE* 14:229.
11. Bonhoeffer, *DBWE* 14:230.

ask the Lord Christ to step in."[12] When he did find the words, Bonhoeffer spoke in terms reminiscent of what the brothers had heard earlier in the session regarding personal confession: "I hardly even know now what I said then, something about the status of the Christian, about desires that pass away, about personal confession and conversion, about our joy in Christ, and about the easy yoke."[13] There in Misdroy, on the beach, late at night, the brothers were confronted again with their continual conversion towards the theme of discipleship. In the frustration, humiliation, guilt, and confusion of the students, Bonhoeffer helped point the way to Jesus: "At the conclusion, we all prayed together. Jesus was the stronger one. At the end, we hardly knew what had happened."[14] The confession was difficult, even confusing. Were the brothers indeed asking for forgiveness, or seeking a way to justify their feelings and actions? In offering absolution, was Bonhoeffer himself willing to absolve, or, as Bethge later wrote in the *Biography*, was he "harsh to the point of injustice"?[15] In any case, Bonhoeffer recognized that more prayer was needed, both for discernment, as well as for strength and mercy. In the end, some brothers would not find the strength to continue standing against a corrupted German state—against the world—and others would remain faithful disciples to their death. Bonhoeffer understood that following Jesus Christ was not just about avoiding worldly temptations; discipleship was about whole-life surrender to the word of God, whether cloistered off in a seminary in a corner of northern Germany, or out enjoying the pleasures of the Baltic coast. He certainly held the brothers to a high standard; but the ultimate stakes were even higher.

It can be easy to idealize Bonhoeffer's work at the Confessing Church preachers' seminary in Finkenwalde. We read lectures about the way of discipleship and the wonders of confession, and can too easily picture a community with unrealistic insulation from the world. But life in the community of disciples was (and is) not easy. Making the connection from theory to actually living in community rarely is. This chapter aims to illuminate that realistic connection by describing how Bonhoeffer both developed and sought to live out his emerging theology of discipleship. In this way, an abstract theology can become alive, and can contain real implications for life in the world. As with Abraham Kuyper, the four principle movements of discipleship develop and resonate with Bonhoeffer's life and thought during this time. As such, this chapter aims first to establish Bonhoeffer's unique

12. Bonhoeffer, *DBWE* 14:230.
13. Bonhoeffer, *DBWE* 14:230.
14. Bonhoeffer, *DBWE* 14:230.
15. Bethge, *Dietrich Bonhoeffer*, 542.

understanding of discipleship in terms of *revelation, reality, action*, and *possibility*, concentrating specifically on how these themes play out in his influential book *Discipleship*; then, it explores how Bonhoeffer's experiment in theological education at Zingst and Finkenwalde worked to prepare ministers who were uniquely equipped to confront the world with the profound grace of Jesus Christ. In the second half of the chapter, the period of theological education underground is examined in light of the recurring theme of simple obedience to the Sermon on the Mount. As the grip of the Reich Church closed tighter around the Confessing Church, we see how Bonhoeffer continued to minister to and lead his brothers in the church struggle. The chapter traces this struggle within the Confessing Church up until the outbreak of the war in September 1939. At that point in time, everything changed.

Theological Movements in *Discipleship*

This book argues that a particular paradigm of discipleship can be traced throughout the life and work of both Kuyper and Bonhoeffer. As with Kuyper, these chapters also argue that Bonhoeffer's concept of discipleship can be understood and examined as occurring in four distinct yet interweaving movements: *revelation* is the *foundation* of discipleship; *Jesus Christ* is the *reality* of discipleship; *belief-obedience* is the *action* of discipleship; and, ultimately, the *possibility* of discipleship is being in and for the *common good of the world*. A previous publication has argued that these four movements can be traced throughout the development of the entire corpus of Bonhoeffer's professional life and work—from *Sanctorum Communio* through *Discipleship* and into *Ethics* and *Letters and Papers from Prison*.[16] While it is still vital to see this theme of discipleship as a unifying theme throughout his work, this chapter will focus on how these themes work themselves out in the key publication of this 1935–1939 period, *Discipleship*.

It is largely because Bonhoeffer's life and thought are so characterized and shaped by his extraordinary journey that a theological hermeneutic of discipleship is appropriate. *Nachfolge* (discipleship/following-after) not only defines Bonhoeffer's concept of discipleship, it also serves to describe his life-response to his historical situation. At each step on his path, Bonhoeffer sought to follow-after Jesus Christ. His life is in many ways a case study in Christian response and responsibility. He often could not anticipate the outcomes of his choices, but he always believed in the faithfulness of God to lead and shine enough light to allow him to take the next step of the journey.

16. See Himes, "Discipleship as Theological Praxis."

Bonhoeffer's life was marked by a steady commitment to follow-after Christ. Certainly an interpretive framework which seeks theologically and historically to describe this phenomenon can do much to further illuminate and explain Bonhoeffer's legacy.

Revelation: The Foundation of Discipleship

Bonhoeffer's theology was, through and through, a theology of revelation. In the vein of Karl Barth, Bonhoeffer espoused a theological program that was ever and always grounded in God's act of self-revelation.[17] His understanding of discipleship was no exception. For Bonhoeffer, the foundation and starting point of discipleship was not in the human possibility, but rather in the revelation of God manifest in the gracious call of Jesus Christ: "Come to me, all who are weary and heavy laden, and I will give you rest. Take my yoke upon you, and learn from me; for I am gentle and humble in heart, and you will find rest for your souls. For my yoke is easy, and my burden is light" (Matt 11:28–30).[18]

There are many ways to approach Bonhoeffer's understanding of revelation.[19] But in the context of exploring the development of Bonhoeffer's theology of discipleship, it is important to take note of the central place of the call of Jesus Christ in God's revelation. Indeed, Bonhoeffer's book *Discipleship* was an exercise in hearing, discerning, and responding to the ultimate revelation of God in Jesus Christ. By grounding his theology of discipleship in the revelatory act of Jesus' call, Bonhoeffer set a clear tone for what it meant to follow-after Jesus Christ: all Christian understanding and action could only come from the power and grace of Jesus Christ himself. Bonhoeffer took great pains to make this point.

The opening chapter of Bonhoeffer's *Discipleship* contains the famous treatise on cheap and costly grace. The opening lines were startling: "Cheap grace is the mortal enemy of our church. Our struggle today is for costly

---

17. See Pangritz, *Karl Barth*.

18. See Bonhoeffer, *DBWE* 4:40.

19. For example, Bonhoeffer wrote about revelation and the church in *Sanctorum Communio*: "*The reality of the church is the reality of revelation, a reality that essentially must be* either believed or denied" (127); he also equated revelation with the person and work of Jesus Christ in the "Lectures on Christology" when he described the three-fold form of Christ as Word, Sacrament, and Church-Community (see Bonhoeffer, *DBWE* 12:315–24); Bonhoeffer also addressed the question of revelation in *Creation and Fall*, writing, "Thus the Bible begins with the free confirmation, attestation, or revelation of God by God: In the beginning God created" (Bonhoeffer, *DBWE* 3:29).

grace."[20] With this statement, Bonhoeffer drew a clear line in the sand: cheap grace was the siren call of a human-centered religion; costly grace was the merciful call to follow-after Jesus Christ. The distinction was stark, and ultimately a matter of a theology of *revelation*. Bonhoeffer juxtaposed the natures of cheap and costly grace as a commentary between the differences of human-driven religion and of God's self-revelation in Jesus Christ: "Cheap grace means grace as doctrine, as principle, as system. It means forgiveness of sins as a general truth; it means God's love as merely a Christian idea of God. Those who affirm it have already had their sins forgiven."[21] Cheap grace was a human construct, a human effort to contain God in a submissive and watered-down religion: "Because grace alone does everything, everything can stay in its old ways."[22] Nothing had to change; the sinner could be self-justified. "Cheap grace is the grace we bestow on ourselves," Bonhoeffer wrote.[23] But this was not discipleship; this was not following-after Jesus Christ. This was "grace without the cross, grace without the living, incarnate Jesus Christ."[24] For Bonhoeffer, cheap grace was a false religion by the world, for the world, and so empty to the world.

In costly grace, Bonhoeffer identified the call of Jesus Christ as the gracious call of transformative mercy that was in—and for—the very heart of the world. This call was God's self-revelation in Jesus Christ, and it was the call to leave human-made religion in favor of life that emanated solely from God's word. But the call demanded nothing less than the relinquishment of a self-made life. What God revealed in Jesus Christ was "the treasure hidden in the field, for the sake of which people go and sell with joy everything they have."[25] The call to discipleship—to following-after Jesus Christ[26]—costs everything; indeed "it costs people their lives."[27] But it was the call of ultimate grace because it was the call to follow *Jesus Christ*—and it thereby called to true life. More so, Bonhoeffer explained,

> It is costly, because it condemns sin; it is grace because it justifies the sinner. Above all, grace is costly, because it was costly

---

20. Bonhoeffer, *DBWE* 4:43.
21. Bonhoeffer, *DBWE* 4:43.
22. Bonhoeffer, *DBWE* 4:43.
23. Bonhoeffer, *DBWE* 4:43.
24. Bonhoeffer, *DBWE* 4:44.
25. Bonhoeffer, *DBWE* 4:44.
26. Bonhoeffer's original German title of this book was *Nachfolge*, which can be translated into English as "discipleship" or—more literally—as "following after." See Bonhoeffer, *DBWE* 4:4, 39.
27. Bonhoeffer, *DBWE* 4:45.

to God, because it costs God the life of God's Son—"you were bought with a price" [1 Cor 6:20]—and because nothing can be cheap to us which is costly to God. Above all, it is grace because the life of God's Son was not too costly for God to give in order to make us live. God did, indeed, give him up for us. Costly grace is the incarnation of God.[28]

... Thus, it is grace as living word, word of God, which God speaks as God pleases. It comes to us as a gracious call to follow Jesus; it comes as a forgiving word to the fearful spirit and the broken heart. Grace is costly, because it forces people under the yoke of following Jesus Christ; it is grace when Jesus says, "My yoke is easy, and my burden is light" [Matt 11:30].[29]

God's act of revelation in Jesus Christ changed everything. It eliminated the need for human efforts to reach God; in Jesus Christ, God came near to all humanity. But in annihilating religious constructs, God's revelation also made a distinct claim on human life: "Leave your nets, leave your life. Follow me and you will find true life."

In this way, the *call* of Jesus Christ was a unique and foundational aspect of God's revelation—and this served as a key aspect of Bonhoeffer's theological understanding of discipleship. The disciples did not call themselves; they could not follow apart from the call of Jesus himself: "As Jesus was walking along, he saw Levi son of Alphaeus sitting at the tax booth, and he said to him, 'Follow me.' And he got up and followed him" (Mark 2:14). Bonhoeffer explained that Jesus called and the disciple followed because Jesus was the Christ; the revelation of God carried authority and the gracious promise of life. Yet God's revelation was not to a series of principles. The content of discipleship was simply to follow, to walk behind Jesus Christ. The disciples followed not out of their own constructs of who God was, but rather out of whom God revealed himself to be in Jesus Christ. And their world was righted by being turned upside down: "The disciple is thrown out of the relative security of life into complete insecurity (which in truth is absolute security and protection in community with Jesus); out of the foreseeable and calculable realm (which in truth is unreliable) into the completely unforeseeable, coincidental realm (which in truth is the only necessary and reliable one); out of the realm of limited possibilities (which in truth is that of unlimited possibilities) into the realm of unlimited possibilities (which in truth is the only liberating reality)."[30] God did not reveal an idealistic pro-

---

28. Bonhoeffer, *DBWE* 4:45.
29. Bonhoeffer, *DBWE* 4:45.
30. Bonhoeffer, *DBWE* 4:58.

gram or a legalistic boundary—these were human constructs. God revealed Jesus Christ in a gracious call and a gracious commandment: follow me. God's revelation was in the call to follow-after Jesus Christ.

Jesus Christ: The Reality of Discipleship

Jesus Christ's breaking into the world—through his life, death, and resurrection—defined a new *reality*. In *Discipleship*, Bonhoeffer argued that the living presence of Jesus Christ, manifest today in the church-community, meant that the call to discipleship remained an active force. Jesus Christ was not dead but alive, and was still speaking today in bodily form and with the preaching of the word. Indeed, for Bonhoeffer, "the preaching and the sacrament of the church is the place where Jesus Christ is present. To hear Jesus' call to discipleship, one needs no personal revelation. Listen to the preaching and receive the sacrament! Listen to the gospel of the crucified and risen Lord!"[31] The call of Christ was made real in the present word and sacrament, and the present-reality of Christ was manifest in the continuing existence of the church-community.

For Bonhoeffer, the church-community found its movement and being in the for-otherness of Jesus Christ. From *Sanctorum Communio* through *Life Together*, Bonhoeffer connected his understanding of ecclesiology with the concept of personal-relatedness.[32] Just as Jesus Christ existed as the man-for-others, the church-community realized its potential when relationships between church members and towards the world were defined as being-for the other. And this was the reality of Jesus Christ existing as the church-community. A community that existed as being rescued and set apart from the world was in fact, at its core, only set apart from the world in order to be for the world. In *Discipleship*, Bonhoeffer described the nature of baptism into the body of Christ in similar terms.

Baptism was initiation into the reality of Jesus Christ. "In baptism," Bonhoeffer explained, "we become Christ's possession. The name of Jesus is spoken over baptismal candidates, they gain a share in that name; they are baptized "into Jesus Christ" (εἰς, Rom 6:3; Gal 3:27; Matt 28:19). They now

---

31. Bonhoeffer, *DBWE* 4:202.

32. Bonhoeffer wrote extensively about the I-You relationship in *Sanctorum Communio*, and this concept manifested itself in *Life Together* particularly through the juxtaposition of the practices of solitude and communal living. Bonhoeffer described the nature of personhood in terms of the I-You relation in *Sanctorum Communio*, especially in pages 49–57. In *Life Together*, he argued, "*Whoever cannot be alone should beware of community*. . . . But the reverse is also true. *Whoever cannot stand being in community should beware of being alone*" (Bonhoeffer, *DBWE* 5:82).

belong to Jesus Christ. Having been rescued from the rule of this world, they now have become Christ's own."[33] This meant the old life was gone, and a new life was born; and this new life was added to Christ's own body in the church-community. At this point, Bonhoeffer emphasized a stark break from the world: "Those who are baptized no longer belong to the world, no longer serve the world, and are no longer subject to it. . . . The break with the world is absolute."[34] His view of the church-community here could come across as sectarian;[35] but his argument should not be abandoned to sectarianism. The baptized no longer belonged to the world; instead, Bonhoeffer insisted "they belong to Christ alone, and relate to the world only through Christ."[36] That was the key—those in the church-community related to the world only through Christ; that was to be their reality. And Christ's relation to the world, arguably, was anything but sectarian.[37]

In the section on "The Body of Christ," Bonhoeffer explained that, in addition to the preaching of the word, God accepted humanity in the body of Christ. God saw it fit to relate to the world through the reality of the human body: "God's mercy sends the Son in the flesh, so that in his flesh he may shoulder and carry all humanity."[38] What's more, in relating to the world in bodily form, the Son of God marked his acceptance of "all of humanity in bodily form, the same humanity which in hate of God and pride of the flesh had rejected the incorporeal, invisible word of God."[39] Humanity rejected what it could not touch and see. And so God came near: "In the body of Jesus Christ humanity is now truly and bodily accepted; it is accepted as it is, out of God's mercy."[40] Jesus Christ, as the new human being (1 Cor 15:47), stood in our stead. He was "for-us," and so for the world. In so being for the world, Jesus Christ sought to draw those in the world into his

---

33. Bonhoeffer, *DBWE* 4:207.

34. Bonhoeffer, *DBWE* 4:208.

35. Indeed, Bonhoeffer himself admitted that danger in a July 21, 1944, letter from Tegel to Bethge (the day of the failed assassination attempt on Hitler): "I thought I myself could learn to have faith by trying to live something like a saintly life. I suppose I wrote *Discipleship* at the end of this path. Today I clearly see the dangers of that book, though I still stand by it. Later on I discovered, and am still discovering to this day, that one only learns to have faith by living in the full this-worldliness of life" (Bonhoeffer, *DBWE* 8:486). Bonhoeffer could still stand by what he wrote because the foundations for this-worldliness were present even in *Discipleship*, and even through the contextual pressure to be set-apart (see note below).

36. Bonhoeffer, *DBWE* 4:208.

37. See Jackson, "Church, World, and Christian Charity."

38. Bonhoeffer, *DBWE* 4:214.

39. Bonhoeffer, *DBWE* 4:214.

40. Bonhoeffer, *DBWE* 4:214.

own visible and tangible body, the church-community. "On the cross, in the word, in baptism, and in the Lord's Supper,"[41] Jesus Christ was calling the world into himself. This was the new reality. This was Jesus Christ existing as church-community, yes, Bonhoeffer argued, set apart from the world—but not called to abandon the world. Such a posture would be counter to the very being of Jesus Christ existing for-others.[42]

Belief and Obedience: The Action of Discipleship

When the call came to follow-after Jesus Christ, there was a decisive moment of decision: "[Jesus] said to him, 'Follow me.' And he got up and followed him" (Mark 2:14). Bonhoeffer made a poignant observation here: "The call goes out, and without further ado the obedient deed of the one called follows. The disciple's answer is not a spoken confession of faith in Jesus. Instead, it is the obedient deed."[43] Resolute obedience to the call of Jesus Christ marked the movement to discipleship. The call came, in the reality and physicality of Jesus Christ, and the response was a simple obedience. But surely there could be no obedience without belief. Where was the movement to faith?

This is where Bonhoeffer closely linked God's revelation in the call of Jesus Christ with faithful and obedient action. He argued that only the call of Jesus Christ (as the revelation of God) could qualify a situation where faith was possible. That is, "a situation where faith is possible is never made by humans. Discipleship is not a human offer. The call alone creates the situation.... The call alone justifies it."[44] So from this call, a situation of faith was created which itself enabled faith. Apart from the call of Christ, faith was not possible; but the call not only beckoned faith, it demanded obedience. Bonhoeffer described it this way: "The concept of a situation in which faith is possible is only a description of the reality contained in the following two statements, both of which are equally true: *only the believers obey,* and *only the obedient believe.*"[45] The first statement was easy to affirm. Certainly, only those who believed the Christ obeyed him. Bonhoeffer argued that this was a natural conclusion: "Of course, obedience follows faith, the way good

---

41. Bonhoeffer, *DBWE* 4:217. See also Bonhoeffer's "Lectures on Christology" (*DBWE* 12:310–24).
42. See Green, *Bonhoeffer*.
43. Bonhoeffer, *DBWE* 4:57.
44. Bonhoeffer, *DBWE* 4:63.
45. Bonhoeffer, *DBWE* 4:63.

fruit comes from a good tree."[46] However, there was a catch: "If this meant only that faith alone justifies us and not deeds of obedience, then it is a firm and necessary precondition for everything else." But it could also, mistakenly, have alluded to something else: "If it meant a chronological sequence, that faith would have to come first, to be later followed by obedience, then faith and obedience are torn apart, and the very practical question remains open: when does obedience start?"[47] Here, Bonhoeffer was steadfast: obedience cannot remain separated from faith.

This is why Bonhoeffer juxtaposed the first statement with the second, *only the obedient believe*. In the first statement, faith was the precondition for obedience; in the second statement, the opposite was claimed: obedience was the precondition for faith. When Bonhoeffer claimed that only the obedient believed, he was affirming that the concrete commandment of Jesus Christ must be obeyed. Apart from getting up and following, faith could not take hold. "A first step has to be taken," Bonhoeffer wrote, "so that faith does not become pious self-deception, cheap grace."[48] Without the first step of obedience, faith became just a cheap religious construct. But true faith—faith in following-after Jesus Christ—became possible in the new state of existence created by obedience.[49]

Bonhoeffer offered a critical caution: "it is not the *works* which create faith."[50] Instead, Jesus' call presented a situation in which faith was possible, and Bonhoeffer implored his readers not to insist on faith coming before obedience: "You believe—so take the first step! It leads to Jesus Christ. You do not believe—take the same step; it is commanded of you!"[51] In so placing faith and obedience together, Bonhoeffer sought to remove barriers to discipleship:

> Jesus says to anyone who uses their lack of faith to excuse their acts of disobedience to his call: First obey, do the external works, let go of what binds you, give up what is separating you from God's will! Do not say, I do not have faith for that. You will not have it so long as you remain disobedient, so long as you will not take that first step. Do not say, I have faith, so I do not have to

---

46. Bonhoeffer, *DBWE* 4:63.
47. Bonhoeffer, *DBWE* 4:63.
48. Bonhoeffer, *DBWE* 4:64.
49. See Bonhoeffer, *DBWE* 4:64.
50. Bonhoeffer, *DBWE* 4:67.
51. Bonhoeffer, *DBWE* 4:67.

take the first step. You do not have faith, because and so long as you will not take that first step.⁵²

The goal, indeed, was true faith in Jesus Christ. Bonhoeffer realized that apart from concrete action, faith was humanity's own creation of cheap grace. By insisting on the faithful response of obedient action, Bonhoeffer continued to point to the possibilities and potentialities of following Jesus Christ. Only in the juxtaposition of belief and obedience could Bonhoeffer affirm the potentiality of true discipleship.

The Possibilities of Discipleship

Bonhoeffer's book *Discipleship*, and its companion *Life Together*, created a picture that, admittedly, focused on the potentialities of discipleship within a particular church-community context. He often wrote in ways that placed the church over and against the world, to such an extent that his later work in *Ethics* and *Letters and Papers from Prison* can seem to contradict some of the driving forces of *Discipleship*. Bonhoeffer scholarship, too, is often critical of how *Discipleship* created a sense of the church walling itself off from the world.⁵³ And a few years after its publication, writing from prison, Bonhoeffer himself "saw the dangers of that book."⁵⁴ But Bonhoeffer still stood by what he wrote.⁵⁵ So the question is, how? He could still stand by *Discipleship* because the underlying theology was sound. *Discipleship* was grounded in revelation, Jesus Christ and the church-community, and the juxtaposition of belief and obedience—and these led to a myriad of possibilities. In Finkenwalde, as we will see later in this chapter, the possibility of discipleship was the cloister. In the next chapter, we will see how the possibility of discipleship thrusts Bonhoeffer squarely into the political resistance against Adolf Hitler. What changed was not the foundation of his theology, but the context and the concrete call of Jesus Christ. However, even though *Discipleship* was written for the Finkenwalde context, Bonhoeffer did provide clear openings in his theological concept of discipleship for direct engagement with the world. For example, the final chapter of *Discipleship* was titled "The Image of Christ," and it invited the disciple into the fullest possibilities of faithfully engaging the call of Jesus Christ.

---

52. Bonhoeffer, *DBWE* 4:66.
53. See, for example, Jackson, "Church, World, and Christian Charity," 92–94; Pugh, *Religionless Christianity*, 103–4; and Rasmussen, *Dietrich Bonhoeffer*, 28.
54. Bonhoeffer, *DBWE* 8:486.
55. See Bonhoeffer, *DBWE* 8:486.

Bonhoeffer concluded *Discipleship* with stunning insight into the potentiality of what it meant to follow-after Jesus Christ: "To those who have heard the call to be disciples of Jesus Christ is given the incomprehensibly great promise that they are to become like Christ. They are to bear his image as the brothers and sisters of the firstborn Son of God. To become "like Christ"—that is what disciples are ultimately destined to become."[56] The goal of discipleship was to bear the image of God's own Son—"to be shaped into the entire *form* of the *incarnate*, the *crucified*, and the *transfigured one*."[57] In taking on human form, Jesus Christ lowered himself to the earth so that the human race could recognize itself in him; he became like humanity so that humanity could become like him. Jesus' taking on the image of humanity was a reminder that humanity was first created in the image of God. And in Christ, in this second Adam, the image of God had been restored for all humanity.[58] The implication here was great: "Whoever from now on attacks the least of the people attacks Christ, who took on human form and who in himself has restored the image of God for all who bear a human countenance."[59] What was more, as the body of Christ, the church-community was transformed, and God's love for every human being on earth was manifested in the call of Christians to treat everyone as a brother or sister. The church on earth bore the human image of Christ by seeing the world through the human eyes of Jesus.

Jesus also saw the world through the eyes of the cross. Bonhoeffer explained: "The form of Christ on earth is the *form of the death* of the crucified one. The image of God is the image of Jesus Christ on the cross. It is into this image that the disciple's life must be transformed."[60] This was the significance of baptism—in baptism, the disciple took on the death of Jesus Christ in a daily dying to the world. The ultimate identification with the suffering and death of Jesus Christ was martyrdom, but only a few did Jesus call to this. For the rest, the death of Christ meant a daily surrender to the suffering and persecution that the world would inflict. Further, in identifying with the image of Christ in all humanity, bearing the image of the crucified one meant bearing the suffering and sin of the world—not in the place of Jesus Christ, but alongside and with him.

The image of Christ culminated in resurrection and glorification. Bonhoeffer proclaimed: "All those who remain in community with the incarnate

---

56. Bonhoeffer, *DBWE* 4:281.
57. Bonhoeffer, *DBWE* 4:285.
58. See Bonhoeffer, *DBWE* 4:282.
59. Bonhoeffer, *DBWE* 4:285.
60. Bonhoeffer, *DBWE* 4:285.

and crucified one and in whom he gained his form will also become like the *glorified and risen one*."[61] Those who bore Christ's image were continually being changed into the fullness of Christ's form. "Already on this earth," Bonhoeffer wrote, "we will reflect the glory of Jesus Christ. The brilliant light and the life of the risen one will already shine forth from the form of death of the crucified one in which we live."[62] As Jesus Christ was dwelling in the heart of disciples, they reflected his human, crucified, and risen form because Christ continued to live on earth in the life of the church-community. Christ's glory was reflected for the entire world to see and to experience. As the church displayed this image of Christ, more people were drawn into his shape and form. The world became a place of witness and possibility, because of who Christ was and because of how he related to—and for—the world. The followers of Jesus Christ, then, looked only to the one they followed—and they followed Christ to become imitators of Christ, in his incarnation, death, and glory.[63]

Summary: The Four Movements

Revelation, reality, action, and possibility, then, are principle markers along the movements of Bonhoeffer's theology of discipleship. His book *Discipleship* affords the opportunity to take a snapshot at a significant juncture of some of the unique nuances and characteristics of his understanding of discipleship during the height of his involvement in theological education, from 1935 through 1939. *The call of Jesus Christ* does not define his complete understanding of God's *revelation*, but it does describe how revelation remained at the foundation of his concept of discipleship. Similarly, there is much to describe about Bonhoeffer's theology of *Jesus Christ existing as church-community*. But taking it as a key perspective on how Bonhoeffer viewed *reality* provides a necessary orientation to how he would work to overcome the sacred/secular split worldview so common in Lutheranism.[64] The relationship between *belief and obedience* provides a distinct call to *action* in the life of the disciple, while limitless *possibilities* for engagement emerge when disciples seek to bear *the full image of Christ*, as the crucified and risen one. But what did these four movements look like in the life of the seminary at Finkenwalde? How did Bonhoeffer's developing theology

---

61. Bonhoeffer, *DBWE* 4:286.
62. Bonhoeffer, *DBWE* 4:286.
63. See Bonhoeffer, *DBWE* 4:288.
64. Bonhoeffer explicitly argued for this in *Ethics* in the chapter "Christ, Reality, and Good," *DBWE* 6:47–75.

of discipleship take shape and form in his life among the seminarians and in his involvement with the Confessing Church? His ideas would certainly be tested.

Preparing Disciples for a Broken World

By the spring of 1935, the Confessing Church in Germany was decisively losing in the church struggle. The Reich Church had taken over all theological training and examinations, so that the seminaries of the newly constituted Confessing Church (which had emerged out of the Barmen Declaration) were considered illegal. There was now a clear line to be taken between receiving either state-sanctioned training for ministry or unlawfully participating in a Confessing Church preachers' seminary. But the Confessing Church did not let up. Bonhoeffer, as an outspoken leader in the Confessional movement, was called upon to direct one of the five seminaries that the Confessing Church established throughout Germany for training their own evangelical pastors. Initially, Bonhoeffer was assigned as the director of the last intact preachers' seminary of the Old Prussian Union, in Düsseldorf. However, upon the advice of a wise attorney, the Council of Brethren decided it would be better to move the seminary away from such a large city and industrial area to a place that was not so conspicuous. By the start of the first session in April 1935, a suitable permanent location still had not been found. However, Bonhoeffer did manage to arrange accommodations for the twenty-three ordinands at the Westphalian School Bible Club youth holiday camp in Zingst, on the Baltic Sea. The camp could only host them for the first two months of the session, but, by that time, the school had secured a building on an estate in Finkenwalde, near the Baltic Sea port of Stettin, in Pomerania.

Bonhoeffer's seminary was unique in its program and design. Having spent intentional time at Protestant monasteries in Britain, he wanted to explore how Christian communal living could play a part in the final preparations of candidates for church ministry in his own context. While Bonhoeffer sometimes received criticism that his practices were too "monastic," he was steadfast in his commitment to the personal, theological, and spiritual formation that his fellow brothers would undergo while in his care.[65] As mentioned at the beginning of this chapter, personal confession played a crucial part in the life of the community. But confession was just one piece of a comprehensive program that Bonhoeffer implemented into the curriculum at Zingst and Finkenwalde.

65. See Bonhoeffer, *DBWE* 14:268, 931.

In a report from the Pomeranian Members of the Preachers' Seminary, four of the brothers described their initial experience of Bonhoeffer's program. Writing on August 5, 1935, the brothers first recounted their initial landing in Zingst, "where on April 26 we were greeted by rather raw spring winds." They continued: "But after walking half an hour through impenetrable darkness and finally reaching the "Zingsthof," and once we had steaming fried potatoes on the table before us, once we had our first communal devotion with communal reading of the Psalms, readings from the Old and the New Testaments, and had sung some hymns, we knew we would be well taken care of in Zingst. Admittedly, Pastor Bonhoeffer—as he recently divulged to us—was at first a bit uneasy at the sight of so disparate a group."[66]

From the beginning, the brothers were enfolded into a new perspective of theological education. Sermons were prepared together, for example, with significant discussion and collaboration; and alongside sermon preparation, Bonhoeffer delivered lectures on homiletics and the doctrine of preaching. There were also classes on catechesis and on the question of pastoral office. There were Old and New Testament study groups, times of personal meditation and corporate singing, and free time for recreation. However, the brothers reported that the course that made the biggest impression was the one on discipleship in the New Testament. They provided an apt summary of this central theme: "Dr. Bonhoeffer presents an exegesis of the call stories, of Jesus's statements concerning discipleship, and currently also of the Sermon on the Mount. Probably no one is unaffected by the seriousness with which these New Testament findings have drawn our attention to the phenomenon of discipleship."[67] And then they gave a most telling definition:

> Discipleship is the unconditional, sole commitment to Jesus Christ and thus to the cross, a commitment whose content cannot wholly be articulated. The place to which the church is called is the cross, and the only form in which the church can exist is discipleship. A church in a worldly form of existence, of *iustita civilis*, is no longer the church of Jesus Christ. The multitude assembled around the word and sacrament is visible; the city on Golgotha cannot be hid.[68]

The brothers in the first session of the preachers' seminary at Zingst and Finkenwalde were already faced with the most pressing questions of discipleship

66. Bonhoeffer, *DBWE* 14:87.
67. Bonhoeffer, *DBWE* 14:89.
68. Bonhoeffer, *DBWE* 14:89.

and the church. Bonhoeffer's methods of theological education—with all its aspects of Scripture, study, personal meditation, recreation, and communal living—were helping to set a paradigm of whole-life discipleship amongst the ordinands. The preachers' seminary was not just a place to acquire the necessary head knowledge to pass an ordination exam; this was a place to discover and then live out the call to discipleship.

The House of Brethren

To help foster the spiritual and practical matters of the Finkenwalde experiment, Bonhoeffer initiated the creation of a House of Brethren. This group of six or so brothers would stay on site through each of the six-month sessions, so as to provide continuity, leadership, and direction when a new set of ordinands descended upon the house for this unique season of their theological education.[69] In September of 1935, Bonhoeffer wrote to the Council of the Evangelical Church of the Old Prussian Union seeking official approval for the establishment of the House of Brethren. In the letter, Bonhoeffer outlined key considerations, tasks, and requests for the Council to review. The letter's contents provide a first-hand perspective on the meaning and purpose of this unique ministry. First, Bonhoeffer argued that pastors—especially young ones—could suffer from isolation. The heavy weight of the national church struggle was an especially taxing burden, particularly on those individual pastors who were called as ministers, not prophets. As a result, "both in terms of content and the actual way they preach, they need the help and fellowship of their brothers."[70] At this time, when the struggle for church survival was at risk, Bonhoeffer argued that "a proclamation that derives from a community that is lived and experienced in a more practical fashion will, in its own turn, be more objective and imperturbable and will be less likely to run aground."[71] In other words, it would take the strength of the extended church-community to deliver the true message of gospel proclamation. In this sense, Bonhoeffer dismissed as mere "excuses" those objections that called such communal life "Enthusiasm" or "un-Lutheran behavior."[72] On the contrary, Bonhoeffer argued that the question of the

---

69. In the Old Prussian Union, theological education generally took place at the hands of state-appointed professors at the university. During the two years between the first and second theological exams, ordinands were to participate in a six to twelve month period of seminary education with a regional church's training program—like Finkenwalde. See Bethge, *Dietrich Bonhoeffer*, 419–24.

70. Bonhoeffer, *DBWE* 14:95.

71. Bonhoeffer, *DBWE* 14:95.

72. Bonhoeffer, *DBWE* 14:95.

Christian life "can no longer be abstract and instead can be articulated only by actually living and reflecting together on the commandments in a concrete, objective fashion."[73] The House of Brethren was designed to meet such a need.

The purpose of the House was not only to provide a sense of communal continuity in Finkenwalde, but also to keep a group of pastors at the ready for immediate service when emergency situations arose as part of the church struggle. Bonhoeffer argued that having the stability of the brotherhood would allow for the ministers to come and go when needed for the service of the Confessing Church. Bonhoeffer was clear: "The goal is not monastic isolation but rather the most intensive concentration for ministry to the world."[74] The brothers would not be isolated from the world, but rather they would be prepared to focus their work and ministry out in the community. At the outset, therefore, the House was established to include caring for the Confessing Church community in Finkenwalde and in the surrounding area of Stettin, and also to provide evangelization ministry in and beyond Pomerania.[75] In Bonhoeffer's estimation, effective ministry to the world required a firm theological and ecclesial foundation. The House of Brethren was to provide the continuity for such a communal framework at Finkenwalde.[76]

The Practice of Meditation

One of the most important—and personally challenging—features of life at the preachers' seminary in Finkenwalde was the admonition to set aside time each day for meditation. In this regard, the House of Brethren's example and guidance in the practice provided a measure of comfort for the newly arriving ordinands. But the practice was not an easy one to follow. From the first days of the seminary in Zingst, Bonhoeffer introduced the practice of meditation into the rhythm of daily life. By late spring of 1936—a year into the seminary's existence—the practice had become such a unique and hallmark feature of the seminary that a "Guide to Scriptural Meditation" was penned and sent out in a circular letter to past ordinands, and to others in the Confessing Church.[77] Bonhoeffer had worked with his friend and fellow brother in the House of Brethren, Eberhard Bethge, to prepare the

---

73. Bonhoeffer, *DBWE* 14:95.
74. Bonhoeffer, *DBWE* 14:96.
75. See Bonhoeffer, *DBWE* 14:96.
76. See Bonhoeffer, *DBWE* 14:97.
77. See Bonhoeffer, *DBWE* 14:931.

guide. The result was a concise document that not only provided a practical guide to meditation, but also offered tangible insight into the theological underpinnings of this important practice at Finkenwalde.

The guide was organized into four sections, with the first addressing the question, "Why do I meditate?" "*Why do I meditate?*" the guide begins, "*Because I am a Christian* and because for that very reason every day is lost to me in which I have not deepened my knowledge of God's word in Holy Scripture."[78] Bonhoeffer believed that a deeper knowledge of Scripture came in two ways, through the sermon and through personal meditation. As Finkenwalde was training Christian preachers, Bonhoeffer felt it was imperative that the brothers came to a place in their personal lives of profound love, trust, and understanding of the Scriptures. He argued that, as a preacher, he could not interpret the Scriptures for others "if I have not myself allowed them to speak to me each day."[79] What was more, "if I am no longer genuinely experiencing the word, then I have doubtless gone too long without letting that word genuinely speak to me."[80] The pastor held a great responsibility to both know and experience the Scriptures, and meditation provided the firm discipline for Bible reading and prayer that was so necessary to the office. Finally, Bonhoeffer explained, meditation forced the brothers to slow down in their haste to pray and to give generously a service of worship to God.

Bonhoeffer next addressed the goal of meditation. "In any event, we always want to come away from meditation differently than we go to it. What we want is to encounter Christ in his own word."[81] Bonhoeffer instructed the brothers that the goal of meditation was to experience Christ, to meet him at the start of the day even before meeting others. Meditation was about right-orientation to Christ. As he wrote, "the goal is Christ's community, Christ's help, and Christ's guidance for the day through his word. It is thus that you will begin the day strengthened anew in your faith."[82] True to Bonhoeffer's theological understanding of discipleship, meditation was about putting Christ at the center of life.

The final two sections of the guide addressed the practical matters of meditation, "How do I meditate?" and perhaps the more pressing question, "How can we overcome the problems of meditation?" To answer the first question, Bonhoeffer explained that there were two forms of meditation:

78. Bonhoeffer, *DBWE* 14:931.
79. Bonhoeffer, *DBWE* 14:932.
80. Bonhoeffer, *DBWE* 14:932.
81. Bonhoeffer, *DBWE* 14:932.
82. Bonhoeffer, *DBWE* 14:933.

free meditation and meditation that was bound to Scripture. He strongly advocated for the second form: "To ensure the certainty of our prayer, but also to discipline our thinking, we recommend meditation bound to Scripture. Finally the consciousness of our community with others who are meditating on the same text will also endear scriptural meditation to us."[83] The community would meditate on the same ten to fifteen verses for a week, thus providing continuity and encouragement. This also gave immense time and space for the Scripture to sink deeply and personally into one's heart. Bonhoeffer advised that the brothers each ask, "What are they saying to me! Then ponder these words for a long time in your own heart until they completely enter into you and take possession of you."[84] The goal was complete submersion into the text, but they need not even get through the entire text each day. He explained that sometimes we may linger for days over a single word. However, in this sense, practically speaking, Bonhoeffer warned, "do not flee to philology. This is the place not for the Greek New Testament but for our familiar Luther text."[85] Meditation was not the time for word studies, but for prayerful petitions to the Holy Spirit, for intercession, and for thanksgiving. And under no circumstances were they to use their coming sermon text for the meditation. That text received separate times of meditation and study.

Bonhoeffer also explained that the morning was the best time for personal meditation, and all in the seminary were to observe this practice at the same time. "A half hour will be the minimum requirement for proper meditation. Self-evident prerequisites include complete external peace and quiet as well as the resolve not to allow oneself to be distracted regardless of how important something else may seem."[86] But distractions were, in fact, inevitable.

The final section of the guide acknowledged the pressing challenges of meditation. Bonhoeffer admitted, "Those who seriously engage in the daily practice of meditation will quickly encounter great difficulties."[87] This was a discipline that required long patience and earnestness. Bonhoeffer's advice was genuine and understanding: "Do not become impatient with yourself. Do not get tied up in despair about being distracted. Simply sit down again each day and wait patiently."[88] Certainly, Bonhoeffer recog-

---

83. Bonhoeffer, *DBWE* 14:933.
84. Bonhoeffer, *DBWE* 14:933.
85. Bonhoeffer, *DBWE* 14:933.
86. Bonhoeffer, *DBWE* 14:933.
87. Bonhoeffer, *DBWE* 14:935.
88. Bonhoeffer, *DBWE* 14:935.

nized that thoughts would wander, minds would get anxious, and feelings of guilt and incompetency would arise. But he encouraged the brothers to turn these wanderings into prayers, which would help them find their way back to the text, "and the minutes spent in such digressions will not be lost, but neither will they torment you any longer."[89] Bonhoeffer also offered some advice and aids in helping the brothers to meditate. He suggested that one might read the same word over and over, write down thoughts, or memorize verses. But he warned that these practices might soon usurp the call to simple meditation. Meditation was about learning to pray, and, he explained, "basically, the backdrop to all our problems and helplessness is our own trouble with prayer; for too long many of us simply had no real help or guidance."[90] In this case, there are no tricks to quick success—just a resolve to begin again, with patience and faith. There was comfort and help in knowing that other brothers and Christians were meditating, and also that, "the entire holy church in heaven and on earth is always praying along with us. This provides comfort to us in our weakness in prayer. For even if we genuinely do not know what we should be praying, and even if we quite despair, we nonetheless still know that the Holy Spirit intercedes for us with sighs too deep for words."[91] Meditation was an integral part of the life of the seminary, one that could not be neglected. It helped each brother to know and experience the hope and faithfulness of Jesus Christ, in his own life, and in the life of the world.

What was significant about the practice of daily meditation at Finkenwalde was not merely that Bonhoeffer instituted such a practice in the first place, but rather that he did so for the sake of preparing the seminarians for ministry in and for a hostile world. Finkenwalde was a distinct place of preparation, a site for a final six-months of practical training and spiritual formation before the new ordinands would be sent out to lead and care for a Confessing Church congregation. But soon, even Finkenwalde would have its doors shuttered by the Gestapo, and Bonhoeffer's drive at theological education would have to go even deeper underground.

When Ministry Is Illegal

On September 28, 1937, almost two and a half years after it was established, the Confessing Church preachers' seminary in Finkenwalde was closed by the Gestapo. The Himmler Decree of August 29, 1937 had banned most

89. Bonhoeffer, *DBWE* 14:935.
90. Bonhoeffer, *DBWE* 14:935.
91. Bonhoeffer, *DBWE* 14:936.

activities of the Confessing Church, and thus made Finkenwalde and the other four preachers' seminaries illegal under state law. At their establishment, these seminaries had already been considered "illegal" by the Reich Church authorities, but the Himmler Decree now solidified their fate in the state's eyes.[92] A communication from the Office of the Gestapo in Berlin to Reich Church Minister Hanns Kerrl described Finkenwalde's matter-of-fact fate. The letter read, in part:

> In accordance with the decree of August 29, 1937, from the SS Reichführer and head of the German Police—S-PP (11 B) 4431/37—the preachers' seminary in Finkenwalde, under the leadership of Director of Studies D. Bonhoeffer has been closed. Decisive for my decision was the fact that the entire teaching staff of the seminary belonged to the confessional front and the purpose of this teaching institution clearly was to educate the vicars in the spirit of the confessional front and to equip them with the tools to complete the second theological exam before the examination offices of the confessional front.
>
> In order to prevent the influence of the Confessing Church on theological education, I find it necessary that above all the preachers' seminaries that are under the direction of the confessional front and guided by its spirit should be closed.[93]

The fate of those on the "confessional front" was now even more dire. Bonhoeffer's ability to teach at Berlin had been revoked in August 1936, and now his teaching for the Confessing Church had been made illegal.[94] But his commitment to preparing confessional pastors for ministry would not be diminished. Instead, his efforts at theological education would go underground, with the establishment of a series of collective pastorates to replace the official Confessing Church seminaries. From the winter of 1937 through the start of the war and into the spring of 1940, Bonhoeffer helped to coordinate and continued to participate in the training of Confessing Church pastors. As the Reich's grip continued to tighten around everything in Germany, Bonhoeffer kept a firm focus on what he could control—including the clandestine teaching of ministers who might stand above all else for the church of Jesus Christ.

With the closing of the seminaries by the Gestapo, the Confessing Church was able to continue the training of its ministers by establishing a program of collective pastorates. Although Bonhoeffer had argued that a

---

92. See Bonhoeffer, *DBWE* 15:19.

93. Bonhoeffer, *DBWE* 15:19. See also Bethge, *Dietrich Bonhoeffer*, 584.

94. See Bethge, *Dietrich Bonhoeffer*, 585; and Bonhoeffer, *DBWE* 14:1019.

new seminary should be defiantly opened again in Stettin, he finally agreed that an apprenticeship model of clergy training could be effective. Other minority church groups, like the West German Reformed Church, were using a model whereby the training of new ministers was taking place under the tutelage of then legal pastors. Pairing "apprentice vicars" with existing pastors who were sympathetic to the Confessing Church thus allowed for the continuation of ministerial education. Each ordinand would register with the local police that he was working under a parish vicar (whom they hardly knew), and then seven to ten would live together in a house within the district. In this way, the ordinands were able to keep a Finkenwalde-esq ethos to their theological training program. Bonhoeffer took up residence as an "assistant pastor" in Schlawe, and traveled the forty miles between vicarages in Köslin and Gross-Schlönwitz twice a week to provide directorship and instruction to the ordinands. In this way, he was able to add five more six-month sessions in these collective pastorates to the five sessions he had held at Finkenwalde. It was not until March 1940—six months into the war—that most of the ordinands were conscripted into the military, and the police shut down the secluded collective pastorate program in eastern Pomerania.[95]

Although the political situation had initiated a re-imagining of theological education, Bonhoeffer was able to maintain a program which contained the same central elements of the features in Finkenwalde. Much of the education was now further dispersed and more remote, but Bonhoeffer continued to focus on (among others) the themes of the Sermon on the Mount and belief and obedience in the life of discipleship. These two themes were central in his 1937 book *Discipleship*, and their out workings were further explored in the short book from 1938, *Life Together*. During the years in the collective pastorates, a unique perspective on these themes can be discerned from the circular letters that Bonhoeffer sent out to the past and present brothers. As the political tensions rose, and as the church situation became more dismal, Bonhoeffer continued to press upon the brothers the central importance of following-after Jesus Christ with every part of their existence—and their decision to follow this call often came down to the consequences of their very own lives.

After the Himmler Decree, twenty-seven of the seminarians who had studied under Bonhoeffer at Finkenwalde were arrested. As his 1937 Christmas letter to the Finkenwalde brothers revealed, cryptically, "this is a time of testing for us all."[96] No one individual was being spared from

---

95. See Bethge, *Dietrich Bonhoeffer*, 589–91.
96. Bonhoeffer, *DBWE* 15:21.

the tumultuous impact on life and work. If not present imprisonment, the threat remained imminent because of the "increasingly impatient attacks of the anti-Christian forces."[97] Further, now that Finkenwalde had been taken away, the work of the community had become that much more difficult—and that much more important: "Particularly now, the great task is to ensure that those among us who are isolated are not left alone. More than ever, the responsibility for this falls upon each of you. Please don't neglect it."[98] Dispersed and under greater pressure to conform to the state, the brothers now needed each other more than ever. Bonhoeffer pleaded with them: "Pray that the service to our young brothers will be done properly; lend a hand wherever you can."[99] This help included the intercession and accountability that the daily meditations provided the dispersed community. Additionally, in each of his circular letters, Bonhoeffer provided the meditation texts for the coming weeks. There was comfort and strength in the continuation of this most sacred practice, and Bonhoeffer implored the brothers to support each other in the meditations. These, he argued, were a key ingredient in mustering the strength and resolve to respond with belief and obedience to Jesus' call in the Sermon on the Mount.

The Sermon on the Mount

Bonhoeffer's ordinands had an intimate understanding of the Sermon on the Mount. It was a key aspect of Bonhoeffer's teaching on the call of simple obedience to follow-after Jesus Christ; his exegesis on Matthew 5–7, for example, made up by far the longest chapter in his book *Discipleship*. In his December 20, 1937 circular letter to the Finkenwalde brothers, Bonhoeffer expressed that he would have liked to give each of them a copy of the book for Christmas, writing, "When it was published I often dedicated it in spirit to you all. I did not do this on the title page, because I did not want to claim you for my thinking and theology. Our fellowship is grounded in something else. The thought of giving the book to each of you for Christmas unfortunately had to be dropped due to finances. Anyway, you know what is in the book."[100]

Indeed, the brothers did know what was in the book. Bonhoeffer had challenged them—and would continue to challenge them through his letters and correspondence—to take seriously Jesus' teachings in the Sermon

97. Bonhoeffer, *DBWE* 15:21.
98. Bonhoeffer, *DBWE* 15:21.
99. Bonhoeffer, *DBWE* 15:21.
100. Bonhoeffer, *DBWE* 15:21.

on the Mount and to follow them with unhindered obedience. Much of his pushing, prodding, encouraging, and rebuking of the brothers throughout this season of theological education can be tied back to a key theme of the Sermon on the Mount: the extraordinary, hidden nature of a disciple's life was set apart from the world in order to bear faithful witness of God's love and grace for the world. Bonhoeffer's careful exegesis of Matthew 5–7 in *Discipleship* revealed a theology of discipleship that demanded simple and complete obedience to the fullness of Jesus Christ's call. He explored this theme in three stages, corresponding to Matthew chapters 5, 6, and 7.

Matthew 5, Bonhoeffer explained, described the "extraordinary" of Christian life. This extraordinariness, first, came from Jesus' pronouncement of blessing upon the group of disciples gathered there together on the mountain. The disciples were blessed because theirs was the kingdom of heaven; they were called and chosen by Jesus to be poor in spirit because they were needy in every way. In following this call, the disciples were set apart from the crowd, and yet Jesus' call to discipleship remained an open invitation to all who would listen. Indeed, the beatitudes described a small band of disciples set apart to live an extraordinary life—a life of renunciation, mourning, suffering, mercy, purity, peace, and persecution. In short, Bonhoeffer explained that the place of discipleship was "the place where the poorest, the most tempted, the meekest of all might be found, at the cross on Golgotha."[101] This was the place of blessing and the place of identity with the one who had called: "With him they lost everything, and with him they found everything."[102]

In addition, the life of discipleship was extraordinary because of the nature of the extraordinary call. The call of Jesus, Bonhoeffer continued (and reiterated from chapter 3), was to simple obedience. In truth, the disciples were the salt of the earth and the light of the world, and so in obedience the community of disciples lived visibly in the world. This meant that, in obedience, they understood the "better righteousness" of the law to be about both teaching and doing. The call of Jesus was not a mental exercise; it required a physical response: reconciliation of anger, a posture of love and respect toward women and the body, truth-telling, suffering, and even love of the enemy. The "extraordinary" was "the way of self-denial, perfect love, perfect purity, perfect truthfulness, perfect nonviolence."[103] Bonhoeffer continued: "It is the love of Jesus Christ himself, who goes to the cross in suffering and obedience. It is the cross. What is unique in Christianity is the

---

101. Bonhoeffer, *DBWE* 4:109.
102. Bonhoeffer, *DBWE* 4:109.
103. Bonhoeffer, *DBWE* 4:144.

cross, which allows Christians to step beyond the world in order to receive victory over the world. The passio in the love of the crucified one—that is the "extraordinary" mark of Christian obedience."[104] The community of disciples gave witness to this call in profound visibility to the world. Set apart in their extraordinariness, the disciples nonetheless do and teach for the purpose of bearing witness to the passion of Christ. Being extraordinary was not about exclusivity; it was about the integrity of the blessed call for the witness of the community.

Bonhoeffer's exegesis of Matthew 6 helped to illustrate the danger of a one-dimensional understanding of "extraordinariness." He explained that the call to live an extraordinary, set apart life could quickly denigrate into a dangerous sectarianism: "The danger is that the disciples will completely misunderstand this [extraordinariness] as a command to start building a heavenly kingdom on earth, despising and destroying the world order. The danger is great that in enthusiasts' indifference to this age they will think it their duty now to achieve and make visible the extraordinariness of this new world, separating themselves from the world radically and with no willingness to compromise, in order to force into being what is Christian, what is appropriate to discipleship, what is extraordinary."[105] Piety made it too easy to disregard the world and to attack it with a righteous rage. Being extraordinary—which was Jesus' call!—could quickly lead to the kind of spiritual arrogance and enthusiasm that traded humility for pride, and grace for legalism. No, Bonhoeffer explained, "the extraordinariness is not supposed to happen in order to be seen."[106] Disciples were not called to extraordinary deeds as if being extraordinary was an end to itself. True, discipleship was visible, but if the goal was the visibility of pious action, then the nature of the gracious call of Jesus Christ would be smothered.

In this way, Bonhoeffer believed that Matthew chapters 5 and 6 collided hard against each other: "What is visible should be hidden at the same time; at the same time both visible and not to be seen."[107] So, in this seeming contradiction, disciples needed to discern the nature of their extraordinariness as being fully grounded in Jesus Christ alone. As disciples followed Jesus and kept their eyes fixed on him, their eyes remained off of themselves; in looking forward towards Jesus, their own righteousness was hidden.[108] The extraordinariness, of course, is not kept from them; they

---

104. Bonhoeffer, *DBWE* 4:144.
105. Bonhoeffer, *DBWE* 4:146.
106. Bonhoeffer, *DBWE* 4:148.
107. Bonhoeffer, *DBWE* 4:149.
108. Bonhoeffer, *DBWE* 4:149.

see that it exists. But they do not see themselves in it; they see the grace and power of Jesus Christ. In this way, the content of discipleship remained extraordinary, and it kept disciples under the cross of Jesus Christ. In their simple obedience to Jesus Christ, the disciples remained exclusively committed to the will of God: their extraordinary actions remained shockingly visible to the world and yet hidden to themselves. Bonhoeffer summarized the principle: "In simple obedience disciples do the will of the Lord who bids them do something extraordinary, and they know in everything that they can do nothing else, that they are, therefore, doing what is simply a matter of course."[109] Through their prayers, through their piety, through the simplicity of their carefree life, disciples abided in the communion of Jesus Christ, and lived extraordinary lives hidden from themselves, though shining brightly to the world.

Set apart in this way, the community of disciples bore witness to a gospel of transformation and grace in the world. Bonhoeffer thus understood Matthew chapter 7 as a call to confront the world not in violence, but in the peace and power of Jesus Christ. The essential connective thread woven through Mathew chapters 5, 6, and 7, Bonhoeffer argued, was the definitive relationship that disciples held with Jesus Christ. Having been separated from their community and called into an extraordinary life, disciples now were to hold a distinct posture towards each other and towards the world: "Do not judge, so that you may not be judged" (Matt 7:1). Bonhoeffer explained here that "the gap which divides them from others, as the just from the unjust, even divides them from Jesus."[110] Judgment was a matter of one's relationship not only with the world, but also with Jesus Christ. The barriers that were erected between disciples and those outside the community also served to divide disciples from Jesus himself. In this sense, it was not for the disciples to decide the bounds of righteousness. Instead, Bonhoeffer argued, "what makes them disciples is not a new standard for their lives, but Jesus Christ alone, the mediator and Son of God himself."[111] The disciples related to the world as Jesus related to the world—as mediator, as Son of God, and as the one who judged and justified by grace alone.

Bonhoeffer continued: "If the disciples judge, then they are erecting standards to measure good and evil. But Jesus Christ is not a standard by which I can measure others. It is he who judges me and reveals what according to my own judgment is good to be thoroughly evil."[112] Having such an

---

109. Bonhoeffer, *DBWE* 4:150.
110. Bonhoeffer, *DBWE* 4:170.
111. Bonhoeffer, *DBWE* 4:170.
112. Bonhoeffer, *DBWE* 4:171.

unreliable capacity for judgment, the disciples were called instead to love. However, Bonhoeffer explained, "love does not prohibit my having my own thoughts about others or my perceiving their sin, but both thoughts and perceptions are liberated from evaluating them. They thereby become only an occasion for that forgiveness and unconditional love Jesus gives me."[113] While judging made disciples blind, love provided sight. Love viewed the world as Jesus viewed the world—through the gracious power of the cross.

To be sure, there would be a great separation. It would be Jesus himself who could proclaim, "I never knew you." But the Sermon on the Mount, Bonhoeffer explained, held together from beginning to end with the simple call of Jesus, "come, and be known by me." The word of grace would carry disciples through, and the response to Jesus knew only one possibility: "simply go and obey. Do not interpret or apply, but do it and obey. That is the only way Jesus' word is really heard."[114] Bonhoeffer was adamant: doing something was not an idealistic wish, but rather the disciples' obedient reality. The Sermon on the Mount was the call to simple obedience, and it was the call to action. To ponder these lessons, to idealize or relativize them, outside of the place of obedience and action, was to miss the extraordinary call. It was still possible to hear from afar, and like the crowd gathered on the mountain, to be astonished at his words. But the disciples, the blessed ones, stood beside and with Jesus—the one who "took the judgment of the world into his hands."[115]

The Question of Legalization

From the end of 1937, the issue of simple obedience found a concrete expression in the increasing pressure put upon Confessing Church ordinands to take the path of "legalization." It was during this time that the Confessing Church as a whole lost its resolve to stand firmly against the Reich Church. Many Confessing Church pastors did not see a future for their ministries in a country where they were excluded from official posts and pastorates. Select confessional churches were privately donating funds for pastoral salaries and operations to the Council of Brethren, but, as of September 1, 1938, the Council in Pomerania was only taking in half of the needed monthly 9,000 Reich marks. The additional statistics in Pomerania were grim: "Years ago 318 of the 600 Pomeranian clergy in office had signed a commitment to the Confessing church; of those 318, only 60 pastors still

113. Bonhoeffer, *DBWE* 4:171.
114. Bonhoeffer, *DBWE* 4:181.
115. Bonhoeffer, *DBWE* 4:182.

held to the Council of Brethren. There were 57 young illegal theologians; only 17 of them held regular pastorates, 22 were in positions that were not legal, and 15 could not be placed at all."[116] As the theological drive to follow "in simple obedience" the declarations at Barmen and Dahlem diminished, so did the Confessing Church's ability to maintain a significant stand against the relentless forces of Nazi and Reich Church ideology. In this increasingly marginalized ecclesial context, Bonhoeffer continued to speak boldly and directly to the responsibility of the Confessing Church, and he urged his ordinands to remain faithful to the clear call of Jesus Christ.

Legalization proved to be a flashpoint between theological and practical matters for Bonhoeffer's ordinands. The practical offer from the Reich Church was enticing, and the choice stark: remain an illegal presence in the Confessing Church and face the increasing reality of arrest and, at the least, the diminishing possibility of being able to carry out any ministry at all in a parish setting; or, submit your papers to the local consistory, pass a Reich Church screening process, and then receive a pastoral placement, with a parish house, a state salary and pension, and the security to continue on in ministry. A great debate thus ensued within Bonhoeffer's ranks, with more and more of the Finkenwalde brothers opting for the safety of legalization. But Bonhoeffer did not let go of anyone easily.

Many of Bonhoeffer's circular letters to the Finkenwalde brothers during the collective pastorate years contained direct arguments and pleas to follow the path of simple obedience. In a January 3, 1938 letter to the brothers, for example, Bonhoeffer wrote an extensive excurses on the "severe temptations" of legalization currently facing their ranks. He reminded them of their great joy and unity in affirming the Barmen and Dahlem synodal confessions of 1934, and asked them what had changed? "Was this an illusion?" he wrote. "No, it was the most certain faith, it was the biblical truth itself, that was made known before the entire world. It was the witness to Christ that overcame hearts, created joy, and called to the obedient deed."[117] Yet that joy had crumpled under the weight of the pressing circumstances of the church struggle, and the Pomeranian church sat paralyzed, "as if in a spell."[118] Bonhoeffer attributed this paralysis, this, "lack of gladness, the weakness of the witness,"[119] to the disobedience of the Confessing Church. From the scandal surrounding the loyalty oath to Hitler,[120] to the steady

---

116. Bethge, *Dietrich Bonhoeffer*, 613.
117. Bonhoeffer, *DBWE* 15:30.
118. Bonhoeffer, *DBWE* 15:31.
119. Bonhoeffer, *DBWE* 15:31.
120. See Bethge, *Dietrich Bonhoeffer*, 599–605.

stream of Confessing pastors and theologians capitulating to the state, Bonhoeffer concluded: "that which, done in obedience, is a gentle and light yoke, becomes an unbearable burden for the disobedient."[121] For many, following the call of Christ to stand firm in the line of Barmen and Dahlem had become too unbearable of a burden in light of the present political reality; the risks to life and ministry were becoming too great. But Bonhoeffer held firm. This was the time and place for simple, clear obedience.

As strong as Bonhoeffer levied his arguments, he battled a steady stream of ordinands opting for legalization. This clearly wore on him, as described in a letter of January 28, 1939 to his brother, Karl-Friedrich: "It has been at times very depressing in the last few weeks, when one must see how many people are seeking quiet and security at all costs and using all kinds of pretexts and reasons."[122] One of the Finkenwalde brothers who eloquently argued against Bonhoeffer's view on legalization was Gerhard Krause. He claimed, in part, that the present path of the Confessing Church was no longer theologically correct because of its rejection of what came to be known as "Way B"—the arrangement with provincial church consistories in support of legalization. Bonhoeffer insisted on "Way A," which prohibited Confessing Church ordinands taking the path of legalization through the Reich consistories. Krause, and others like him, believed that the ministry of the Confessing Church could be continued if they just took the path of legalization; they could not bear to see their ministry barred because of a "church dispute." He argued, "But they [the consistory] require nothing for legalization that I would have to reject as 'against the faith' or 'against the truth.'"[123] Krause found nothing in legalization that would hinder him neither from proper preaching nor from confessing. And he even expressed his "good cheer and conscience"[124] to Bonhoeffer. But he did pose a stark question to his mentor: "Whether I remain *in* the CC is for the CC to decide; whether I remain in the Finkenwalde brotherhood, that is my request and question to you."[125]

Over the next several months, as Germany intensified its preparations for war, the Confessing Church in Pomerania continued to struggle for unity and strength. Even with a resolution at the end of February 1939 proclaiming "that we all wish to try to remain together, despite the different

---

121. Bonhoeffer, *DBWE* 15:32.
122. Bonhoeffer, *DBWE* 15:115.
123. Bonhoeffer, *DBWE* 15:151.
124. Bonhoeffer, *DBWE* 15:151.
125. Bonhoeffer, *DBWE* 15:151.

ways, though Way A is generally preferred,"[126] disunity and confusion prevailed in regards to the legalization question. But the problems never had an opportunity to be fully resolved. In the late spring of 1939, Bonhoeffer left for England and America, and men from all over the country—and from the Confessing Church—were called into military service. "The war created a new situation," Bethge recounted. "Bonhoeffer had no misgivings about including Krause and his friends in the circle of the Finkenwalde brethren. Once they were on the front, he even intensified his correspondence with them, without any further mention of Way A and Way B."[127] In this new situation, Bonhoeffer discerned pathways of simple obedience that continued to return to Jesus Christ's work of mediation in the world. The imminence of war had squelched the internal arguments of church struggle. Now the brothers were dispersed in all different capacities throughout the front, and bearing witness to the gospel of grace and reconciliation took on a more universal tone. Bonhoeffer sent prayers of peace and strength to all the brothers, while he himself was drawn into a completely new side of ministry and witness: the conspiracy against Hitler himself.

Conclusion: What Discipleship Becomes

Viewing Bonhoeffer's theological understanding of discipleship in terms of the four movements described above is admittedly just one hermeneutical option for Bonhoeffer interpretation. But it is not an ambiguous one. Bonhoeffer's theological program throughout *Discipleship* is clearly marked by a deliberate commitment to *revelation*, *Jesus Christ*, *action*, and *possibility*. Placing these four movements together in a unified program provides an opportunity to discover the complexities and nuances of Bonhoeffer's concept of theological discipleship—both within and beyond the years of 1935 to 1939. It is important to see Bonhoeffer's understanding of discipleship in the broader sense of his theological commitments and developments because it can be too easy to dismiss "discipleship" as a passing phase in his theological and ethical life. But *Discipleship*, its companion *Life Together*, and Bonhoeffer's work as a director of theological education for the Confessing Church were not isolated events, separated from what came before and after in his life. The developments in *Discipleship* of revelation and Christology, for example, were in clear continuity with the rest of his theological program, and the following chapter will solidify this claim even more so. But the purpose of this chapter was to establish the theological

126. Bethge, *Dietrich Bonhoeffer*, 619.
127. Bethge, *Dietrich Bonhoeffer*, 619.

underpinnings that supported Bonhoeffer's developing concept of discipleship. The four movements provide theological weight to an understanding of discipleship, and they account for Bonhoeffer's continued personal and theological development in the final phase of his life. From the practices of confession and meditation, to New Testament teachings on the beatitudes and following-after Jesus Christ, to confronting issues of church legality and brotherhood, Bonhoeffer's concept of discipleship provides unwavering theological commitment while expecting the call of Christ to push forth into new potentialities. Bonhoeffer sought to equip his ordinands with the theological, spiritual, and personal acumen to follow-after Christ with unwavering clarity and commitment. Ultimately, the lessons were also deeply personal for Bonhoeffer himself. It was because Bonhoeffer was grounded in a theology of revelation that found its reality in Jesus Christ existing as church-community, and because he acted with unwavering responsibility for belief-obedience, that he would have the freedom to explore new possibilities and potentialities for discipleship throughout the remainder of his life. From this foundational framework, even—no, especially—the bars of Tegel prison could not stifle his creativity and commitment to discover anew the meaning and ever-expanding possibilities of following-after Jesus Christ. The more Bonhoeffer pressed into this foundational framework, the clearer the implications became for the meaning of Jesus Christ's work in and for the world.

Chapter 4

Discipleship In and For the World, 1939–1945

Those who wish even to focus on the problem of a Christian ethic are faced with an outrageous demand—from the outset they must give up, as inappropriate to this topic, the very two questions that led them to deal with the ethical problem: "How can I be good?" and "How can I do something good?" Instead they must ask the wholly other, completely different question: what is the will of God?

—Dietrich Bonhoeffer, *Ethics*

The Difficult Path of Simple Obedience

IN JUNE OF 1939—as the church struggle grew ever hopeless, and as Hitler's Germany marched steadily toward launching an aggressor's war—Bonhoeffer boarded a ship for New York. There were several factors involved. First and most pressing, Bonhoeffer had been trying to forestall the military orders that he report to the recruitment office for duty. When he was ordered to report for call-up on May 22, arrangements had to be made carefully and in haste for legitimate foreign travel. If he could secure a leave of absence, then he could put off the military decision for a year. Otherwise he would be forced either to join an army unit or else appear before a court-martial as a conscientious objector. The latter decision would certainly lead to arrest, and likely the death penalty. Thus, May was spent securing invitations for theology and church work in America from Reinhold Niebuhr and Paul Lehmann, who worked quickly to arrange lectureships and church work, and send official invitations and wires to the necessary authorities.

But avoiding military service out of personal conviction was not Bonhoeffer's only motive for the trip to America. He also had the Confessing Church in mind. In a March 25, 1939 letter to his friend and mentor George Bell, the Bishop of Chichester, Bonhoeffer wrote:

> I am thinking of leaving Germany sometime. The main reason is the compulsory military service to which the men of my age (1906) will be called up this year. It seems to me conscientiously impossible to join a war under the present circumstances. On the other hand, the Confessional Church as such has not taken any definite attitude in this respect and probably cannot take it as things are. So I should cause a tremendous damage to my brethren if I would make a stand on this point which would be regarded by the regime as typical of the hostility of our church towards the state. Perhaps the worst thing of all is the military oath which I should have to swear. So I am rather puzzled in this situation, and perhaps even more, because I feel, it is really only on Christian grounds that I find it difficult to do military service under the present conditions, and yet there are only very few friends who would approve of my attitude.[1]

Bonhoeffer was keenly aware that any decision to object officially to military service would not only put his own life in danger, but it would also endanger the Confessing Church itself. Bonhoeffer did not want to give the state officials even more reason to seek out and persecute the Confessing Church and its pastors; he did not want his personal decisions to damage his brothers. While he felt very strongly about the idea of military service, he did not feel it right to force this conviction unnaturally onto others.

Third, Bonhoeffer sought out opportunities in America on professional grounds. He urged the Council of Brethren to grant him a leave of absence because he felt it was critical that the Confessing Church continue to build international and ecumenical ties. Though the church struggle was losing its luster and its members to the war efforts, Bonhoeffer was still committed to the training of confessional pastors and to further theological reflection. His ties to America could provide a measure of sustainability and growth for the movement. Bonhoeffer's arguments and efforts paid off; he was granted a

---

1. Bonhoeffer, *DBWE* 15:156–57.

leave of absence by the Council of Brethren, and was subsequently approved for foreign travel. The requirement to enlist was postponed for a year. It was with great relief that he crossed the German border, and then set sail on a ship for America on June 2.

As was often his custom, Bonhoeffer kept a diary of his travels. The American diary, from June and July 1939, provided Bonhoeffer with the space to work through one of the most difficult decisions of his life: when and whether he should remain in America, or return to Germany and face its destiny. As early as June 9, he began to reflect on the nature of discipleship and on his decision to go to America. In responding to Isaiah 41:9 and John 12:26 and the nature of servanthood, Bonhoeffer wrote:

> God chooses the sinner as the servant, in order that God's grace becomes entirely clear. The sinner is to do God's work and spread God's grace. Whomever God has forgiven, God gives this person as service to do. But this service can consist in nothing other than discipleship. Great programs always lead us only to where we ourselves are; we, however, should be found only where God is. We cannot be anywhere other than where God is. Whether you work over there or I work in America, we are both only where God is. God takes us along. Or have I indeed evaded the place where God is *for me*? No, God says: You are my servant.[2]

Bonhoeffer's written reflections on discerning God's distinct call for him had begun. He started out on the trip certain of his current direction in life, but he also admitted the beginning rumblings of an internal struggle. He was seeking the path of simple obedience to the call of Jesus Christ, but as the days and weeks unfolded, particularly after landing in New York, the internal uncertainty gave way to a full-fledged personal battle.

First, there was the disappointment of the work that had been arranged for him. There were a smattering of lectures and seminars for the summer and beyond, but the main task was not what he had been expecting: a three year appointment working with German refugees. Neither the timing nor the work seemed to suit him. At first, he was firm that he could only commit to one year. Then, as the days wore on, and he battled the quite unfamiliar anxieties of homesickness and doubt about being in America at all, he realized he was simply not up to the task. The situation in Germany was also deteriorating, and so there became a real fear of being stranded outside of his homeland if war broke out. As he was to write to Niebuhr about his decision not to remain in America, "I will have no right to participate in

---

2. Bonhoeffer, *DBWE* 15:218.

the reconstruction of Christian life in Germany after the war if I do not share the trials of this time with my people."[3] But Bonhoeffer's thinking on the issue required much effort to come together. Some days he felt it was weakness and cowardice to run away from America, yet he also questioned if he would ever be able to do meaningful work there.[4] He was constantly distracted by thoughts of the brothers in Germany, wondering what he was missing and even lamenting the difficulty of sharing prayer at the same time, due to their different time zones. On June 20, Bonhoeffer made the decision to return home as quickly as possible. He realized he could never be completely clear about his motives, while also wondering if that was "a sign that we are *led* beyond that which we can discern."[5] Bonhoeffer had made the decision, but he knew that "in the end one acts out of a level that remains hidden from us."[6]

This proved a difficult lesson of discipleship. In *Discipleship*, following God was described as responding in simple obedience to the call of Jesus Christ. Now, in New York, with very real issues of personal safety and faithfulness to God's call on the line, the simple call did not sound so straightforward and clear. There were conflicting motives, unfamiliar surroundings, and awkward feelings of confusion and homesickness. On the one hand, his American hosts had gone out of their way to provide a fulfilling life for him; on the other hand, the work back in Germany could not leave his mind. So, a simple act of discipleship for Bonhoeffer became a complex and protracted decision to trust God's lead. The act of simple obedience was more than discerning a choice; it was a reliance on the grace of God. Bonhoeffer did not know what lay ahead for him in Germany, but through the remainder of his life, he refused to look back and did not regret the decision to return.[7]

By leaving the safety of America, Bonhoeffer took a decisive step into the unknown possibilities of discipleship. He knew his life would not be the same, and that his convictions would likely lead him only into danger. But he was willing, even eager, to follow Jesus Christ into the unknown. As his life shifted from the role of pastor, teacher, and theologian to one of involvement in the political and military drama of Germany, Bonhoeffer embraced new opportunities to push—both personally and theologically—the boundaries of his understanding of discipleship.

---

3. See Bethge, *Dietrich Bonhoeffer*, 655.
4. See Bonhoeffer, *DBWE* 15:223.
5. Bonhoeffer, *DBWE* 15:223.
6. Bonhoeffer, *DBWE* 15:223.
7. See Bonhoeffer, *DBWE* 8:517.

The Conspiracy

On July 27, after a brief stop in London to see his sister and brother-in-law, Bonhoeffer was back home in Berlin. He quickly resumed his post directing the collective pastorates in eastern Pomerania, even taking groups of brothers to the Baltic coast in celebration of his return. As it became clear that war was imminent near the end of August, however, Bonhoeffer broke off the sessions and returned to his parent's home in Berlin. The war began on September 1 with Hitler's invasion of Poland.

With the German war machine churning at full capacity, the church struggle received less attention and seemed less important to the public. Confessing Church pastors were being called to the front in large numbers, and the questions of pastoral legality and church organization were being subsided with the concern for personal survival. Bonhoeffer himself continued to look for means to avoid being drafted into a combat role. He applied for military chaplaincy, but was denied because chaplains were required to have had previous active service. However, as Bonhoeffer navigated through the complexities of the application process during the fall and winter months of 1939, the Confessing Church had eight ordinands ready for a final session of training. In October, the group moved to the primitive pastorate in Sigurdshof, and Bonhoeffer had one last opportunity to teach and guide seminarians.[8]

It was also during this time that Bonhoeffer began to meet more frequently with the individuals who were preparing to stage a *coup* against Hitler. In particular, Bonhoeffer found himself in the company of Colonel Hans Oster and Hans von Dohnanyi (his brother-in-law). Oster and Dohnanyi were among the key conspirators plotting the overthrow of Hitler from within the Military Intelligence Foreign Office. It was Dohnanyi who compiled and kept the files of atrocities being committed by the Nazis for use as evidence of war crimes in future trials, and when Bonhoeffer's name was discovered in Dohnanyi's files it was to prove decisive in sealing his fate.[9]

Bonhoeffer's decision to join the Oster-Dohnanyi conspiracy ring set in motion a deeper period of self-exploration regarding the possibilities and potentialities of discipleship. As early as 1938, Bonhoeffer himself was aware of the group's plans to stage a *coup d'état*, and in October 1939 he began to take on a more active role within the circle. Further, it was through these connections that Bonhoeffer was finally able to avoid his call up to the military by being appointed as a foreign intelligence officer in Oster's

---

8. See Bethge, *Dietrich Bonhoeffer*, 664–66.
9. See Bethge, *Dietrich Bonhoeffer*, 935.

office—work that called on him to exploit his ecumenical church contacts in the gathering of foreign intelligence for the benefit of Nazi Germany. In reality, however, he acted as a double-agent. Working with his co-conspirators, Bonhoeffer officially served as a courier for the Military Intelligence Foreign Office; in actuality, his frequent trips to countries like Switzerland and Sweden were designed to provide information to foreign dignitaries ahead of a planned overthrow of Hitler's government.

With such a dramatic change of vocation—from pastor/theologian to co-conspirator—it is appropriate to ask how Bonhoeffer's decision to act as a double-agent was motivated by his theological understanding of discipleship. Does this turn represent a stark departure from the theology of Finkenwalde? Or was it its fulfillment? Most likely, it was an act of simple obedience to the call of Christ. Though his involvement with the conspiracy was indeed couched in many layers, throughout this experience Bonhoeffer remained confident in his Christian responsibility and clear in his theology. The four movements of discipleship—revelation, Christ existing as church-community, belief-obedience, and possibility—all brought Bonhoeffer to this place; and importantly, they brought him to further theological explorations and developments even while in Tegel prison. While all four movements are present in this period of Bonhoeffer's life, the remainder of this chapter will focus exclusively on the final movement, the possibility of discipleship.

At this juncture, further investigation of the development of Bonhoeffer's theology of discipleship during the Tegel prison years would prove helpful. More specifically, exploration of the concept of the possibility and potentiality of discipleship in *Letters and Papers from Prison* will reveal the scholarly emphasis that is often placed on this period of "new" and creative theology. Bonhoeffer did indeed spend much time in theological development while at Tegel, as he did also while writing the initial draft of *Ethics* prior to his arrest. Bonhoeffer's theological work during his imprisonment, however, is of particular interest in further conceptualizing the theological notion of "possibility" in discipleship. In *Letters and Papers from Prison*, Bonhoeffer engaged in innovative and cross-disciplinary research that fueled his emerging understanding of God's work in and for the world. It is both the model of engagement and the insights themselves that help point the way forward in understanding and applying the four movements of discipleship being proposed in this book. In this way, having a sense of how Bonhoeffer deliberately constructed a theology of the possibility of discipleship will help in conceptualizing the uniqueness and power of his theological potentialities.

Bonhoeffer's Tegel Prison Studies

Bonhoeffer's writings from Tegel prison are often described as "the new theology."[10] His *Letters and Papers from Prison* contain wonderful and fresh theological insights, and represent a serious attempt to reconcile the reality of the revelation of Jesus Christ with the growing effects of secularization on Western religion and culture. Though fragmented in nature, the *Letters and Papers* represent some of Bonhoeffer's most creative work. They were the result of focused study and reflection on an impressive array of scholarship, including drama, literature, music, history, philosophy, and physics. He scoured the prison library for material and he managed to receive a regular supply of books from his family and friends, often smuggled into Tegel by a friendly prison guard. Of the dozens of authors that Bonhoeffer read while in prison, three had a particularly strong influence on the development of his new theology: Wilhelm Dilthey, José Ortega y Gasset, and Carl Friedrich von Weizsäcker.

Bonhoeffer's letters from the spring and early summer of 1944 represented the height of his theological reflections. During this time he was giving particular attention to questions of the philosophies of history, human life, and worldview and was looking to Dilthey, Ortega y Gasset, and Weizsäcker for insight. Dilthey and Ortega y Gasset provided a framework for Bonhoeffer to engage critically the historical emergence of science and its perceived companion, secularization. Their philosophies of the radical reality of human life in the interpretation of history offered Bonhoeffer a compelling hermeneutic for interpreting God's place in the rise of human autonomy. Weizsäcker, a physicist, argued that our evolving scientific view of the world has determined our perception of, and belief in, God; this led to an ever-retreating God of the gaps. From these authors (and certainly others) Bonhoeffer was able to refine and articulate the central aspect of his new theology. He refused to flee from the modern world, but embraced it, referring to it as "a world come of age," and declaring that Jesus Christ has and always will be in its very midst. The false claims of religion, exposed by secularization, far from destroying religious faith, opened wide the possibilities of the recognition of God's nearness and grace, for Bonhoeffer understood that the church could only truly follow Jesus Christ when religious constructs were shed from Christianity. He called this separation "religionless Christianity," and for him it was the very possibility of discipleship in a world that had come of age. Bonhoeffer's understanding of this "possibility" emerged in part from his study of human life, history, and

---

10. See Bethge, *Dietrich Bonhoeffer*, 853–91.

worldview in the writings of Dilthey, Ortega y Gasset, and Weizsäcker. Each of these three figures will be examined in terms of how their particular writings influenced this key development of Bonhoeffer's emerging theology. The possibility of discipleship, then, is seen as a culmination of Bonhoeffer's theological developments within his concepts of revelation, Jesus Christ, and belief-obedience. Bonhoeffer's Tegel theology uniquely illuminated his ever-expanding notions of living into the radical reality of Jesus Christ in a much-altered world. It was only from this place, Bonhoeffer discovered, that the possibility of discipleship could truly spring to life.

The Influence of Wilhelm Dilthey

Wilhelm Dilthey (1833–1911) was one of the nineteenth century's most prominent philosophers of ideas. His work not only shaped Continental thought during his lifetime, but reached far into the twentieth century—to Bonhoeffer, for example—and, arguably, its influence continues to this day. A student of historical methodology, biography, psychology, literature, or philosophy would be hard pressed to avoid the confluence of his ideas. Dilthey's complete writings currently appear in German in over twenty edited volumes; even the six volumes of selected writings in English show the scope of his work, ranging from the human sciences, historicity, and hermeneutics to poetry, experience, and aesthetics.[11]

Dilthey was the son of a Protestant minister in Germany's rural Rhineland, and his pietistic surroundings helped cultivate a sense of inwardness and self-experience. He prepared for a career as a philosopher and historian of ideas at the University of Berlin, where he assisted in the editing of the letters of Friedrich Schleiermacher. Schleiermacher certainly left his mark on Dilthey, whose later work led him to the belief that "the immediacy of our inner life is the authentic ground of all philosophy."[12] But it was the quest for authentic historical understanding that preoccupied Dilthey's work. He was especially concerned with separating history from metaphysical dogma and prejudice, and believed that only with such objectivity could humanity be freed for creative activity.[13]

---

11. See Dilthey, *Selected Works*.
12. See Tuttle, *Human Life*, 13.
13. See Rickman, "General Introduction," 14.

Major Streams of Dilthey's Thought

To make any sort of meaningful connections between Dilthey and Bonhoeffer, it is necessary first to understand the major contours of Dilthey's thought. The present study is limited to introducing two of Dilthey's most prominent contributions to the wider intellectual arena: historicism and the philosophy of life. Once the foundation for Dilthey's thought is set, we can explore his more specific (and nuanced) influence on Bonhoeffer's theology.

Undoubtedly, Dilthey's most important achievement was his work in the field of history. His philosophy and methods still serve as the basis for modern historical research and interpretation. While Dilthey was not the founder of German historicism (whose most famous figure was Leopold von Ranke, 1795–1886), he sought to further its credibility by laying a strong philosophic foundation for historical research and writing. The German historical school pioneered practices that are quite conventional today, including a commitment to rigorous scholarship based in primary sources and the often tedious searches of archives, registers, and various collections.[14] Dilthey worked further to support a second aim of the historical school: hermeneutics.

Dilthey and others in the historical school came to reject presuppositions that were common in seventeenth and eighteenth-century historical research. At that time, history was interpreted in terms of natural law and natural theology—with the notion that there were fixed concepts of law, morality, religion, and the nature of humans. Instead, the historicists argued that even such basic concepts as these were subject to historical change.[15] Further, they argued, strict empiricism was not a valid method for understanding history, for in history, contended Dilthey, "We want to understand human beings. Regarding all other objects there is an interest to explain; regarding human beings, an interest to understand."[16] Understanding came when the historian could accurately interpret human life in terms of its experienced reality. Dilthey's work on Schleiermacher's biography helped to illustrate this concept.

In the preface to the first edition of *The Life of Schleiermacher* (1870), Dilthey wrote: "The biography of a thinker or artist has to solve the great historical question how dispersed elements of culture—given through general conditions, social and moral presuppositions and the influence of predecessors and contemporaries—are absorbed and moulded into an

---

14. See Rickman, *Dilthey Today*, 21.

15. See Rickman, *Dilthey Today*, 21.

16. Dilthey, "On Understanding and Hermeneutics," in *Hermeneutics and the Study of History*, 229.

original whole by an individual who, in turn, influences the creative life of the community."[17] Understanding the given reality of Schleiermacher's life could only come from drawing on the extensive historical factors that influenced him. His biography, then, would be a comprehensive accounting of all of aspects of life. So, for example, Dilthey examined the beliefs and religious practices of Schleiermacher's formative community, the Christian community at Herrnhut. He then explored the social and cultural atmosphere of Berlin, where Schleiermacher lived for a time. Poets of the Romantic Movement were Schleiermacher's contemporaries, so Dilthey carefully reviewed the influence of Romanticism on Schleiermacher and his theology. Likewise, the influence of Kant, Goethe, and Spinoza (among others) all had to be properly illuminated. In addition, as a professor at the University of Halle, the nature of Schleiermacher's lectures needed exploration. One of those lecture topics, hermeneutics, was especially important to Dilthey.[18] That this particular topic influenced Dilthey's own philosophy proved (to his thinking) the point—the forces of history on a particular life informed the reality and experiences of others in the community. History was located in the reality of the individual, and not in ultimate models of law, religion, or empiricism. Human life became the radical reality of history.

Dilthey inaugurated the philosophy of life (*Lebenphilosophie*) school of thought in Germany with the understanding that human life itself, and not the traditional philosophical category of substance, was the radically real.[19] "*The fundamental idea of my philosophy,*" he wrote, "is that no one, so far, has based his philosophizing on the full, unmutilated whole of experience, and so, on the whole fullness of reality."[20] Dilthey based an understanding of life and what was real in the world on actual lived experience. Abstract philosophical categories and scientific empiricism were not adequate methods for grasping the fullness and immediacy of life. Empiricism especially, Dilthey wrote, "bases itself on mutilated experience, distorted from the outset by an atomistic theoretical view of mental life . . . no complete human

---

17. Dilthey, *Leben Schleiermachers*, xxxiii. Translated by Rickman in *Dilthey Today*, 17.

18. Rickman, *Dilthey Today*, 17–18.

19. Tuttle, *Human Life*, 14–15.

20. Dilthey, *Gesammelte Schriften*, vol. 8, 175. Translated by Rickman in *Dilthey Today*, 133. Note: Historicism is not a universally accepted concept, and many opposed it in the nineteenth century and even today. Even though natural law has fallen out of favor among liberal Protestants, Roman Catholics and a growing number of more conservative Protestants are quite interested in natural law theory, and would not be sympathetic to historicist claims.

being can be confined within this experience."[21] Dilthey believed that only by embracing the totality of human experience could the true nature of reality be understood and subsequently lived.

Feelings then played a key role in the understanding of what was real.[22] Knowledge was not gained only through cognitive reason; feeling and willing were not "just subjective" reactions. Reality was comprehended only in the fullness of experience. Dilthey was adamant:

> What occurs in this contact [with the world] is life, not a theoretical process; it is what we call an experience, that is, pressure and counter-pressure, expanding towards things which in turn respond, a vital power within and around us which is experienced in pleasure and pain, in fear and hope, in grief over burdens which cannot be shifted, in delight over what we receive as gifts from outside. So the I is not a spectator who sits in front of the world's stage, but is involved in actions and counteractions in which the same actualities are overwhelmingly experienced whether kings figure in them or fools and clowns. This is why no philosopher could ever persuade those involved that everything was appearance or show and not reality.[23]

The reality of human life was thus understood in the connectedness of humanity's inner and outer experiences through time. There was an immediacy to life within each unique individual. "Our life is what is happening to us right now, what we are doing right now, what is before us in a now present,"[24] explained the American philosopher Howard Tuttle. As human beings, we simply comprehend life as it is for us here and now.

Dilthey's Influence on Bonhoeffer's Thought

Bonhoeffer scholars have consistently noted the importance of Dilthey for the development of Bonhoeffer's Tegel theology. Often, though, the extent of the discussion is just that—a general note. The influence of Ernst Feil's work may be responsible for much of the generalizations. In *The Theology of Dietrich Bonhoeffer* (1985), Feil carefully outlined the influence of Dilthey on the prison letters.[25] He paid particular attention to the emergence

---

21. Rickman, *Dilthey Today*, 133.
22. Note the connection here to "feeling" in Schleiermacher.
23. Dilthey, *Gesammelte Schriften*, vol. 19, 153. Translated by Rickman in *Dilthey Today*, 135.
24. Tuttle, *Human Life*, 16.
25. Feil, *Theology of Dietrich Bonhoeffer*, 178–91.

of the term "world come of age," and offered a convincing explanation for Bonhoeffer's use of this concept from Dilthey. Feil shows how Bonhoeffer was confronted with the rise of the "autonomy of reason" and the "worldliness" of emerging history, especially in Dilthey's *Das Erlebnis und die Dichtung*[26] and *Weltanschauung und Analyse des Menschen seit Renaissance und Reformation*.[27]

German theologian Ralf Wüstenberg took the discussion further, focusing on the question of Dilthey's influence as a "philosopher of life" on Bonhoeffer's late theology.[28] Wüstenberg examined Bonhoeffer's reading of *Weltanschauung und Analyse* and argued that Dilthey's concept of life then became Bonhoeffer's basic cognitive-theoretical concept. "From the philosophy of life," Wüstenberg wrote, "Bonhoeffer acquired an important impulse for his understanding of life, and the theological understanding of life remains determinative for his reading of Dilthey."[29] This philosophy of life became the major hermeneutic for Wüstenberg's interpretation of Bonhoeffer. Thus, both Feil and Wüstenberg provided an important beginning point for the study of Bonhoeffer and Dilthey. Their work will certainly help inform aspects of what follows.

Bonhoeffer was deep into the writings of Dilthey as he began to formulate his notions of "the world come of age." During the winter and spring of 1944, Bonhoeffer procured and studied three of Dilthey's works. He received *Das Erlebnis und die Dichtung* and *Von deutscher Dichtung und Musik* for the occasion of his February 4 birthday, and, on March 2, he requested *Weltanschauung und Analyse des Menschen seit Renaissance und Reformation* from his parents. The first evidences of *Weltanschauung und Analyse* appeared in the June 8, 1944 letter to his close friend and dialogue partner, Eberhard Bethge. But the influences of the first two works were apparent months earlier, in the March 9, 1944 letter to Bethge.[30]

In this correspondence, Bonhoeffer began to reveal the burgeoning influence of Dilthey with his discussion of the "worldliness" of the thirteenth century. Dilthey discussed how worldliness emerged out of the Middle Ages with such figures as Walther, Nibelungen, and Parsifal.[31] Bonhoeffer responded: "This is no 'emancipated' worldliness, but rather a 'Christian'

26. See Dilthey, *Selected Works*.
27. See Dilthey, *Gesammelte Schriften*.
28. See Wüstenberg, *Theology of Life*, 104–12.
29. Wüstenberg, "Influence of Wilhelm Dilthey," 173.
30. See Bonhoeffer, *DBWE* 8:320.
31. See Dilthey, *Von deutscher Dichtung und Musik*, 72–94, 107–30. See also Bonhoeffer, *DBWE* 8:320.

one, though anti-clerical. Where does this 'worldliness,' which is so different from that of the Renaissance, actually break off?"[32] Bonhoeffer here was confronting Dilthey's own interpretation of "worldliness." Whereas for Dilthey, the Middle Ages represented a breaking off from Christian faith and a turning to secular knowledge and worldliness,[33] Bonhoeffer denied such an "emancipation" and instead wanted to affirm a "Christian worldliness."[34] Still, although he may not have been willing to abandon the finality of Christianity in history, Bonhoeffer found Dilthey's discussion of history pivotal for understanding the development of religious ideas.

In *Von deutscher Dichtung und Musik*, Bonhoeffer read how the German Middle Ages, with its heroic poetry and national epic, cultivated both an inwardness of religious life and a free, worldly reflection about life.[35] As a consequence, a separation of the worldly from the religious ensued: "The focus of life shifts from the transcendent orders, fears and desires to this world. Lady World and her needs, demands, possibilities, ethical structures and ideals govern the new society."[36] In the midst of these readings, Bonhoeffer wrestled with his whole notion of history. He came to understand that historical understanding and interpretation was vital for an accurate assessment of the past, and a viable vision for the future. But, he wondered, was the emergence of worldliness merely a condition of the continuum of "ancient," "medieval," and "modern" history, as in Ranke and Delbrück? Or,

---

32. Bonhoeffer, *DBWE* 8:320. Bonhoeffer is also reflecting in this quote his dislike of medieval Christendom, and his view that it perpetuated itself by compulsion.

33. Heidegger's interpretation of Dilthey is helpful here: "For him, theology had a relation to philosophy and to history, namely, the history of Christianity and its fundamental fact, the life of Jesus. Dilthey planned a history of Western Christianity, but this plan and his whole program of theological studies fell apart during his study of the Middle Ages. In the struggle between faith and knowledge, Dilthey sided with knowledge and this-worldliness. He renounced all closure and finality and was everywhere satisfied only with being able to explore, only with researching and 'dying on the journey.'" See Heidegger, "Wilhelm Dilthey's Research," 151–52.

34. See, for example, Bonhoeffer's earlier conviction in *DBWE* 6:55: "What matters is *participating in the reality of God and the world in Jesus Christ today*, and doing so in such a way that I never experience the reality of God without the reality of the world, nor the reality of the world without the reality of God." For Bonhoeffer, Jesus Christ is the center of all reality, and therefore cannot be removed or "sided over" in favor of "worldliness." This does not mean that "worldliness" is not a historical phenomenon; it is just not a reflection of God's nearness to humanity, as we will see further below.

35. See Dilthey, *Von deutscher Dichtung und Musik*, 66, 70, as cited in Feil, *Theology of Dietrich Bonhoeffer*, 179.

36. Dilthey, *Von deutscher Dichtung und Musik*, 77, as cited in Feil, *Theology of Dietrich Bonhoeffer*, 179.

were cultural domains self-contained, as in Spengler?[37] If the former, then the whole course of history culminated in the arrival of "modernity" (and, Bonhoeffer noted, in the emergence of Hegel's own philosophical system). But the latter choice was insufficient as well: "Spengler's morphology is *biological*, and that is its limitation (what does 'aging' or 'decline' of a civilization mean?)."[38] Thus, Bonhoeffer concluded, "Until we have more insight here, it would be good to base our relationship to the past, and to classical antiquity in particular, not on a general concept of history, but solely on *content* and specific *topics*."[39] So Bonhoeffer would not try and interpret history within a philosophical system, and would instead look to history for insight into specific topics—like the development of worldliness and autonomy.

Bonhoeffer found Dilthey's *Weltanschauung und Analyse* especially helpful in examining the concept of human autonomy. The first evidence of Bonhoeffer's use of this work can be found in a letter to Bethge of June 8, 1944; however the letters of July 8 and July 16, 1944 (also to Bethge) contained Bonhoeffer's most intense and deliberate reflections on Dilthey's concepts. Bonhoeffer acknowledged on July 8 that, "God's being pushed out of the world, away from public human existence, has led to an attempt to hang onto God at least in the realm of the 'personal,' the 'inner life,' the 'private' sphere."[40] He then explained that people then began to go about hunting down the secrets of others' private spheres for exploitation—as if people could only be addressed as sinners after having spied out their weaknesses.[41] Such suspicion and bifurcation of human life into "outer" and "inner" experiences further perpetuated the false assumption that only a person's "inner life" and most intimate depths were to be the domain of God.

In Dilthey, Bonhoeffer was therefore reminded of the biblical concept of human life. Dilthey traced the discovery of the inner life to Petrarch, in the Renaissance: "so he could grasp the idea of wanting to be a full, whole human being."[42] Bonhoeffer agreed: "the Bible does not know the distinction that we make between the outward and the inward life. How could it, actually? It is always concerned with the *anthropos teleios*, the *whole* human

---

37. See Bonhoeffer, *DBWE* 8:320–21.
38. Bonhoeffer, *DBWE* 8:321.
39. Bonhoeffer, *DBWE* 8:321.
40. Bonhoeffer, *DBWE* 8:455.
41. See Bonhoeffer, *DBWE* 8:455–56.
42. See Dilthey, *Weltanschauung und Analyse*, 20, as quoted in Bonhoeffer, *DBWE* 8:457.

being."[43] In the midst of this discussion we find one of Bonhoeffer's most well-known quotes:

> What I am driving at is that God should not be smuggled in somewhere, in the very last, secret place that is left. Instead, one must simply recognize that the world and humankind have come of age. One must not find fault with people in their worldliness but rather confront them with God where they are strongest. One must give up the "holier-than-thou" ploys and not regard psychotherapy or existential philosophy as scouts preparing the way for God.[44]

With Dilthey, Bonhoeffer affirmed the radical beauty and wholeness of human life; he now wanted to look to the fullness of human life for a proper understanding of God. Dilthey also contended that the understanding of others did not come from mere logical construction or psychological analysis, but rather from an epistemological standpoint. He insisted that human beings were always expressions of their complete life, including their concepts, judgments, thought structures, and emotions.[45] This whole human being had now come of age and lived autonomously in the midst of the world.

Bonhoeffer traced the development of the world's autonomy from religious constructs with careful detail in the July 16, 1944 letter to Bethge. Largely following Dilthey's historical account in *Weltanschauung und Analyse*, Bonhoeffer took time to explicate the origins and implications of the modern autonomous society. Especially potent was the recognition of Grotius, who "sets up his natural law as an international law, which is valid *etsi deus non daretur*, "as if there were no God."[46] When Bonhoeffer reexamined the nature of the world, from the vantage point of Montaigne, Machiavelli, and Grotius, and through Descartes, Spinoza, Kant, Fichte, and Hegel, he realized that God as a working hypothesis for morality, politics, the natural sciences, philosophy, and even religion had been overcome. "And we can't be honest unless we recognize that we have to live in the world—'*etsi deus non daretur*.'"[47]

Here, as Naozumi Eto pointed out, was where Bonhoeffer most drastically differed from Dilthey. "[Bonhoeffer] accepts the relativity of religion which Dilthey proved in his historical study, but never accepts the relativity

43. Bonhoeffer, *DBWE* 8:456.
44. Bonhoeffer, *DBWE* 8:457.
45. See Dilthey, *Pattern and Meaning*, 116–18.
46. Bonhoeffer, *DBWE* 8:476.
47. Bonhoeffer, *DBWE* 8:478.

of Christ or Christian faith."[48] Living as if there were no God may be the historical development of society, but this in turn led to a truer recognition of our situation before God, and affirmed the immanence of the cross: "God consents to be pushed out of the world and onto the cross; God is weak and powerless in the world and in precisely this way, and only so, is at our side and helps us."[49] The world's coming of age, according to Bonhoeffer, had cleared the way by eliminating a false notion of God, "and frees us to see the God of the Bible, who gains ground and power in the world by being powerless."[50] This was the beginning point for a "worldly interpretation" of Christianity, a Christianity that in its religionlessness affirmed the entire human being Christ created in us. The possibility of discipleship then begins with the recognition that the world has come of age, and it finds momentum in the affirmation of human life.

The Influence of José Ortega y Gasset

José Ortega y Gasset (1883–1955) was a prolific writer, his work covering numerous aspects of Spanish and European culture. His twelve-volume *Obras Completas* contains books and essays on philosophy, literary criticism, pedagogy, painting and sculpture, politics, sociology, music, and even hunting and golf.[51] Nora de Marval-McNair noted that Ortega y Gasset is "regarded as the intellectual leader of a whole generation," and that through him, "Spaniards became better acquainted with the rest of Europe, and Europe with Spain."[52] Like Dilthey, Ortega y Gasset's philosophical system focused especially on the profoundly human; the idea of human life formed his basis for historical understanding.

Ortega y Gasset was born in Madrid, the son of an editor and lawyer, and enjoyed the culture and privilege of the liberal upper classes.[53] He obtained a bachelor's degree at fourteen, a *licenciado* in philosophy and letters from the University of Madrid at nineteen and a doctorate two years later. The next year, in 1905, he began postdoctoral studies in Germany, convinced that European culture and governance needed to be brought to Spain. By 1910, he was a professor in metaphysics at the University of Madrid, from where he became an advocate for the reformation of Spain.

48. Eto, "Bonhoeffer's Idea of Religion," 288.
49. Bonhoeffer, *DBWE* 8:479.
50. Bonhoeffer, *DBWE* 8:479.
51. Ortega y Gasset, *Obras Completas*. See De Marval-McNair, "Preface," xi.
52. De Marval-McNair, "Preface," xii.
53. Tuttle, *Human Life*, 26.

This lasted until 1936, when the Spanish Civil War forced him into exile to Buenos Aires.[54] It was in this year that Ortega y Gasset penned "History as a System," an essay that Bonhoeffer read in 1944 while in prison and which offers important insights into Bonhoeffer's thinking and development.

"History as a System"

Ortega y Gasset himself recommended "History as a System" for readers to see the major contours of his philosophy of history and human life. Calling it a "good example of what I want to say," he noted that "it contains a few insights which, in view of the time when they were gained, are perhaps not undeserving of consideration."[55] His humility is quaint, but this statement affirms the essay's ability adequately to characterize and summarize some of Ortega y Gasset's more formative ideas. As such, a brief outline of some of his principle ideas allows for a discussion about the influence of Ortega y Gasset's thought on the formation of Bonhoeffer's ideas of religionless Christianity and worldly discipleship.

Though Ortega y Gasset described the essay as "a good example" of his thought, a leading contemporary scholar, John Graham, offered a word of caution: "Merely *reading* "History as a System" will not get one very far, because it is a schematic distillation of Ortega's historical *thinking* as a whole, without a corresponding overall unity clearly imposed on its thematic variety."[56] Graham went on to argue that, in order to interpret and understand the essay adequately, a full comprehension of its larger relationships and background was necessary. This is certainly the case, and Graham dedicated a chapter to "History as a System" in the midst of an entire book on Ortega y Gasset's theory of history. Overall, Graham has produced a dense three-volume work on Ortega y Gasset, which also covers his philosophy and social thought.[57] So, while acknowledging fully Graham's cautions and our indebtedness to his comprehensive research and interpretation, the following summary is intended to provide a basic familiarity with some of Ortega y Gasset's key concepts from "History as a System" for the purpose of illustrating its contribution to Bonhoeffer's intellectual development.

Following Dilthey, Ortega y Gasset proposed that human life was the impetus for understanding all reality: "Human life is a strange reality concerning which the first thing to be said is that it is the basic reality, in

---

54. See Tuttle, *Human Life*, 26–28.
55. Ortega y Gasset, "Author's Forward," 10–11.
56. Graham, *Theory of History*, 130–31.
57. See Graham, *Pragmatist Philosophy*; and Graham, *Social Thought*.

the sense that to it we must refer to all others, since all others, effective or presumptive, must in one way or another appear within it."[58] Human life was concrete reality; so that when speaking of ontology, it refers to what is actually happening around us. Ortega y Gasset understood this as the liberation from naturalism and idealism. So, he concluded, Hegel's system of progress and Comte's theory of three epochs, while intellectually creative, were not representative theories of reality. While historically they may have demonstrated the progression of human life and thought, ontologically their claims of utopian progress were simply unfounded.[59] Such things, explained Ortega y Gasset, "are the ideas that come out of our heads and are taken by us as reality."[60] Independent and authentic reality, on the other hand, "is only real when functioning in the human life."[61] Ortega y Gasset thus described human life pragmatically: "Man is not his body, which is a thing, nor his soul, psyche, conscience, or spirit, which is also a thing. Man is no thing, but a drama—his life, a pure and universal happening which happens to each one of us and in which each one in his turn is nothing but happening."[62] Human life was what one made of it. An idea or ontological presupposition did not reveal reality. Humans were not static beings that could have idealistic concepts placed upon them. Ortega y Gasset was clear: a human "lives" rather than "is."[63]

As such, the idea of narrative reason became central to Ortega y Gasset's conceptions. A human life made sense only in light of the past and the present. "To comprehend anything human, be it personal or collective," claimed Ortega y Gasset, "one must tell its history." He continued: "This man, this nation does such a thing and is in such a manner, *because* formerly he or it did that other thing and was in such another manner."[64] The actual story of human life, and not the mere idea of human life, was the central hermeneutic. Humans were granted the ability to "invent for themselves" a pattern of life, and yet they recognized that they were only who they are because of who they were. His conclusion was frank: "*Man, in a word, has no nature; what he has is . . . history.*"[65] The system of history was the experience

---

58. Ortega y Gasset, "History as a System," 165.
59. Ortega y Gasset, "History as a System," 188.
60. Ortega y Gasset, "History as a System," 198.
61. Ortega y Gasset, "History as a System," 198.
62. Ortega y Gasset, "History as a System," 200.
63. Ortega y Gasset, "History as a System," 213.
64. Ortega y Gasset, "History as a System," 215.
65. Ortega y Gasset, "History as a System," 217.

of human life, "linked in a single, inexorable chain."[66] Each life-event was only understood in light of what had come before. History, ever a science of the present because it always looked to the past, then brought meaning and purpose to the radical reality of human life.

Ortega y Gasset's Influence on Bonhoeffer's Thought

Wüstenberg has rightly connected Bonhoeffer's reading of Ortega y Gasset with his interest in Dilthey during the time he served in Tegel prison. Ortega y Gasset himself regarded Dilthey as "the most important figure in the second half of the nineteenth century," and was especially indebted to his work concerning the idea of human life.[67] Wüstenberg has argued that Bonhoeffer read Ortega y Gasset in an effort to clarify Dilthey's concept of the interdependence between human life and history, with particular attention given to the concept of life.[68] Indeed, Wüstenberg's entire project traced Bonhoeffer's "theology of life" to the interplay between Dilthey and Ortega y Gasset. He speculated that Bonhoeffer's reading of Ortega y Gasset's *On the Roman Empire* in the autumn of 1943 "quite possibly" led to the view of religion as a historical phenomenon.

Wüstenberg then reviewed F. W. Kantzenbach's study on the connections between Bonhoeffer's prison letters and Ortega y Gasset's *The Nature of Historic Crisis* in order to deepen his thesis. Here, he explained how Ortega y Gasset overcame the determinative concept of religion in the nineteenth century: "For Dilthey, religionlessness is historically incomprehensible" because religion was an anthropological phenomenon. By contrast, for Ortega y Gasset, religionlessness was quite possible because religion, he argued, "is a matter of behavioral expression manifesting itself in different ways in different historical epochs, and which can even be completely absent."[69] Finally, Wüstenberg summarized *History as a System* and illustrated how Ortega y Gasset picked up Dilthey's concept of life experience. As he concluded: "the thrust of the entire study, the rejection of rationalism, corresponds to a typical, basic feature of Dilthey's historical philosophy of life."[70]

While Wüstenberg's study looked to Dilthey and Ortega y Gasset for the foundations of Bonhoeffer's "theology of life" in the Tegel correspondence, this study is interested in investigating specific points of connection

---

66. Ortega y Gasset, "History as a System," 221–23.
67. Ortega y Gasset, "History as a System," 216.
68. Wüstenberg, *Theology of Life*, 104.
69. Wüstenberg, *Theology of Life*, 102.
70. Wüstenberg, *Theology of Life*, 103.

between Bonhoeffer's critical study of primary sources and the emergence of his "new" theology, focused on the "possibility of discipleship." A close look at Bonhoeffer's June 27 and 30, 1944 letters to Bethge allow some of the connections between Ortega y Gasset's essay "History as a System" and Bonhoeffer's emerging theological ideas to be drawn out. Bonhoeffer's particular concern in these letters continued to be the "worldliness" of Christianity.

Tracing specific reference of Ortega y Gasset in Bonhoeffer's letters is more difficult than finding examples from Dilthey and Weizsäcker. While quotes and direct references to the latter can be found in the letters, Bonhoeffer's only direct mentions of Ortega y Gasset come in the form of requests for his books, and not in quotations or even in explicit recitation of his ideas. However, this does not bar investigating probable occurrences of influence; it simply renders the task more speculative.

Bonhoeffer first requested a copy of *History as a System* in a letter of October 4, 1943 to his parents; by April 26 of the following year the book still had not arrived and he asked for it a second time: "Could you perhaps try to get me Ortega y Gasset's new book, *Das Wesen geschichtlicher Krisen* (Deutscher Verlagsanstalt Stuttgart-Berlin), and if possible also his previous one, *Geschichte als System*?"[71] These books must have arrived soon after, as Bethge noted that Bonhoeffer read them both in May of 1944.[72] By the end of June, it was evident that Bonhoeffer was working some of the ideas from the essay "History as a System" into his theological thoughts.

In the June 27, 1944 letter, Bonhoeffer addressed the Old and New Testament notions of redemption to make a case for worldly Christianity. He described how the Old Testament differed from other oriental religions in not being a religion merely of transcendent redemption; for Israel redemption was *within history*, "that is, *this side* of the bounds of death, whereas everywhere else the aim of all other myths of redemption is precisely to overcome death's boundary. Israel is redeemed out of Egypt so that it may live before God, as God's people on earth."[73] Bonhoeffer was now connecting his foundational biblical and theological concepts to the philosophy of life he found in Dilthey and Ortega y Gasset. Redemption was the ultimate affirmation of human life in that it recognized the pragmatic reality of life. The principle danger Bonhoeffer saw in his day was that redemption "now means being redeemed out of sorrows, hardships, anxieties, and longings, out of sin and death, in a better life beyond."[74] The Christian hope of resur-

---

71. Bonhoeffer, *DBWE* 8:360.
72. See Bethge, *Dietrich Bonhoeffer*, 944.
73. Bonhoeffer, *DBWE* 8:447.
74. Bonhoeffer, *DBWE* 8:447.

rection, rather, referred people to their present life in a whole new way, and the New Testament needed to be interpreted in such a way that affirmed the worldliness of the Old Testament.

The hope of the resurrection inaugurated with Christianity was tragically limited when redemption came to mean flight from the jagged edges of this world into the glory of the next. The proclamation of Christ in the Gospels and in Paul's epistles reached beyond these desires. Affirming the baseness of life Bonhoeffer remarked, "Christians do not have an ultimate escape route out of their earthly tasks and difficulties into eternity. Like Christ ("My God . . . why have you forsaken me?"), they have to drink the cup of earthly life to the last drop," and only then were they "crucified and resurrected with Christ."[75] Drinking the cup of earthly life to the last drop meant embracing and living in the full reality of existence. It meant affirming the "history" of one's present life and not just living for the next life; God's work of redemption was both for this world and for the next. On this, noted Bonhoeffer, the Old and New Testaments were united. Our tendency was to look beyond our circumstances and life for redemption, but "this-worldliness must not be abolished ahead of its time."[76]

Instead, the reality of life in Jesus Christ needed to be realized. Christ was interested in this life, here and now; he even "takes hold of human beings in the midst of their lives."[77] To affirm otherwise would be to regard happiness as disastrous, health as sickness and vitality as an object of despair. This might be the triumph of existential philosophy and psychotherapy, chided Bonhoeffer, but this was not the gospel. "When Jesus made sinners whole, they were real sinners, but Jesus didn't begin by making every person into a sinner. He called people from their sin, not into it."[78] Jesus certainly accepted people from all corners of society, including prostitutes and tax collectors, but "never did [he] question anyone's health and strength or good fortune as such or regard it as rotten fruit. . . . Jesus claims all of human life, in all its manifestations, for himself and for the kingdom of God."[79] All of life was affirmed, embraced, and redeemed in Jesus Christ.

Bonhoeffer now had transformed the humanism in Ortega y Gasset by placing it into a proper christological context. This-worldliness was affirmed and the reality of human life was embraced through the redeeming work of Jesus Christ. While Ortega y Gasset's system of history (working from

75. Bonhoeffer, *DBWE* 8:448.
76. Bonhoeffer, *DBWE* 8:448.
77. Bonhoeffer, *DBWE* 8:448.
78. Bonhoeffer, *DBWE* 8:450.
79. Bonhoeffer, *DBWE* 8:451.

Dilthey), with its scientific study of the human being and human drama, and the philosophy of life had affirmed the maturity of the world, Bonhoeffer recognized that Jesus was always in the midst of the world. Religion may have been a fading social construct, but Jesus was in relationship with the world, and may have been even closer to this world that has come of age. Human life was the radical reality, but human life was not the center of reality; Jesus Christ was. And Jesus remained in the midst of this-worldliness, even as he was pushed out.

Ortega y Gasset allowed Bonhoeffer to press forward with a new theology, a theology that explored the far reaches of the possibility of discipleship. By affirming the reality of human life, Bonhoeffer could now describe a theology of presence and engagement. The experience of human life, as the new hermeneutic, described what was real; idealism and its accompanying historical religiosity no longer relied on God for antagonism or support. However, in the midst of the world, Jesus Christ remained for the world. Those who follow Jesus Christ now had a renewed model of discipleship. As those in world scraped away the remaining remnants of religion in an effort to find their true selves, they would be better able to discover that Jesus Christ had been next to them all along.

The Influence of Carl Friedrich von Weizsäcker

Bonhoeffer was aided in his endeavor to describe religionless Christianity in a third source. The final figure in this brief study was a young German physicist, a contemporary of Bonhoeffer's. Although he was not a "philosopher of life," like Dilthey and Ortega y Gasset, the scientific writings of Carl Friedrich von Weizsäcker (1912–2007) furthered the development of Bonhoeffer's concept of worldliness and his emerging form of Christianity. Especially significant was Bonhoeffer's adoption of the concept of God of the gaps from Weizsäcker.

Bonhoeffer was introduced to Weizsäcker through his eldest brother Karl Friedrich, himself a physical chemist. Bonhoeffer kept up a fervent reading schedule while in prison, and his letters showed the constant flow of books back and forth between him and the members of his family.[80] A June 12, 1943 letter from Karl Friedrich piqued Bonhoeffer's interest. His brother offered to send "a freshly published collection of lectures on modern phys-

---

80. Bonhoeffer uses this passing of reading material to continue his participation in the conspiracy against Hitler; the conspirators had devised a prearranged plan for passing information by making inconspicuous markings in the books that were exchanged. See Bethge, *Dietrich Bonhoeffer*, 812.

ics, or rather the philosophy of nature; but I first have to read it a little more carefully myself in order to decide whether you would get something from it."[81] Some months later, Bonhoeffer still remembered the offer: "At some point K. Friedrich mentioned a generally comprehensible physics book that he wanted to send to me."[82] He was clearly anxious to expand his exposure to the sciences as revealed on February 2, 1944 to Bethge: "I greatly regret my lack of knowledge of the natural sciences, but it's too late for that."[83] However, by the end of May, the book had arrived, and Bonhoeffer was pleasantly surprised at its impact: "I'm now reading, with great interest, Weizsäcker's book on the "worldview of physics" and hope to learn a good deal from it, even for my own work."[84] Bonhoeffer's venture into physics was quite a departure from the philosophy and history of Dilthey and Ortega y Gasset (among others); however, he managed to integrate Weizsäcker into his work. A brief introduction of Weizsäcker and his *World View of Physics* will provide a deeper context and appreciation for Bonhoeffer's synthesis.

The World View of Physics

Weizsäcker was six years younger than Bonhoeffer and obtained his Ph.D. from the University of Leipzig in 1933. He taught at the universities of Leipzig, Berlin, and Strasbourg between 1933 and 1945, and quickly became a leading research scientist and astrophysicist.[85] Yet Weizsäcker was also interested in working through some of the philosophical implications of modern science. His collection of lectures and essays, *The World View of Physics*, tackled questions of physical reality and worldview, perception and the atomic theory, the implications of the law of conservation, the relation of quantum physics to the philosophy of Kant, the infinity of the world, natural law, theodicy, and fundamental questions of experimentation. The book wonderfully weaved the leading questions of science with philosophical reflections. Bonhoeffer was especially taken with the ideas in the fifth

---

81. Bonhoeffer, *DBWE* 8:104.
82. Bonhoeffer, *DBWE* 8:155.
83. Bonhoeffer, *DBWE* 8:285.
84. Bonhoeffer, *DBWE* 8:401.

85. See *Oxford Dictionary of Scientists*, s.v. Weizsäcker, Baron Carl Friedrich von. During the war effort in Germany, Weizsäcker was a leader of the team working to develop the atomic bomb. They never succeeded. Weizsäcker later said that they did not figure out how to make the bomb because there was a general "lack of motivation" among the scientists working on the project. "I don't think we ought to make excuses now because we did not succeed, but we must admit that we didn't want to succeed." See Frank, *Operation Epsilon*, 78.

chapter, "The Infinity of the World: a Study of the Symbolical Element in Natural Science."

Weizsäcker framed his discussion of infinity around the question of natural science and symbolism. He described how the scientific question of infinity came to bear on human imagination and perceptions. When people asked, "Does the world stretch without limit into space?" or "Is it of everlasting duration?," they sought not only scientific answers, but at the same time they betrayed a symbolic attitude of the mind, "a feeling for life," in Weizsäcker's words. He then examined the linked scientific-symbolic pursuit of this question of infinity throughout Western cultural history, and was especially interested in its implications for today.[86] "To many of us," he wrote, "precisely the physical discoveries of our century appear to be the expression of a spiritual change which extends far beyond the limits of physics."[87] Yet, were these physical discoveries the cause of such spiritual change? What was the relationship between scientific discovery and the spiritual expression of our own time? Weizsäcker showed that throughout history perceptions of the cosmos have always symbolized and expressed perceptions of God and the spiritual.

Antiquity held that the cosmos were finite. The earth was a round disc, surrounded by the stream of the ocean, and the physical world had defined, finite boundaries, which symbolized spiritual order. What lay beyond the grey, immeasurable boundary of the ocean was inconsequential. To look beyond it was not only impossible, but impious, for to do so would be to abandon the measure which the gods had set for human beings. One could not, and must not, ask what lies beyond the vast expanse of water.[88]

Greek science soon left behind the notion of the world disc and instead described the earth as a sphere in the center of the world. The world had expanded, but was still finite because it was ordered. The seven planets all orbited around the earth on fixed spheres, and the outer sphere held the stars. To be sure, Greek philosophy now meddled in questions of the infinite, but resolved that there could not be "empty space" out there, because there *is* no empty space—there is only place. Every-body had a place; an empty place would be the place of nothing, and therefore no place. Such logic was "a necessary consequence of Aristotelian logic which is oriented to being, and according to which a proposition is false, precisely if there is no thing of which it is true," explained Weizsäcker.[89]

86. See Weizsäcker, *World View of Physics*, 136-37.
87. Weizsäcker, *World View of Physics*, 137.
88. See Weizsäcker, *World View of Physics*, 141-43.
89. Weizsäcker, *World View of Physics*, 144.

For the Middle Ages, the world remained finite; but an infinite God stood over and against it. The world was finite in space, yet created by a God that was beyond the world and even non-spatial. The world was finite in time—having a first day of creation and a last day of judgment—but before the creation and after the judgment there was no time. God, however, was omnipotent, omniscient, omnipresent, and eternal; God was infinite. The language of "infinite" was not conceptual, though; instead "it is the symbol of experience which language can only suggest."[90] The finite world looked beyond to the infinite for salvation and grace. But this meant that the world could also forget and neglect God.

By the middle of the fifteenth century, Nicolas of Cusa began to teach the concept of infinity of the world. He began, to be sure, with a symbolic religious view, but this quickly led to the mathematical natural science of modern times. For Nicolas, God infused into the creation of the world all but the last measure of God's infinity—just enough to keep the world different from himself. Though not 'absolutely' infinite, the world was in fact 'concretely' infinite. This meant that while God remained unknowable, much could be known about God through mathematically studying and understanding the infinite world. Within two hundred years, Johannes Kepler formulated his laws of planetary motion with two set conditions of scientific inquiry: undeviating agreement with experience and mathematical simplicity. As scientific observation and methodology continued to develop, the possibility again arose of a turning back from God to the world for symbolic expression and meaning. "[And] once the symbolic relation between God and world is broken," wrote Weizsäcker, "a material relation cannot well be salvaged." He continued, with a passage that certainly set Bonhoeffer's mind spinning:

> The step from Kepler to Newton is historically intelligible, that from Newton to Laplace objectively necessary. For Kepler the positive knowledge of science points to God, while for Newton it is just the gaps in this knowledge which leave room for God. But such gaps are usually filled in in further development, and science cannot rest satisfied until they are filled in. Even if the hypotheses of Laplace had been false in some particulars, still every scientist must certainly set for himself the goal of making the hypothesis 'God' superfluous in his field. God and the faded, half-religious concepts which have often been substituted for him in recent times, always designate, as scientific hypotheses for the explanation of particular facts, only incomplete points in

90. Weizsäcker, *World View of Physics*, 147.

science, and therefore with the advance of knowledge they find themselves in continuous and dishonourable retreat.[91]

The modern world was now understood as infinite. Modern science ceaselessly explored this infinite depth. Whether investigating the farthest of distances or the smallest of particles, the symbolic language of scientific discovery had continually filled in the gaps, without God. How were we now to face the reality that our substitute symbolism for God had broken down? We must admit that it failed not because it was merely symbolism, but because it was a substitute. And now that we are left in silence, asked Weizsäcker, did God no longer speak to us? The answer was striking: the silence which has taken the place of our symbolism "is eloquent enough, for it puts us before our real situation. We must in fact know only whether we want to hear God at all—not where we wish to hear him, but where he really speaks to us."[92] Bonhoeffer picked up this exciting development and quickly worked it into his theological reflections.

Weizsäcker's Influence on Bonhoeffer's Thought

Scholars have long recognized the significance of Weizsäcker on the development of Bonhoeffer's prison theology, noting the clear reference Bonhoeffer makes to Weizsäcker and *The World View of Physics* in his adoption of the "God of the gaps" concept. An article by Rodney Holder explores science and religion in the theology of Bonhoeffer, and takes particular notice of Weizsäcker's influence. Holder argues that Bonhoeffer looked to Weizsäcker to combat the ambiguity of natural theology.[93] Yet, instead of responding to natural theology with a simple positivism of revelation (as in Karl Barth), Bonhoeffer advocated a radical appropriation of the centrality of Jesus Christ.[94] In what follows, Holder's observations are more fully explored and Weizsäcker's "God of the gaps" observation is directly connected to Bonhoeffer's emerging theological synthesis with the philosophies of history and life from Dilthey and Ortega y Gasset.

From an early date, Bonhoeffer referred to God as a "stopgap." He mentioned the concept several times in his habilitation, *Act and Being*, and then again when referring to Paul Tillich's *Religious Situation* during his lectures

---

91. Weizsäcker, *World View of Physics*, 157.
92. Weizsäcker, *World View of Physics*, 178.
93. See Holder, "Science and Religion," 116–25.
94. See Bonhoeffer, *DBWE* 8:424–31.

in the winter semester of 1931–32.[95] However, he admitted in a May 29, 1944 letter to Bethge that reading Weizsäcker had brought the concept back to the forefront of his thoughts: "[Weizsäcker's book] has again brought home to me quite clearly that we shouldn't think of God as the stopgap for the incompleteness of our knowledge, because then—as is objectively inevitable—when the boundaries of knowledge are pushed even further, God too is pushed further away and is thus ever on the retreat."[96] A God of the gaps was useful for explaining what could not be scientifically elucidated. But, as science found more and more answers for more and more mysteries, this God was pushed ever further from relevance. As the world matured and came of age, there was less of a need for the religious God.

Theology had resisted this development in two ways, explained Bonhoeffer. On the one hand, it looked in vain to apologetics to take up arms against scientific developments, like those in Darwinism. "On the other hand, [theology] has resigned itself to the way things have gone and allowed God to function only as a *deus ex machina* in the so-called ultimate questions, that is, God becomes the answer to life's questions, a solution to life's needs and conflicts."[97] Both of these solutions ignored the transcendence of God, and they failed to recognize God's work in the very midst of our lives—through science, art, and literature, for example. A God of the "machine" refused to engage in the full complexities of human life and experience.

Bonhoeffer instead insisted that we must listen from the place where God was actually speaking to us, and not from where we wished God was speaking. And God spoke in what we knew, not in what we did not know: "God wants to be grasped by us not in unsolved questions but in those that have been solved."[98] Scientific discoveries did not threaten God's revelation in Jesus Christ; instead, they affirmed the presence of God in the very midst of our lives. Still further, in the questions beyond science—the universal questions of death, suffering, and guilt—Bonhoeffer admitted that the world could get along just fine without Christianity's answers. So, here too, God was not a stopgap.[99] God was not to be recognized only at the end of our explanations and possibilities, but in health, strength, and action. "God is the center of life and doesn't just 'turn up' when we have unsolved

---

95. See Bonhoeffer, *DBWE* 2:49–53; and *DBWE* 11:177–244. See also *DBWE* 16:641: "It is a misuse when we make God a stopgap in our discomfort"; and *DBWE* 8:405.

96. Bonhoeffer, *DBWE* 8:405.

97. Bonhoeffer, *DBWE* 8:450.

98. Bonhoeffer, *DBWE* 8:406.

99. Bonhoeffer, *DBWE* 8:406.

problems to be solved," Bonhoeffer wrote. "In Christ there are no 'Christian problems.'"[100]

By rejecting the God of the gaps, Bonhoeffer affirmed the radical presence of Jesus Christ that was in and for the world. As long as God was placed over and against the maturing world, and not recognized in its very midst, the revelation of God was misappropriated, and largely denied. But in this secular age, explained the Lutheran scholar Jay Rochelle, where God was discontinuous from the world, the church was finally able to return to its proper task: "to proclaim the inbreaking of God's kingdom into the world."[101] Bonhoeffer was working, then, to define new boundaries for the theological task. The revelation of God in Jesus Christ was the message of grace for the world, and must be guarded by theology, "lest we lose the whole point of grace . . . and we end by reconstructing religion as a means whereby we either assuage or are enabled to disregard God in the world."[102]

Essentially, Bonhoeffer was working to demolish the defensive wall that separated God and the world. Weizsäcker himself commented in a 1976 article that Bonhoeffer's use of his own work was personally very moving because it affirmed the place of theology in the very fiber of every human endeavor.[103] The boundary, erected in large part by the church, could only be removed through the proclamation of Christ's presence here and now. The radical reality of Jesus Christ in the midst of human life called forth belief in a God that was revealed in every triumph, every failure, every discovery, and in every mystery. Bonhoeffer's new theological course placed Jesus Christ at the very center of life, and trusted in the power and grace of God to reveal the ultimate truth of Jesus Christ to the world.

Failure and the Possibility of Discipleship

On July 21, 1944 Bonhoeffer wrote again to Bethge. It was the day after the failed assassination attempt on Hitler's life, and Bonhoeffer's reflections were especially focused and personal. In a very real sense, this letter represented the culmination of Bonhoeffer's Tegel theology, and is thus worth quoting at length:

> In the last few years I have come to know and understand more and more the profound this-worldliness of Christianity. The

---

100. Bonhoeffer, *DBWE* 8:407.
101. Rochelle, "Gospel in a Secular World," 319.
102. Rochelle, "Gospel in a Secular World," 320.
103. Weizsäcker, "Thoughts of a Non-Theologian," 168–69.

> Christian is not a *homo religiosus* but simply a human being, in the same way that Jesus was a human being—in contrast, perhaps, to John the Baptist. I do not mean the shallow and banal this-worldliness of the enlightened, the bustling, the comfortable, or the lascivious, but the profound this-worldliness that shows discipline and includes the ever-present knowledge of death and resurrection.... [I] am still discovering to this day that one only learns to have faith by living in the full this-worldliness of life. If one has completely renounced making something of oneself—whether it be a saint or a converted sinner or a church leader (a so-called priestly figure!), a just or an unjust person, a sick or a healthy person—then one throws oneself completely into the arms of God, and this is what I call this-worldliness: living fully in the midst of life's tasks, questions, successes and failures, experiences and perplexities—then one takes seriously no longer one's own sufferings but rather the suffering of God in the world. Then one stays awake with Christ in Gethsemane. And I think this is faith; this is *metanoia*. And this is how one becomes a human being, a Christian.[104]

The possibility of discipleship, of following Jesus Christ, was in recognizing the radical presence of Jesus Christ in the very midst of human life and experience. The ultimate revelation of God was discovered in this world through participating in Christ's sufferings for the world. The church thus had a new posture, one that was completely for the world because Jesus Christ was for the world.[105] And the possibility of discipleship was the journey of faith, the journey of becoming fully human in Jesus Christ.

The philosophical ideas of history, human life, and worldview that Bonhoeffer encountered in the writings of Dilthey, Ortega y Gasset, and Weizsäcker encouraged serious reflection on the implications of the Christian faith. From these thinkers, Bonhoeffer gained significant insight on the historical marginalization of Christianity and discovered creative, and more christocentric, responses. The secularized world that had now come of age had increasingly less use for a God of the gaps. Meanwhile, the interpretation of this history from a hermeneutic of the reality of human life inspired Bonhoeffer to take seriously the fullness of God's revelation. Following after Jesus Christ in this context revealed the unending possibilities of discipleship. Christ was to be recognized in our very midst, in the suffering and success of this-worldliness. Faith then emerged, because Christ was for the

---

104. Bonhoeffer, *DBWE* 8:485–86.
105. See Bonhoeffer, *DBWE* 8:499–504.

world; and Christ was proclaimed, because the people of faith were for the world.

Confession: The Practice of Possibility

While Bonhoeffer's theological developments in Tegel prison added greater definition and nuance to his conception of the possibility of discipleship, he was already thinking of the practical implications of this possibility in the years and months leading up to his arrest. Specifically, Bonhoeffer was contemplating the necessity of confession within the church's (and Germany's) attempt to process the atrocities of Nazi complicity. For Bonhoeffer, the practice of personal confession had been a pillar of the seminary experience at Zingst and Finkenwalde, and in Tegel prison he continued to write about the necessity of personal confession to Bethge.[106] But beginning in the summer of 1940, while working on *Ethics*, Bonhoeffer also recognized the importance of corporate confession for the witness of the church and renewal of the world.

By the latter half of 1940, Bonhoeffer solidified his duties with the conspiracy as part of the Military Intelligence Foreign Office, and he began writing what he considered would be his *magnum opus*, *Ethics*. Between trips as a double-agent of the Foreign Office, Bonhoeffer—somewhat surprisingly—found time and space for quiet theological work.[107] It was thus in the middle of 1941 that he came to write a manuscript titled "Guilt, Justification, Renewal." Here, he speculated about how Christ took form as the real, judged, and renewed human being. Grounding his concept of the human in Jesus Christ, Bonhoeffer wrote, "Falling away from Christ is at the same time falling away from one's true nature."[108] This was the situation in Germany—the people, having fallen away from Christ, had turned their backs on humanity as a whole. The consequence was disastrous, and even worse—murderous. Bonhoeffer knew that there was only one way back: "acknowledgment of guilt toward Christ." He wrote, "The guilt we must acknowledge is not the occasional mistake or going astray, not the breaking of an abstract law, but falling away from Christ, from the form of the One who would take form in us and lead us to our own true form."[109] Renewal, then,

---

106. See, for example, Bonhoeffer, *DBWE* 8:200, 216, 296.

107. For example, from November 17, 1940 until February 1941, Bonhoeffer was a guest at the Benedictine monastery in Ettal, with access to the library. See Bonhoeffer, *DBWE* 6:453.

108. Bonhoeffer, *DBWE* 6:134.

109. Bonhoeffer, *DBWE* 6:135.

was only possible by looking towards the form that Christ himself took—on the cross. "Therein lies the miracle," Bonhoeffer explained. "How can those who have fallen away from Christ still have community with Christ, except by the grace with which Christ holds fast the fallen and preserves that community with them?" Acknowledgment of guilt, then, was only possible in and through Jesus Christ.[110]

Certainly it was the church-community that held the responsibility for this admission of guilt. While the fallout was in no means limited to the church, the church was not only complicit in its support of Nazi Germany, it also had failed to prophetically call the world back to its true nature, in Christ. Without diminishing the necessity of personal confession, Bonhoeffer identified the startling reality: the guilt was shared by society as a whole, and as Christ was the vicarious representative for the sins of the world so now the church was responsible for emulating Christ's representative action on behalf of the world.[111] Bonhoeffer explained: "The church is today the community of people who, grasped by the power of Christ's grace, acknowledge, confess, and take upon themselves not only their personal sins, but also the Western world's falling away from Jesus Christ as guilt toward Jesus Christ. The church is where Jesus makes his form real in the midst of the world. Therefore only the church can be the place of personal and corporate rebirth and renewal."[112] In the midst of a war-torn world, it was the church which held the responsibility for the acknowledgment, confession, and repentance of the world's sins. The grievous abandonment of humanity to the vices of war-lust was not an action that could be deflected to another party. Just as Jesus Christ stepped in for humanity, so the church must step in for the world. Although in this case, while the church represented Christ on earth, the church also needed the grace of Christ to cover its own sins. Under the judgment of Christ, there could be no hiding; however, under the grace of Christ, forgiveness and renewal were quite possible.

---

110. See McBride, *Church for the World*, 57–146, for further discussion of the implications of Bonhoeffer's christological grounding for confession and repentance.

111. Bonhoeffer used *Stellvertreter* beginning in *Sanctorum Communio* and continuing through *Life Together* to describe Jesus as the "vicarious representative," "substitute," or "deputy"—"as one who acts on behalf of and for others, especially representing humanity before God" (see *DBWE* 5:55; and *DBWE* 1:107, 113–14, 136). Stassen argues that a translation of *Stellvertretung* should contain an explicitly incarnational element. He thinks it important to understand Bonhoeffer's usage of the term to mean "empathetic representative action" and "incarnational representation"—"intending a depth of incarnational meaning that no translation can completely convey." See Stassen, *Thicker Jesus*, 29, 152–53, 233.

112. Bonhoeffer, *DBWE* 6:135.

Conclusion: Discipleship for the World

In the final years of his short life, Bonhoeffer discovered that following-after Jesus Christ culminated in faithful actions that were ultimately in and for the world. Bonhoeffer had this sense in *Discipleship*, but it was under-articulated. He felt the implications of this in his *Ethics* fragments, but the concepts were incomplete. Remarkably, it was Bonhoeffer's arrest and imprisonment at Tegel that afforded him the opportunity to reflect deeply on the very possibilities of discipleship in a world that had come of age. By entering into dialogue with key thinkers such as Dilthey, Ortega y Gasset, and Weizsäcker, Bonhoeffer was able to articulate a theological understanding of discipleship that took into account the possibilities and reality of history, human life, and worldview. When Bonhoeffer grounded these concepts in the christological reality of Jesus Christ, the result was a form of discipleship that was free to be in and for the world—as Jesus Christ was free to be in and for the world. The confinement of a self that had been caught up in pride— "I want to be for myself; I have a right to myself"[113]—was finally freed in the reality of Christ's decision to be in the midst of the world. When the disciple shifted his or her gaze from inward toward the self, to outward toward the world, the barriers of possibility were finally removed. Now, Bonhoeffer discovered, the disciple could serve the world, confess on behalf of the world, repent for the sake of the world, and bear witness to the reality of Jesus Christ in and for the world. The foundation of revelation remained; Jesus Christ could still only exist as church-community; action still required the dedication to belief-obedience; but now the possibility of discipleship embraced the fullness of Jesus Christ's being in and for the world. This meant that in the darkest night of a world chaotically and destructively at war with itself, there was hope—hope for the world because Jesus Christ gave himself for the sake of the world. In history, human life, and through ever-changing worldviews, Bonhoeffer recognized the constant reality of God's pursuit of humanity. To participate in that pursuit only meant life, so that even on his way to the gallows, Bonhoeffer could proclaim: "This is the end—for me, the beginning of life."[114]

---

113. Bonhoeffer, *DBWE* 5:111.

114. See Bethge, *Dietrich Bonhoeffer*, 927, 1022. See also Best, *Venlo Incident*, 200. Best was a fellow-prisoner of Bonhoeffer's and recorded these words as Bonhoeffer left the schoolhouse in Schönberg for transport to his court martial (and the gallows) at Flossenbürg. In a letter to Bishop Bell, Best recounted a more complete account of Bonhoeffer's words: "Will you give this message from me to the Bishop of Chichester, 'tell him that this is for me the end, but also the beginning—with him I believe in the principle of our Universal Christian brotherhood, which rises above all national hatreds and that our victory is certain—tell him, too, that I have never forgotten his

words at our last meeting.' He gave me this message twice in the same words, holding my hand firmly in his and speaking with emotional earnestness." See Bonhoeffer, *DBWE* 16:468–69.

Part 3

Discipleship for a Better Worldliness

Chapter 5

Discipleship for the Common Good in Kuyper and Bonhoeffer

How do we go about being "religionless-worldly" Christians, how can we be ἐκ-κλησία, those who are called out, without understanding ourselves religiously as privileged, but instead seeing ourselves as belonging wholly to the world?

—Dietrich Bonhoeffer, *Letters and Papers from Prison*

THIS STUDY HAS TRAVELED a long way with Kuyper and Bonhoeffer, and now it will attempt to place the historical and theological insights to use in a constructive, comparative, and ethical manner. Admittedly, there is a marked shift in methodology and intention in this final chapter. The historical/theological lens will remain, but the ethical dimension will be added as Kuyper's and Bonhoeffer's theology is synthesized in order to construct a theology of discipleship for the common good. To start, the chapter unpacks a definition of discipleship that draws deliberately on the unique insights of both Kuyper and Bonhoeffer. The main part of the chapter then explores the four movements of discipleship that have been a unifying theme throughout the book—revelation, Jesus Christ, belief-obedience, and possibility—and investigates particular areas of both convergence and divergence between Kuyper and Bonhoeffer. Finally, it argues that followers of Jesus Christ can come to the place of care and concern for the common good when their discipleship culminates in the notion of unhindered possibility and potentiality.

A New Definition Discipleship

Our study of the four movements—revelation, reality, action, and possibility—yields a new definition of discipleship: *Discipleship is the response to the call to follow-after Jesus Christ in all aspects of human life and endeavor, from the inner personal disciplines to the deliberate shaping of culture—in the very midst of the world.* This definition synthesizes Kuyper's and Bonhoeffer's unique theological concepts of discipleship, while providing an ethical framework for contemporary engagement. The definition is a *synthesis* in that it draws on concepts from both Kuyper and Bonhoeffer in an effort to describe discipleship in a way that neither would necessarily do so by himself. It is not an attempt to conflate the unique theological convictions of Kuyper and Bonhoeffer into one statement. Rather, this definition seeks to pull from the unique historical and theological insights of Kuyper and Bonhoeffer in a way that encourages a holistic conception of the notion of Christian discipleship—a conception that is not bound by particular historical or theological traditions. Further, this definition encompasses all four movements of discipleship that have been described throughout the book: revelation, reality, action, and possibility. These concepts find their function and momentum in this new, holistic definition and description of discipleship.

First and foremost, *discipleship is the response* to something God has done. It requires action, a step of faith. It is, in Bonhoeffer's conception, the response of belief-obedience and obedience-belief—the juxtaposition of a spiritual response and a physical one.[1] Left in the spiritual realm, discipleship is a mirage, a fantasy, and a wish-dream that requires only an intellectual assent. But conversely, discipleship cannot be action devoid of faith. It is, instead, faithful action and faithful response to the movement of God in one's life. What is more, and more importantly, discipleship is always and can be only initiated by God. It is God's own act of self-revelation. In Kuyper's imagery, God's self-revelation is a gold mine, and discipleship is the obligation to mine it.[2] Indeed, faith is required to enter in and explore the mine—but the mine is put there by God and no one else. Apart from God, humankind only explores itself, and then only becomes more self-absorbed. But theology, as the revelation of God, in and of itself, is character forming—disciple-making—because what is discovered from the revealer

---

1. See Bonhoeffer, *DBWE* 4:63–65.
2. See Kuyper, *Encyclopedia*, 58.

transforms one from the inside-out.³ Discipleship is foremost the result of God's act of self-revelation.

Discipleship, in the New Testament context, is also the response to a particular manifestation of God's revelation—it is the response *to the call to follow-after Jesus Christ*. To hear the call of Jesus Christ is to be confronted with God's own self-revelation, and the expectation is that one will follow. Bonhoeffer quotes from Mark 2:14 to explain: "As Jesus was walking along, he saw Levi son of Alphaeus sitting at the tax booth, and he said to him, 'Follow me.' And he got up and followed him." Bonhoeffer then comments: "The call goes out, and without any further ado the obedient deed of the one called follows."⁴ The disciple hears the call and follows. In this instance, Levi does not weigh his options; he does not ask for a miracle; he does not yet even confess his faith in Jesus. He hears the call, stands up, and follows. There is not even a program for his life or "content" for his discipleship. He is simply asked to follow; and he obeys. Disciples cannot call themselves to Jesus. When they attempt to, like the person in Luke 9 who declares, "I will follow you wherever you go," they overlook the reality of life with Jesus. As Bonhoeffer explains, Jesus speaks as "the one who is going to the cross, whose life is described in the Apostles' Creed with the one word "suffered." No one can want that by their own choice. None can call themselves, says Jesus."⁵

The call that comes to follow-after Jesus Christ is the call to follow *in all aspects of human life and endeavor*. Kuyper and Bonhoeffer demonstrate this reality beautifully. Not only did Kuyper declare that Jesus Christ is Lord over every square inch of this world, his life task was an exercise in realizing this potential. From the pulpit, to politics, to journalism, to education, to diplomacy, to social justice, and beyond, Kuyper was relentless in his pursuit of God's rule and glory in every crevice of life. Bonhoeffer, too, recognized that the reality of Jesus Christ's presence in the world demanded a posture of surrender to God's will. Bonhoeffer grappled with the very real implications of defiance against the state for the truth of the gospel. Ultimately that truth led him to the gallows—with dignity and peace.

The ability to follow Jesus Christ faithfully wherever he calls does not appear out of a vacuum; it requires a conviction and clarity of God's will that can only come *from* the cultivation of *the inner personal disciplines*. Bonhoeffer looked to the monastic traditions of solitude, meditation, community,

3. See Kuyper, *Encyclopedia*, 171.
4. Bonhoeffer, *DBWE* 4:57.
5. Bonhoeffer, *DBWE* 4:60. For his part, Kuyper emphasized the role of the Holy Spirit in mediating the call of Jesus Christ through the Scriptures and through the church community.

prayer, confession, and the Lord's Supper for rhythms of the spiritual life. While refusing to be legalistic in the enforcement of these disciplines, he exerted considerable theological and personal energy in demonstrating for his ordinands the utter joy and freedom that resulted in the deliberate fostering of spiritual practices. These disciplines in turn provided Bonhoeffer with the sustenance to remain remarkably faithful during his most trying time in prison. Kuyper also relied on personal spiritual disciplines for clarity and divine intimacy, especially during his tumultuous years as prime minister. It is telling that Kuyper wrote his most personal, transparent, and mystical spiritual reflections, the *Meditations*, while battling labor strikes, navigating foreign policy tensions, and advocating for important domestic initiatives. The more Kuyper engaged the public politically, the more, it seemed, he took shelter in the shadow of God's wings.

Indeed, from this place of the spiritual disciplines, Kuyper and Bonhoeffer were empowered to participate in *the deliberate shaping of culture*. Kuyper especially left behind a formidable legacy, which remains influential to this day in the Netherlands. His Free University continues to thrive in Amsterdam (albeit in an emerged form), his political party played a major role throughout the twentieth century in the leadership of the country, and his journalistic and theological writings not only inspired his Reformed contemporaries, they continue to inform a plethora of public institutions today.[6] For his part, Bonhoeffer elected to return to Germany in 1939 so that he might have a distinct and credible voice in the rebuilding of his culture after the chaos of National Socialism. His post and perspective were located within the Confessing Church, but he did not view the church as isolated and disconnected from the world. Instead, he believed the church had the responsibility to intercede for the world and to model for the world the power of reconciliation. And if it took the removal of a poisoned political figure to initiate this reconciliation, Bonhoeffer was willing to play his part in that also.

Finally, Kuyper and Bonhoeffer did not (and could not) practice discipleship without embracing life *in the very midst of the world*. This was God's creation, meant to be embraced, cultivated, protected, and shared. This was the reality of Jesus Christ, where the barriers of sacred and secular were displaced by the witness of truth and grace. Kuyper understood the lordship of Jesus Christ to permeate each sphere of human life, which meant that Christ could be followed and witnessed to not only in the church, but

---

6. For example, The Center for Public Justice in Washington, DC. It is also important to note that Kuyper changed the organization of Dutch politics from socioeconomy-based to worldview-based, and he initiated the change of societal structures from uniform to pluralist.

also in politics, education, jobs, and social affairs. Bonhoeffer experienced the reality of Jesus Christ in his recognition of Jesus' full embrace of the world—even affirming it to the point of Jesus' own torture, suffering, and death. Jesus' entrance into the world was his turning to the world, his participation in the very midst of the world, and his invitation to his followers to do likewise. Discipleship is the call to do nothing less.

The Four Movements of Discipleship: Convergences and Divergences

To bring together a definition of discipleship that is based upon theological convergences of Kuyper and Bonhoeffer, care must be taken to assert and explain the critical differences between them. While many similarities exist between Kuyper and Bonhoeffer, fundamentally they were very different theologians in two very distinct historical contexts. So, in order to understand how they can contribute to a definition of discipleship such as the one proposed above, it is important to peer into the nuances of their divergent theological convictions. What follows will utilize the four-movement hermeneutic of discipleship to compare and contrast the unique similarities and differences in how Kuyper and Bonhoeffer conceived of the critical elements of revelation, Jesus Christ, belief-obedience, and possibility of discipleship. Note also at this juncture that material from both Kuyper and Bonhoeffer, spanning the breadth of their careers, is incorporated into this investigation, for, in order to define and nuance both their similarities and differences, it is helpful and even necessary to draw upon the entirety of their writings.

Revelation: The Authority at the Foundation of Discipleship

Both Kuyper and Bonhoeffer affirm God's self-revelation—as attested to in Holy Scripture—as the only valid starting point of theology. But they each emphasize different aspects of this revelation: Kuyper's conception draws from a strong emphasis on creation, while Bonhoeffer is decidedly christocentric in his understanding and reasoning. A critical factor in this difference was the volatile historical and theological context of Bonhoeffer's life. Up until the publishing of Karl Barth's commentary on *Romans* in 1919, theologians were largely comfortable with looking to creation as the basis for an understanding of God's revelation. In many ways, Kuyper presented a typical Reformed view that affirmed in Scripture the importance of creation as a foundational starting point for theology. In line with the Belgic Confession, for example, Kuyper could declare that we know God, "First, by the creation, preservation, and government of the universe."[7] This doctrine not only grounded Kuyper in the deep Reformed tradition within the Netherlands, it also allowed him to press forward into new and creative theological formulations. And press forward he did. As early as 1880, he was translating the creation and natural theologies of the Reformed tradition into new expressions of God's authority and revelation—*via* the concepts of sphere sovereignty and common grace.[8] In this way—taking the concept of revelation from the perspective of authority both in Kuyper and in Bonhoeffer—specific comparisons and implications can be drawn into the meaning of revelation for discipleship.

On October 20, 1880, Kuyper delivered the inaugural address at the opening of the Free University in Amsterdam.[9] His address, "Sphere Sovereignty," set out the institutional implications for a fundamental belief in the glory and reign of God. For Kuyper, this concept expressed the Reformed view of God's ultimate rule over all of creation, and thus affirmed that God's sovereignty alone was the basis for the founding of the Free University. "Sphere sovereignty," he proclaimed, "[is] the hallmark of our institution,"[10] and in its distinctly Reformed character, the university affirmed—from the creation—that the sovereignty of God lay above all spheres of life. This, it was argued, was why the Free University—the first university in the Netherlands to exist apart from state or church control—was able to exist and flourish. God's sovereignty, expressed in the very order of creation, affirmed the divine right of this new institution to exist apart from the state. God's rule preceded state sovereignty, or that of any other sphere; all spheres were thus ultimately under God alone.

In Kuyper's Reformed doctrine, creation bore witness to the sovereignty of God over all things. In the beginning, God established a well-ordered creation by his Word. God continually called this creation to order with permanent, universal, and normative structures. Through this order,

7. See Article 2 of the Belgic Confession. See also Bratt, *Abraham Kuyper*, 119–20. Kuyper explicitly made the Belgic Confession, the Heidelberg Catechism, and the Canons of Dort the foundational principles for the establishment of the Free University.

8. VanDrunen argues that while Kuyper reacted critically to what he perceived as an increasing emphasis on natural theology through the centuries in the Reformed tradition—damaging theology and distancing it from Calvin, he nevertheless stood in substantial continuity with Calvin and his Reformed orthodox predecessors. See VanDrunen, *Natural Law*, 278–79.

9. Note that this section of the chapter contains updated material from this author's previously published article, Himes, "Distinct Discipleship."

10. Kuyper, "Sphere Sovereignty," 464.

God manifested his sovereign love and care for all of creation, and the structures of life—such as family, state, and church—became real spheres, each existing in their own domain, "and each [having] its own Sovereign within its bounds."[11] God, whether acknowledged or not, was sovereign over all creation, and Christ, in whom "all things hold together" (Col 1:15–20), was the mediator of all creation. In this way, Christology was not limited to the question of soteriology. Because the order of creation was established before the fall, God's sovereignty over creation—*via* the lordship of Christ—was emphasized before Christ's act of salvation.[12]

Here, argued Kuyper, "is the glorious principle of Freedom! This perfect Sovereignty of the *sinless* Messiah at the same time directly denies and challenges all absolute Sovereignty among *sinful* men on earth, and does so by dividing life into *separate spheres*, each with its own sovereignty."[13] Human life was a complex organism, made up of countless parts; Kuyper referred to these parts as "cogwheels" or "'spheres,' each animated with its own spirit."[14] These spheres are in constant interaction, and some, like the state, hold more authority or responsibility. But no sphere could claim absolute sovereignty over others; the fact remained that Christ reigns and is ultimately sovereign over all.[15] Scholarship, for example, was then affirmed in its own sphere, outside of absolute state or church control. The establishment of the Free University stood for Kuyper as a decisive claim for this principle of freedom. In this way—and just like we will see in Bonhoeffer—Kuyper was fighting against the usurpation of power and absolute authority.

Kuyper was careful, however, to recognize and affirm the unique features of the state's sphere. The state must acknowledge the authority that came directly from God as power to protect the other spheres. The state "gives stability to the land by justice (Prov 29:4)"[16] and, he noted, protects those in the other spheres from internal tyranny. Indeed, "The State is the *sphere of spheres*, which encircles the whole extent of human life," and, on behalf of others, "it seeks to strengthen its arm and with that outstretched arm to resist, to try to break, any sphere's drive to expand and dominate a wider domain."[17] The state ultimately guarded each sphere against the suppression of life and the limiting of freedom. What the state could not do,

---

11. Kuyper, "Sphere Sovereignty," 467.
12. See Kuyper, *Encyclopedia*, 258.
13. Kuyper, "Sphere Sovereignty," 467.
14. Kuyper, "Sphere Sovereignty," 467.
15. See also Kuyper, *Pro Rege*.
16. Kuyper, "Sphere Sovereignty," 468.
17. Kuyper, "Sphere Sovereignty," 472.

however, was infringe upon the unique sovereignty inherent in each separate sphere, for God's absolute sovereignty was conferred only upon Christ, and Christ reigned supreme over all of life.

Bonhoeffer too, early in his career, began working through the responsibility and limits of the state. His explanation of state sovereignty was derived initially from the Lutheran doctrine of the two kingdoms, though the rapid rise of the Nazi regime was cause for deep reflection. Hitler came to power early in 1933, and, on April 17, the Law for Reconstitution of the Civil Service was passed, effectively barring those of Jewish descent from working in any part of the government, including the church. Bonhoeffer leveled his response to this new law in an essay, entitled "The Church and the Jewish Question."

In this essay, Bonhoeffer challenged the Lutheran understanding of the two kingdoms. Around this same time, in his lecture series *Creation and Fall*, delivered in the winter semester of 1932–33, Bonhoeffer replaced the traditional Lutheran notion of orders of creation with the idea of orders of preservation. Since the fall, he argued, humans do not have access to the primal creation and liberation except through Jesus Christ, the mediator. God's orders "have no value in and of themselves; instead they find their meaning only through Christ. God's new action with humankind is to uphold and preserve humankind in its fallen world, in its fallen orders, for death—for the resurrection, for the new creation, for Christ."[18] Bonhoeffer's christocentric interpretation of the orders was quite deliberate. With Karl Barth, he rejected any hint of natural theology which could legitimize the Nazi religious mythology and its claim of divine right through creation. By demanding Christ's mediation with the orders of preservation, Bonhoeffer placed Christ's mediating sovereignty over both the realms of church and state. He worked out the implications for this order of preservation in his article, "The Church and the Jewish Question."

The beginning of this essay sounded the typical conservative Lutheran explanation of the two kingdoms: "There is no doubt that the church of the Reformation is not encouraged to get involved directly in specific political actions of the state. The church has neither to praise nor censure the laws of the state. Instead, it has to affirm the state as God's order of preservation in this godless world."[19] But it soon became clear that Bonhoeffer was after something quite new, even radical, provided by the doctrine of God's order of preservation. True, the church could not "praise nor censure" the laws of the state, but the church was called to keep asking whether the government's

---

18. Bonhoeffer, *DBWE* 3:140.
19. Bonhoeffer, *DBWE* 12:362.

actions could be justified as legitimate, that is, were they "actions that create law and order, not lack of rights and disorder."[20] The church could then be called upon to question the very character of the state. If the state was failing in its responsibility to create law and order by force, the church must intervene. For Bonhoeffer, the so-called Aryan paragraph in the April 17 law effectively delegitimized the Nazi government. His discussion throughout the remainder of the essay was thus not the typical conservative Lutheran stance of separation and distance; instead, he grappled with the church's responsibility in working to re-establish the true state.

After the church questioned the state as to the legitimacy of its actions, it was next called to serve the victims of the state's misdeeds. The church, in its freedom, served the interest of a free state by "binding up the wounds" of those wronged by the state. "The church has an unconditional obligation toward the victims of any societal order, even if they do not belong to the Christian community,"[21] explained Bonhoeffer. Even the deprivation of rights of one group of citizens was enough to call the church to action. Any act of creating either too much or too little law led the state to the act of self-negation, and the church was called to intervene.

In such a case, the church had the possibility of exercising a third option, "not just [to] bind up the wounds of the victims beneath the wheel but to seize the wheel itself."[22] Bonhoeffer envisioned an "evangelical council" that would make such a decision for direct political action on the part of the church. Moreover, the call to seize the wheel itself eventually became a personal mandate through his participation in the conspiracy against Hitler. From the beginnings of Nazi power, then, Bonhoeffer had a heightened awareness of the fragile balance between the two realms of church and state, and he was particularly quick to call on the church to be ready for political action against the state.[23]

Now, it is clear that both Kuyper and Bonhoeffer were working in their respective theological and historical traditions to articulate the implications of God's sovereignty through the revelation of Jesus Christ. As such, there

---

20. Bonhoeffer, *DBWE* 12:364.
21. Bonhoeffer, *DBWE* 12:365.
22. Bonhoeffer, *DBWE* 12:365.
23. Notably, Bonhoeffer recognized that the Nazi law that removed baptized Jews from Christian congregations placed the church in *status confessionis*—"a state of confessional protest in which such matters as church membership and rules are no longer matters of convenience and doctrinal indifference. Rather, they are matters in which the 'very truth of the gospel and Christian freedom are at stake.'" See Bonhoeffer, *DBWE* 12:366. What Bonhoeffer and the church were not as outspoken about was the state of the non-baptized Jews.

are some significant differences in each of their doctrines of revelation that should be highlighted. Kuyper's concept of sphere sovereignty was based on the Reformed doctrine of creation. The cultural mandate that he found in Genesis 1 (to be fruitful and multiply, to have dominion, and to fill the earth) was rooted in the sovereign act of creation.[24] Jesus Christ's role in creation was sovereign, and so Jesus Christ ruled over the mandate to create culture. Kuyper could then affirm Christ's rule over all of the spheres of life while also encouraging the creative development of each of the various cultural spheres, from church and education to media and politics. Bonhoeffer, for his part, lived and worked in a context that was marked by the emerging abuse by theologians of the doctrine of creation.[25] Scholars like Paul Althaus, Gerhard Kittel, and Emanuel Hirsch had corrupted the biblical notion of creation ordinances, in part, to justify and support the pagan ideology of Nazism.[26] The concept of the creation order was wrongly used by some theologians to argue that the Aryan race in Germany was chosen to usher in the new millennium. The result of such thinking was the atrocity of the Holocaust. Dissenting theologians like Barth and Bonhoeffer saw how the doctrine of creation was being twisted by Nazi ideology and thus reacted very strongly against any idea of natural theology and creation orders.[27] The emergence of Bonhoeffer's orders of preservation was an attempt to salvage the Lutheran doctrine of creation. He argued—from a Christ-centered redemptive framework—that creation orders and mandates were to be understood as a means of God's preserving work, which occurred distinctly through redemption and reconciliation in Jesus Christ. For Bonhoeffer, creation was christological in its connection to redemption; for Kuyper, Christ was sovereign first and foremost in creation. These were, to be sure, significant theological differences and should not be glossed over in comparisons between Kuyper and Bonhoeffer.

However, while recognizing the importance of these doctrinal and historical differences, it is important to note that both Kuyper and Bonhoeffer came independently to a similar conclusion regarding the implication of God's sovereignty: while the state is a vital sphere of God's order, God, through Jesus Christ, is definitively sovereign over all. In Kuyper's booming rhetoric, "no single piece of our mental world is to be hermetically sealed off from the rest, and there is not a square inch in the whole domain of our human existence over which Christ, who is Sovereign over *all*, does not cry:

---

24. See Mouw, *Abraham Kuyper*, 6–7.
25. See Spykman, *Reformational Theology*, 179–80.
26. See Ericksen, *Theologians Under Hitler*.
27. See, for example, Brunner and Barth, *Natural Theology*.

'Mine!'"[28] For Kuyper, this meant that the sphere of scholarship was free to flourish apart from state or ecclesial control. For Bonhoeffer, this meant that the individual and the Christian community had a mandate to respect and hold the state to its responsibility. For both, this meant that Christians were called upon to participate in the very public realm of social engagement and political critique. More than mere critique, however, "Sphere Sovereignty" and "The Church and the Jewish Question" revealed how Kuyper and Bonhoeffer found themselves drawn into an intense cultural battle. Just like Bonhoeffer was fighting against the usurpation of power and absolute authority for the state, so also Kuyper was fighting against the power of the modern, centralized nation-state—who wanted to extend its dominion into the sphere of religion and the church, as the first half of the nineteenth century clearly showed. To combat the tendency of the state towards absolute control, Kuyper and Bonhoeffer relied on the foundation of God's revelation, as attested to in Scripture. So, while "Sphere Sovereignty" and "The Church and the Jewish Question" were just one aspect of Kuyper's and Bonhoeffer's developing theology of discipleship, their statements here lead to much greater theological and practical implications.

The Reality of Discipleship: Common Grace, the Church, and Jesus Christ

Kuyper's concept of common grace emerged naturally and immediately out of the idea of sphere sovereignty. Kuyper spent six years developing and bringing a high degree of nuanced argument to the doctrine of common grace in the pages of his weekly periodical, *De Heraut*, and he published the compiled constructions as *De Gemeene Gratia* in three volumes, in 1902, 1903, and 1904. Despite the cries from his conservative opponents that he was inventing a new teaching, Kuyper insisted he was only expanding and systematizing "what earlier Reformed theologians have left as hints and pieces."[29] Additionally, the development of Kuyper's theology of common grace played a practical purpose. At its core, common grace enabled a very public theology, reaching out to the larger society and culture, and so was an excellent political tool; Kuyper completed the series on common grace at the height of his political career, occurring simultaneously with his election as prime minister to the Netherlands.[30]

28. Kuyper, "Sphere Sovereignty," 488.
29. Bratt, "Editor's Introduction," 165.
30. See Bratt, "Editor's Introduction," 165.

Kuyper developed the significance of common grace in light of the fall of human history described in the first chapters of Genesis. Before *and* after the fall, he explained, grace abounds: "To every rational creature, grace is the air he breathes."[31] Yet, since the fall, death, in its full effect, had not set in. Thus, he observed, "Reformed theologians have consistently pointed out how in this non-arrival of what was prophesied for ill we see the emergence of a saving and long-suffering grace."[32] God, solely in his sovereignty and majesty, extended this grace through restraining, blocking, or redirecting the consequences of sin. This grace was both saving and restraining, and distinguished itself in two manifestations. First, there was a *saving* grace, "which in the end abolishes sin and completely undoes its consequences." Second, there was a *temporal restraining* grace, "which holds back and blocks the effect of sin" in the wider world. These manifestations of God's grace flow from his sovereignty and election: "The former," explained Kuyper, "that is saving grace, is in the nature of the case *special* and restricted to God's elect. The second, that is *common* grace, is extended to the whole of our human life."[33] It was this second expression of God's grace, common grace, that had such a profound impact on public theology, for without common grace history could not have developed for God's purposes.

The connection between God's saving, special grace and restraining, common grace was of vital importance. Had the full effects of sin set in at the fall of Adam and Eve, contended Kuyper, Seth would not have been born, and thus humanity and society would not have been established and developed. Further, had hell been released on earth at the time of the fall, the church simply could not have existed; "it would be massacred in less than no time."[34] Without common grace, special grace simply could not function. But Kuyper was also clear that common grace did not simply exist solely for the salvation of the elect. With such an assumption, "people focus more on *their own salvation* instead of on the *glory of God*."[35]

In reality, it was for God's glory when societies developed, creative arts flourished, and science magnified God's truth. As a result, there was in common grace a call to Christian action in political and cultural affairs. Since, Kuyper explained, there was grace operating outside the church, and grace even where it did not lead to eternal salvation, we were duty bound to

---

31. Kuyper, "Common Grace," 167.
32. Kuyper, "Common Grace," 167.
33. Kuyper, "Common Grace," 168.
34. Kuyper, "Common Grace," 169.
35. Kuyper, "Common Grace," 169.

honor the operation of divine grace in civic life.[36] Here, then, lay the heart of Kuyper's theological basis for engagement in education, politics, and public debate. God was glorified in the quest for truth in the academic halls, in the building of civic society, and in the free and open communication of ideas. To focus all one's attention in the church was not only short-sighted, it denied the existence of God's grace beyond the walls of the church.[37]

The church, therefore, held a special and unique place in the manifestation of God's glory and grace. The church remained true to itself by recognizing and living by special grace in distinction from common grace. The lamp of the Christian religion that burned within the walls of the church "shines out through its windows to areas far beyond, illuminating all the sectors and associations that appear across the wide range of human life and activity." As Kuyper argued in more detail: "Justice, law, the home and family, business, vocation, public opinion and literature, art and science, and so much more are illuminated by that light, and that illumination will be stronger and more penetrating as the lamp of the gospel is allowed to shine more brightly and clearly in the church institute."[38] A strong confessional church, therefore, did not and could not make for a confessional state. Rather than co-opt, the church—not as an institution, but through its members acting in society—aimed to influence. The Christian character of society was only gained as the light of the gospel shined through the church into all segments of society. Common grace allowed Kuyper the confidence not only to engage directly with all aspects of modern society, but also to affirm its pluriform existence.

As such, it was Kuyper's broad christological understanding that enabled his deliberate theology of public engagement. Contrary to those who would focus on their own salvation before the glory of God, Kuyper denied that Christ was exclusively the expiator of sin: "No: Christ, by whom all things exist including ourselves, is before all things."[39] The *savior* of the world, he emphasized, was first the *creator* of the world. This creator was also the re-creator, by the mediation of the Son through the Spirit, and would continue to bestow grace upon history until the world reached its consummation and fulfillment. Common grace emphasized what special grace simply could not: God worked in every fiber of history for his glory. Special election was a vital aspect of God's plan, but God also elected to be

36. See Wolterstorff, "Abraham Kuyper (1873–1920): Commentary," 53.

37. See Wolterstorff, "Abraham Kuyper (1873–1920): Commentary," 53.

38. See Wolterstorff, "Abraham Kuyper (1873–1920): Commentary," 54, for these particular quotes from Kuyper in *Common Grace*. Kuyper also uses this imagery in his second Stone Lecture.

39. Kuyper, "Common Grace," 170.

glorified through the manifold manifestation of his grace in all of cosmic history.

Interestingly, Bonhoeffer took up many of these same themes in two of his later writings, *Ethics* and *Letters and Papers from Prison*. Although he did not write in the same Kuyperian or Reformed terms, he was very much interested in explicating the issues at the heart of Kuyper's notion of common grace. In *Ethics*, Bonhoeffer affirmed the sovereignty of God in the revelation of Jesus Christ with his understanding of the nature of reality. Christ's presence for the world, as described in *Ethics*, in turn made possible a kind of "common grace" that was explored in his theological reflections from Tegel prison.

Ethics remains Bonhoeffer's great unfinished work. His working manuscripts were left mid-thought on his desk when he was arrested on April 5, 1943 by the Nazi military legal branch with the help of the Gestapo. In the manuscript "Christ, Reality, and Good," he continued the work that he began ten years earlier, in "The Church and the Jewish Question," to redefine a notion of reality that was over and against the traditional Lutheran doctrine of the two-kingdoms. He pointedly described the fallacy of the contemporary understanding of Luther's sacred and secular realms: "This division of the whole reality into sacred and profane, or Christian and worldly, sectors creates the possibility of existence in only one of these sectors: for instance a spiritual existence that takes no part in a worldly existence, and a worldly existence that can make good its claim to autonomy over against the sacred sector."[40] Such a bifurcated understanding of reality was detrimental to the call and possibility of Christian engagement with the world. What is more, the division of life into these conflicting realms signaled a forfeited view of reality. Bonhoeffer commented that we have given up on reality when we place ourselves in one of the two realms, "wanting Christ without the world or the world without Christ." Or, worse yet, we try and stand in the two realms at the same time, "thereby becoming people in eternal conflict."[41]

These views, however, bypassed both biblical and Reformation Christian thought. With images reminiscent of those employed by Kuyper, Bonhoeffer explained that the whole reality of the world has already been drawn into and is held together in Christ. The theme of two realms was foreign to the biblical concern for "the realization of the Christ-reality in the contemporary world." This was a reality that embraced and inhabited the entirety of the world. Indeed, "history moves only from this center and towards this

---

40. Bonhoeffer, *DBWE* 6:57.
41. Bonhoeffer, *DBWE* 6:58.

center."⁴² There were thus not two realities, the sacred and the secular, "but *only one reality*, and that is God's reality revealed in Christ in the reality of the world."⁴³ Reality existed only in and through Jesus Christ, and it was from this center of all reality that Bonhoeffer was equipped to engage fully in and for the world.

In *Letters and Papers from Prison*, Bonhoeffer offered compelling theological implications for this radically christocentric understanding of reality. Like Kuyper, he was convinced of the serious call for direct Christian engagement with society. In a May 29, 1944 letter to Bethge, he lamented how traditional religious thought had reduced God to a stop-gap measure. Rather than allowing God to be pushed ever further into retreat every time science offered a new explanation of the natural world, "we should find God in what we know, not in what we don't know."⁴⁴ There was no need to fear the discoveries of science or the cultural expressions of society; God did not forfeit sovereignty when scientific knowledge could replace faith. "God wants to be grasped by us not in unsolved questions but in those that have been solved," including "the universal questions about death, suffering, and guilt."⁴⁵ Echoing his conclusions from *Ethics*, Bonhoeffer explained that the ground for this "lies in the revelation of God in Jesus Christ. God is the center of life and doesn't just "turn up" when we have unsolved problems to be solved."⁴⁶ God was present in the very midst of all of life, and in this way, God's revelation in Jesus Christ affected much more than our personal salvation.

Bonhoeffer took up this matter in a May 5, 1944 letter to Bethge. Here, Bonhoeffer began to explicate his emerging concept of "religionless" Christianity. The danger of thinking religiously, as in a religious realm and a secular realm, was that concepts were limited to either the metaphysical or the individualistic. When Christ was only the Lord of the sacred and not at the center of the entire world, his work in the world was merely a matter of personal salvation. But Bonhoeffer recognized the practical and biblical limits of such a perception. As he wrote, "Hasn't the individualistic question of saving our personal souls almost faded away for most of us? Isn't it our impression that there are really more important things than this question (—perhaps not more important than this *matter*, but certainly

---

42. Bonhoeffer, *DBWE* 6:58. See also Bonhoeffer's development of this concept in the Christology lectures of 1933 in *DBWE* 12:299-360.
43. Bonhoeffer, *DBWE* 6:58.
44. Bonhoeffer, *DBWE* 8:406.
45. Bonhoeffer, *DBWE* 8:406.
46. Bonhoeffer, *DBWE* 8:406.

more important than the *question*!?)?"⁴⁷ Bonhoeffer was convinced that the question of saving one's soul was not by any means the central concern of the biblical message. Rather, the Bible seemed to proclaim constantly God's righteousness and coming kingdom on earth. "What matters," he continued, "is not the beyond but this world, how it is created and preserved"; and "what is beyond this world is meant, in the gospel, to be there *for* this world—not in the anthropomorphic sense . . . but in the biblical sense of the creation and the incarnation, crucifixion, and resurrection of Jesus Christ."⁴⁸ To be there *for* this world was a central concern of Bonhoeffer's theology, and it was grounded in the place of Jesus Christ as the center of all reality.

Kuyper and Bonhoeffer both staked their claims for direct engagement with the world on the cosmic centrality of Jesus Christ. To be sure, however, there were important and significant theological differences in how they understood this reality. For Kuyper, the common grace that resulted from God's sovereignty bore witness to the work of Jesus Christ in all aspects of human life and endeavor. But Kuyper was careful to distinguish between the particular, saving grace of salvation and the temporal, restraining grace that was common to all. Bonhoeffer, on the other hand, would not have used Kuyper's language of "common" and "special" grace because he was intent on emphasizing the one reality of Jesus Christ. There were not different manifestations of God's grace for Bonhoeffer. To combat the traditional Lutheran two-kingdom view, Bonhoeffer stressed that Jesus Christ alone was the center of all reality, and he spoke of God's grace in terms of this one reality of Jesus Christ. So, while Bonhoeffer's christological understanding of reality certainly resonates with the Kuyperian view, his understanding is a distinct critique and re-orientation of a traditional Lutheran doctrine; it is a distinction that is quite unique in its own way apart from the Reformed tradition.⁴⁹

Despite these theological differences, it does remain that both Kuyper and Bonhoeffer worked from a Christ-centered view of reality to correct the short-sightedness that fixation on personal salvation can breed. Kuyper, looking to the biblical record, illustrated how common grace must precede special grace, concluding that God's purposes are much bigger than individual salvation. God is concerned with his glory, and will usher in glory through the consummation of all history in Jesus Christ. Similarly, Bonhoeffer argued that there were more important questions than personal

---

47. Bonhoeffer, *DBWE* 8:372.

48. Bonhoeffer, *DBWE* 8:373.

49. VanDrunen makes a compelling argument for the tradition of the two kingdoms in Reformed thought. See VanDrunen, *Natural Law*.

Discipleship for the Common Good in Kuyper and Bonhoeffer 181

salvation. Because Christ is ultimately for the world, the church must bear witness to the reality of Jesus Christ to all areas of human life. Kuyper's image of the lamp of the gospel shining through the windows of the church out into the world could be an appropriate symbol for Bonhoeffer's thought as well. As Bonhoeffer wrote in *Discipleship*, the church holds the pearl of great mystery, but shines its light as a city on a hill.[50]

Theological Reflection on the Action of Belief and Obedience

There are times in a disciple's life when the action of belief-obedience is most poignantly captured through the particular spiritual practice of theological reflection. In the midst of their varying genres of writings, Kuyper and Bonhoeffer both had a habit of writing quite personally in reflecting on how their personal faith demanded certain actions and responses to life's unyielding circumstances. In late August of 1899, Kuyper faced one the most tragic events of his life—the death of his wife Jo, while on vacation in Switzerland—and he responded, in part, by penning a meditation on death that ran in the very next issue of *De Heraut*.[51] Kuyper would run this series of meditations until his sixty-fifth birthday in 1902, and they would be collected and published in a book as *Asleep in Jesus*. This first reflection captured both the deep mourning and steadfast faith of Kuyper, and in so doing laid bare the crux of his life of discipleship.

Kuyper titled the meditation, "When What Is Mortal Is Swallowed Up by Life."[52] It was a telling title, in how it reversed the perceived triumph of death. But to arrive at his main point, Kuyper did not gloss over the pain and sadness of losing a loved one. To open the meditation, he wrote: "Given what lies before your eyes at the time of death, you can only say that Death, the fearful enemy of God and man, finally succeeds in swallowing up a life so precious to you. . . . When the last bit of breath expired it was as if Death mocked you with all your unheard prayers and pointless anxieties.

---

50. See Bonhoeffer, *DBWE* 4:110–14, 146–52.

51. Johanna Schaay Kuyper died on August 25, 1899 in Meiringen, Switzerland, at the age of fifty-seven. Kuyper did not reveal much publicly about the cause of her death. He did allude to a flare up of her chronic lung problem, but Jo had also been depressed and weak since the death of their nine-year-old son, Willy, six years earlier. See Bratt, *Abraham Kuyper*, 281.

52. The meditation started with a citation from 2 Cor 5:4 (KJV): "For while we are in this tent, we groan and are burdened, because we do not wish to be unclothed but to be clothed with our heavenly dwelling, so that what is mortal may be swallowed up by life."

It whispered derisively: 'I won; your morning of joy will *never* come.'"[53] Kuyper continued, now describing the scene at the deathbed, where one stands broken-hearted staring at your lifeless loved one, in disbelief. She had been swallowed up by death. And this *swallowed up*, it was a hard word: "Devoured, as if by a beast of prey. All at once, gone: the look of the eye, the sweet words, the warm handclasp, the facial expression. Everything clean gone: cold, withered, somber. Life swallowed up by death."[54]

At least, that was the view of those who know only this world; they cannot see it any other way: death snatches the final victory, for those who have no choice. But neither was Kuyper delusional: "And let's be honest: in that first hard moment when a shock passes through the heart, the child of God sees it that way too. . . . Death is there, hauling away its prey before our eyes; we are there, compelled to watch it happen, overcome by pain and helplessness."[55] This is the bitter reality of death in the visible world, Kuyper explained. To ignore the pain and to gloss over the helplessness with wreaths and flowers is a deception; "to imagine that you can comfort the bereaved with generalities about God's providential love is cowardice."[56] The fact is, you prayed, and despite that prayer, death won. And here, Kuyper drives home a point that speaks to the dishonesty of shallow comfort. In reality, death came on account of sin and by sin, and "to babble about providential love when God lets bitter death rob you of the dearest thing you had on earth, when you see a precious life wither, disappear, swallowed up before your eyes—that's lying to yourself. That you cannot do with any sincerity. That is playing with words right up to the grave."[57]

Death, dying, and grieving must be done with honesty; it is a harsh reality. But death, according to God's Word, does not have the final say. While the bodily eye sees death, Kuyper explained, God opens up your spiritual eyesight, and a totally opposite reality unfolds, "a reality which shows you that death does not swallow up life but that in death *what is mortal is swallowed up by life*."[58] This is a mystery, and it is a mystery that can only be unraveled in Jesus. "He, the Marvelous One, took hold of death, forced it to let Him pass into glory, and kept open the road behind Him so that death would also let all his children pass into glory, unhindered and

---

53. Kuyper, "When What Is Mortal," 408–9.
54. Kuyper, "When What Is Mortal," 409.
55. Kuyper, "When What Is Mortal," 409–10.
56. Kuyper, "When What Is Mortal," 410.
57. Kuyper, "When What Is Mortal," 410–11.
58. Kuyper, "When What Is Mortal," 411.

undisturbed."⁵⁹ Here, we are talking about true and authentic life—life that is too powerful to remain trapped in an earthly shell. "In that enclosure it cannot unfurl its wings. Therefore life must finally slough off that which is earthly and mortal to push on to the highest reaches of its potential."⁶⁰ As life breaks free from the mortal body and unfolds into its majesty, only then do you realize that it is not death that swallowed up life, but it is life that first swallowed up that which is mortal.

Kuyper was adamant: the life at work here is none other than Jesus himself. For those who have been incorporated in Him and His life, Jesus accomplishes life in the midst of dying. Those in Jesus do not die and then go to Him, Kuyper wrote. Jesus is present with them in dying, "and when death taunted you as though it had won, in that moment your Savior smiled at you and showed you a crown, the palm of victory."⁶¹ But it is those who do not believe that perish upon dying; "Death keeps him in custody."⁶² Floral wreaths and words of consolation only mask the self-deception of Death's victory. While the heart certainly bleeds upon a loved one's dying, those in Jesus see the reality of a holy joy and heavenly peace. For those who are truly in Jesus, mortality is but a season in the abundant life of discipleship. For those who have Jesus at the center, existing both in life and in death only for God and for his holy Name, the words of hope are not hollow. Matters of life and death are matters of our imperative calling to follow Him. We are here for God's work, and "our life is the Lord's, whether we remain here or whether we enter eternity."⁶³ So, Kuyper concluded, "there is weeping over the acute pain felt by the wounded heart. But from that same heart also rises the sound of rejoicing and praise for what God prepared for the loved one who went away and for what He left in this life by way of consolation, love, and holy calling."⁶⁴ That holy calling is the life of discipleship.

In his following-after Jesus Christ, Kuyper understood and experienced the reality of God's presence and hope in the midst of the pain and sorrow of Jo's death. His meditation was not just an expression of thin piety; there was no denying the hurt and loneliness that he felt at his beloved's passing. But through this theological reflection, there was also no denying the depth and strength of his personal faith and discipleship. Actions are a disciple's test for belief-obedience. Actions reveal the most deeply held

59. Kuyper, "When What Is Mortal," 411.
60. Kuyper, "When What Is Mortal," 412.
61. Kuyper, "When What Is Mortal," 413.
62. Kuyper, "When What Is Mortal," 413.
63. Kuyper, "When What Is Mortal," 415.
64. Kuyper, "When What Is Mortal," 415.

beliefs and they call for the immediate execution of obedience. As such, life's turmoil exposes the nature and state of one's discipleship.

At Jo's death, Kuyper chose to process his own grief in the public pages of *De Heraut*, and in so doing he took on the responsibility of teaching and ministering to his readers about this most crucial aspect of the life of discipleship—death and dying. In many ways, death is the ultimate question in this life, and in penning this meditation and then in compiling *Asleep in Jesus*, Kuyper revealed the firm foundation on which he and his followers could stand. As such, "When What Is Mortal Is Swallowed Up by Life" was not a meditation on the passivity of death; it was a call to embrace the fruitful and abundant life in Jesus Christ here, now, and into eternity. For Kuyper, the action of discipleship was a way of life in as much as it was a way of dying.

Bonhoeffer, in much the same way, utilized theological reflection to meditate on his own journey and to convey his own paradigm of belief-obedience in the midst of the most challenging and trying time of his life. He wrote the letter "After Ten Years" to his co-conspirators Eberhard Bethge, Hans von Dohnanyi, and Hans Oster as a Christmas gift in 1942—just a few months before his arrest and imprisonment. His reflections were not driven by a particular personal event (as in Kuyper's case), but instead looked back at the past decade and provided stark conclusions about the nature of human experience—conclusions that had been reached through the shared concrete experiences of this close group of conspirators, relations, and friends.[65]

In this letter, Bonhoeffer was acutely aware of his place in history. He recognized the gravity of the present terror and the sense of futility that standing against a totalitarian regime can bring. But his stance, and that of his friends, was made with clarity and precision. That did not make the stance any easier, yet knowing one's position provided courage and conviction. Bonhoeffer reflected on this situation with poise and insight; his words are worth quoting at length in order to set the tone and stage for what follows:

> Have there ever been people in history who in their time, like us, had so little ground under their feet, people to whom every possible alternative open to them at the time appeared equally unbearable, senseless, and contrary to life? Have there been those who like us looked for the source of their strength beyond all those available alternatives? Were they looking entirely in what has passed away and in what is yet to come? And nevertheless,

---

65. See Bonhoeffer, *DBWE* 8:37.

> without being dreamers, did they await with calm and confidence the successful outcome of their endeavor? Or rather, facing a great historical turning point, and precisely because something genuinely new was coming to be that did not fit with the existing alternatives, did the responsible thinkers of another generation ever feel differently than we do today?[66]

Bonhoeffer left open these questions in the letter, but surely he spent many a late night wrestling through them in concert with others. And the questions were surely driven by his personal decisions and experiences—particularly to return to Germany from America in 1939 to discover his fate at the outbreak of Hitler's war. In this he found himself facing a great historical turning point, where decisions had to be made and actions had to be taken. Bonhoeffer's own discipleship led him here; the call of Jesus Christ beckoned him to an obedience that relied on a strength that was beyond any and all alternatives. Though tempted to fall into a dream state, he grasped instead onto hope, in calm and confidence and assurance of God's leading. While the world crumbled away around him, while ethical concepts and notions of reason, honor, and duty were obfuscated, there remained the possibility of standing firm. It was God alone who called a person to obedient and responsible action—belief and obedience failed when it was grounded in one's own reason, principles, freedom, or virtue. The only one who stands firm is the one prepared to sacrifice all when God calls. "Such a person is the responsible one," Bonhoeffer wrote, "whose life is to be nothing but a response to God's question and call."[67] But the question remained: "Where are these responsible ones?"[68] As he looked around him, the cohort of the responsible was small indeed.

Bonhoeffer observed Germany sacrificing its own responsibility to God's call, but that did not leave him hopeless. Instead, he encouraged his friends with clear convictions of God's work in history. Again, Bonhoeffer's extended words reveal a commitment to embrace his own journey of belief and obedience:

> I believe that God can and will let good come out of everything, even the greatest evil. For that to happen, God needs human beings who let everything work out for the best. I believe that in every moment of distress God will give us as much strength to resist as we need. But it is not given to us in advance, lest we rely on ourselves and not on God alone. In such faith all fear of the

---

66. Bonhoeffer, *DBWE* 8:38.
67. Bonhoeffer, *DBWE* 8:40.
68. Bonhoeffer, *DBWE* 8:40.

future should be overcome. I believe that even our mistakes and shortcomings are not in vain and that it is no more difficult for God to deal with them than with our supposedly good deeds. I believe that God is no timeless fate but waits for and responds to sincere prayer and responsible actions.[69]

Bonhoeffer's God was active, responsive to the belief and obedience of those whom he had called. God provided the strength to endure, but also looked for partners to demolish the evil and promote the greatest good. Above all, God acted in history itself. When God seemed distant and forgotten, Bonhoeffer reminded his friends that God remained at work in and for the world, responding to the prayers and responsible actions of his followers. While God had not abandoned the world, in too many cases God's people had. Nevertheless, God continued relentlessly to craft good for the world, and he continued to call his people to faith and obedience.

Displaying this faith and obedience in the midst of the world's suffering required Christians to embrace sympathetically the suffering of others. But this sympathy and suffering was done only through the freedom of Jesus Christ. Bonhoeffer explained that, while Christ freely experienced in his own body the suffering of all of humanity, "we are not to burden ourselves with impossible things and torture ourselves with not being able to bear them."[70] The burden remained Jesus Christ's alone. We can be instruments in the hands of the Lord in history, but we share only in a limited way the suffering of others. "We are not Christ," Bonhoeffer continued, "but if we want to be Christians it means that we are to take part in Christ's greatness of heart, in the responsible action that in freedom lays hold of the hour and faces the danger, and in true sympathy that springs forth not from fear but from Christ's freeing and redeeming love for all who suffer."[71] Christians received a call to action, a call to take part, lay hold, and face the danger. Bonhoeffer reminded his friends that "inactive waiting and dully looking on are not Christian responses."[72] Christians heed the call of Christ to act into the immediate experience of others, for whose very sake Christ died.

The result of this action and this faithful response to Christ's call bears the risk of suffering. And not just any kind of suffering, Bonhoeffer noted, but the kind of suffering experienced by Christ: "Christ suffered in freedom, in solitude, in the shadow, and in dishonor in body and in spirit."[73]

69. Bonhoeffer, *DBWE* 8:46.
70. Bonhoeffer, *DBWE* 8:49.
71. Bonhoeffer, *DBWE* 8:49.
72. Bonhoeffer, *DBWE* 8:49.
73. Bonhoeffer, *DBWE* 8:49.

These were the infinitely difficult aspects of suffering; the experiences that were without community, without recognition, and without honor. But, Bonhoeffer wrote, since Christ's sufferings, "many Christians have suffered with him."[74] The pain of suffering, however, was not without the hope and promise of Jesus Christ. Bonhoeffer recalled the Sermon on the Mount, and the command—amplified by their critical situation—to forgo "worrying about tomorrow" (Matt 6:34). What lay ahead was "the very narrow path, sometimes barely discernable, [and] of taking each day as if it were the last and yet living it faithfully and responsibly as if there were yet to be a great future."[75] The optimism was not futile or foolish, but faithful and courageous. For the reality of death could no longer be ignored. In fact, Bonhoeffer wrote, the circumstances of recent years have brought us to a place where we can no longer hate Death so much; "we have discovered something of kindness in his features and are almost reconciled to him."[76] Certainly, he explained, we still love life; but Death can no longer surprise us. In the freedom of Jesus Christ, "it is not external circumstances but we ourselves who shall make of our death what it can be, a death consented to freely and voluntarily."[77] Faithful obedience to the call of Jesus Christ, Bonhoeffer rightly understood, could very well result in suffering and death. But, in Jesus Christ, such suffering need not be marks of a failed life, but a culmination of life fulfilled.

Now, at the end of his letter, Bonhoeffer asked the question: "are we still of any use?" The present realities of war had taken their toll: "We have been silent witnesses of evil deeds. We have become cunning and learned the arts of obfuscation and equivocal speech. Experience has rendered us suspicious of human beings, and often we have failed to speak to them a true and open word. Unbearable conflicts have worn us down or even made us cynical. Are we still of any use?"[78] What was needed now, at this juncture of ethics, action, and obedience, were "simple, uncomplicated, and honest human beings."[79] A shared sense of humanity had to take hold and reaffirm its grip on human life. As Bonhoeffer and his friends were seeing and experiencing life from below, in terms of the suffering, powerless, and outcast, they recognized that an honest sense of humanity would realign values to provide perspective and hope. Personal suffering, he had learned, was a

---

74. Bonhoeffer, *DBWE* 8:50.
75. Bonhoeffer, *DBWE* 8:50.
76. Bonhoeffer, *DBWE* 8:51.
77. Bonhoeffer, *DBWE* 8:51.
78. Bonhoeffer, *DBWE* 8:52.
79. Bonhoeffer, *DBWE* 8:52.

more useful key than personal happiness "for exploring the meaning of the world in contemplation and action."[80] In this way, Bonhoeffer could affirm and embrace life from below while recognizing that only in the reality of life grounded in Jesus Christ was it possible fully to "do justice to life in all its dimensions and in this way affirm it."[81]

Far from being a mode of disengagement from the world, both Kuyper and Bonhoeffer relied on theological reflection to solidify their understanding of the place of active belief-obedience in their own lives of discipleship. In both cases, the documents show disciples hard at work wrestling with the lived implications of their beliefs. Kuyper processed a personal loss in the death of his wife by meditating on the truths of Scripture; and in so doing he advocated for—and demonstrated—an active life of following Jesus Christ into and through all of life's joys and perils. Bonhoeffer, too, having been fully exposed to the darkness and shadows of war and conspiracy, had to find a way to articulate the enduring truth of Jesus Christ. It was his discipleship, his following after Jesus Christ, that allowed him to see his place in the world for what it was—an opportunity to respond to history with faithfulness and obedience. From these places of reality, Kuyper and Bonhoeffer could speak and act in and for the world. Their sights were clear and their purposes definite. Understanding the freedom in Christ of their belief and obedience then allowed for unhindered possibilities and potentialities of their discipleship. They could press forward into new explorations and articulations of the reality of Christ in the world because of the grounding of their faith in obedience; and press forward they did.

Possibilities for Christian Influence: Worldview and Divine Mandates

The implications for Kuyper's earlier concepts of sphere sovereignty and common grace are perhaps most clearly seen in his *Lectures on Calvinism*. Delivered at the annual Stone Lectures at Princeton Seminary in October of 1898, the *Lectures* represent one the most systematic and complete applications of Kuyper's constructive theology. Here, he presented Calvinism as an all-encompassing worldview and demonstrated its superior insights into topics as varied as religion, politics, science, art, and the future. His opening lecture, "Calvinism a Life-system," provided a framework for the rest of the series and is especially useful in approaching his understanding of the ordering of society.

80. Bonhoeffer, *DBWE* 8:52.
81. Bonhoeffer, *DBWE* 8:52.

Kuyper began his first lecture with a lively comparison of the two competing worldviews of the time: modernism and Calvinism. The two life systems, he explained, "are wrestling with one another, in mortal combat."[82] On the one hand, modernism sought to build a world that was solely oriented from and toward the natural human. On the other hand, Calvinism worked from and toward the glory of God, and advocated for the continuation of a Christian heritage. Each life system was based on a set of core principles which had far reaching effects, touching all aspects of life and society, and was therefore fundamentally opposed to the other.

Modernism operated from the principles of atheism and individualism found in the French Revolution, the pantheism of German philosophy, and Darwinian evolution. The rampant unbelief advanced by the Revolution was seen as a particular threat that Kuyper consistently battled throughout his career.[83] Although Kuyper allowed that God may have used the Revolution to destroy the tyranny of the Bourbons, he contended that its goal of eliminating God from the church, state, society, and science left nothing but self-seeking individuals whose only concern was their personal independence.[84] Despite any advantages to Western civilization brought about by the Revolution, Kuyper abhorred the accompanying and dramatic shift in society from a God-centered to a human-centered worldview. This flood of humanism soon swept into Germany, where it took the form of pantheism. For Kuyper, pantheism represented the trend towards a modern paganism that found its concrete expression in Darwin's theory of evolution. Pantheism identified God with human progress and thus removed the distinction between God and the world.[85] Calvinism was Kuyper's response to this fatal worldview.

Kuyper took great efforts in his opening lecture to define Calvinism by first explaining how it was a scientific movement, and not merely an ecclesiastical or dogmatic movement. In his historical context, the term "Calvinism" held three distinct connotations—none of which adequately revealed its scientific definition. First, Calvinism could not merely refer to those constantly stigmatized "Calvinists" who bore the derision of the majority press in official Roman Catholic countries like Hungary and France. Second, Calvinism was not just a confessional label for the outspoken subscriber to the dogma of fore-ordination. The Calvinist, third, was not solely

82. Kuyper, *Lectures on Calvinism*, 11.

83. Kuyper was so opposed to these principles, particularly the atheism of the French Revolution, that he named his political party the Antirevolutionary Party (ARP).

84. See Heslam, *Creating a Christian Worldview*, 98.

85. See Heslam, *Creating a Christian Worldview*, 101–2.

one who affixed the name to a denomination or church (as some Baptists and Methodists were doing). Instead, Calvinism must be understood in the *scientific* sense—of history, philosophy, and politics. As he explained: "Historically, the name of Calvinism indicates the channel in which the Reformation moved, so far as it was neither Lutheran, nor Anabaptist, nor Socinian. In the philosophical sense, we understand by it that system of the conceptions which, under the influence of the master-mind of Calvin, raised to dominance in the several spheres of life. And as a political name, Calvinism indicates that political movement which has guaranteed the liberty of nations in constitutional statesmanship; first in Holland, then in England, and since the close of the last century in the United States."[86] Kuyper leaned on this scientific understanding of Calvinism to formulate his ideas of a life system that could combat what he saw as the false notions of modernism. This highest form of Christian understanding, claimed Kuyper, was the most effective bulwark for an all-encompassing challenge to the prevailing modernistic worldview.

The Calvinistic worldview redefined our fundamental relation to God, to humankind, and to the world. The re-orienting of these relationships in light of the scientific principles of Calvinism fundamentally altered how the Christian understood the ordering of society. For our relation to God, Calvinism offered an immediate fellowship of humans with the divine, apart from the mediation of priest or church. For the relation to our fellow human, Calvinism affirmed the equality of all in God's creation and recognized the inherent value and worth of each individual. And for our relation to the world, Kuyper returned to the notion of common grace, recognizing that the curse upon the world was under restraint, and thus we must "discover the treasures and develop the potencies hidden by God in nature and in life."[87] For Kuyper, then, all of life was affirmed and must be scoured and engaged with the application of these fundamentally Christian principles. With this commitment, he constructed a Calvinistic theology of religion, politics, science, art, and the future in his five remaining Stone Lectures. In lieu of an in-depth study of each of these areas, a short summary of his understanding of the arts provides a compelling case that Kuyper succeeded in creating a comprehensive Christian worldview—where God was sovereign over all, and Jesus Christ's claim of lordship over all was realized.

Kuyper's fifth lecture on Calvinism focused on the arts, and here the full creativity of the concepts of sphere sovereignty and common grace came into view. Kuyper, though not an artist himself, nevertheless teased

---

86. Kuyper, *Lectures on Calvinism*, 14.
87. Kuyper, *Lectures on Calvinism*, 31.

out the Calvinistic implications on painting, architecture, music, poetry, and drama. He did not advocate art for art's sake, but argued instead: "When I plead the significance of Calvinism in the domain of art, I am not in the least induced to do so by the vulgarization of art, but rather keep my eyes fixed upon the Beautiful and the Sublime in its eternal significance, and upon art as one of the richest gifts of God to mankind."[88] Art was one of the clearest manifestations of God's work of common grace in the world. As such, Kuyper lamented the artistic poverty of the Calvinist tradition. In the realm of architecture, he thought that Calvinism ought to have boasted the fullness of its ideal in a structure equal to that of the Parthenon in Athens, Saint Sophia's at Byzantium, or Saint Peter's at the Vatican. Historically, explained Kuyper, Calvinism did not develop an artistic style of its own because art was thought at the time to represent a lower level of religious life and expression. Ultimately, however, Calvinism offered a new base of interpretation and now it could encourage the progress and principle of artistic development. Such a move toward the religious affirmation of the arts was a rarity at the time. Kuyper's discussion was thus a challenge to the prevailing prejudice against the arts, and his appeal to discovering the beauty of the creator in art displayed the potential for the Calvinistic worldview to permeate the vast and unique contours of culture and society.

While Kuyper's *Lectures on Calvinism* offered a compelling application of his concepts of sphere sovereignty and common grace, Bonhoeffer aimed to work out some of the implications of his christological understanding of reality with a structure of divine mandates. His *Ethics* contains the manuscript "The Concrete Commandment and the Divine Mandates." Here, Bonhoeffer offered an alternative to the prevailing pseudo-Lutheran doctrines that were used to legitimize Nazi ideology: the orders of creation, the three estates, and the two kingdoms.[89] His goal was to revise and reclaim these ideas with the doctrine of divine mandates, which "depend solely on God's *one* commandment as it is revealed in Jesus Christ."[90] Although the text remained incomplete due to his arrest and imprisonment, Bonhoeffer nevertheless presented his understanding of a Christian ordering of society that took seriously the ultimate reality of Jesus Christ.

Bonhoeffer approached the concept of social order with four divine mandates: church, state, marriage and family, and culture (also called "work" in some writings). These mandates were key social structures and were given from above, and yet they did not encompass the entirety

---

88. Kuyper, *Lectures on Calvinism*, 143.
89. See Green, "Editor's Introduction," 18–20.
90. Bonhoeffer, *DBWE* 6:390.

of human life (friendship, for example, was not a mandate, but was in a realm of freedom).[91] These four divine mandates gave structure and boundaries to human existence, and were regulated by the commandment of God in Jesus Christ. Bonhoeffer would have agreed with Kuyper that society was not a collection of freewheeling individualists. Instead, it found its form as mandates that were with-one-another, for-one-another, and over-against-one-another.

The commandment of God revealed in Jesus Christ found concrete expression in the divine mandates. This commandment was all-encompassing, and embraced the entirety of the world through and in Jesus Christ. However, God's commandment was not found everywhere—it was not in theoretical speculation, private enlightenment, historical forces, or compelling ideas—but only where God had authorized it.[92] The divine mandates of marriage and family, culture, church, and state were concrete commissions of God's revelation in Jesus Christ and Scripture. These institutions did not gain their authority from the primacy of creation, but were conferred authority by divine command. It was for this particular reason that Bonhoeffer preferred the term "mandates" to that of "orders"—a mandate avoided the inherent danger of "focusing more strongly on the static element of order rather than on the divine authorizing, legitimizing, and sanctioning, which are its sole foundation."[93]

The four mandates were implanted from above as organizing structures of the reality of Christ. They were not an outgrowth of history, or an expression of human power, but witnesses to "the reality of God's love for the world and for human beings that has been revealed in Jesus Christ."[94] Regardless of the particular historical circumstance of a church, family, or government, God had commissioned these ordering structures, and the bearers of these mandates were God's representatives. In this sense, God's commandment recognized the influence of those below, and so the mandates required earthly relationships and organizing structures. But Bonhoeffer was clear: "Even a master has a Master. . . . Master and servant owe one another the respect that springs from their respective participation in God's mandate."[95]

This respect came solely in their being with-one-another, for-one-another, and over-against-one-another. Only in these ways, Bonhoeffer

---

91. See Green, "Editor's Introduction," 18.
92. See Bonhoeffer, *DBWE* 6:388.
93. Bonhoeffer, *DBWE* 6:389.
94. Bonhoeffer, *DBWE* 6:390.
95. Bonhoeffer, *DBWE* 6:391.

explained, "do the mandates of church, marriage and family, culture, and government communicate the commandment of God as it is revealed in Jesus Christ."[96] As he claimed, the four mandates must be with, for, and over-against-one-another because they existed in the reality of Jesus Christ—the one who was ultimately with, for, and over-against the world. It becomes clear now how Bonhoeffer's christocentric theology informed his concept of the mandates. Jesus Christ, as the revelation of God, was the ultimate man-for-others. His life, death, resurrection, and ascension bore witness to his mission of being-for-others, and this defined reality. As God commissioned the structures of society, they were ordered around the for-others reality. The mandates each had their own boundaries and limits, and they only existed in actuality when they appropriately engaged and interacted. A mandate was not self-sufficient; neither could one claim to replace the others, or exist in isolation or separation. Further, in being-with and for-others, the mandates were also limited by the others, by being-over-against-one-another. This three-fold interaction both safeguarded and limited a divine mandate. In this place, a mandate was set free to fulfill its own law; "that is the law inherent in it from its origin, essence, and goal in Jesus Christ."[97]

The core of Bonhoeffer's theological ethics came together here, when he introduced the concept of Christonomy. Although this particular term appears only once in *Ethics*, it encompassed his christocentric understanding of reality and provided the basis for the concrete expression of God's commandment in the divine mandates. With Christonomy, Bonhoeffer navigated the complex waters of autonomous existence and individualistic societal structures, explaining that the commandment of Jesus Christ set each of the mandates free to exercise their respective functions. Speaking of the mandate of the church, he explained, "Jesus Christ's claim to rule as it is proclaimed by the church simultaneously means that family, culture, and government are set free to be what they are in their own nature as grounded in Christ." At this point, he inserted a footnote: "Here the antagonism between heteronomy and autonomy is overcome and taken into a higher unity, which we could call Christonomy." He then continued: "Only through this liberation, which springs from the proclaimed rule of Christ, can the divine mandates be properly with-one-another, for-one-another, and against-one-another."[98] This footnoted concept of Christonomy provided Bonhoeffer with a key hermeneutical principle.

---

96. Bonhoeffer, *DBWE* 6:393.
97. Bonhoeffer, *DBWE* 6:402.
98. Bonhoeffer, *DBWE* 6:402.

Christonomy, at its base, was a way to overcome the conflicting pressures of autonomy and heteronomy. An autonomous view of reality, as Kuyper would also have contended with, found its triumph as each individual acted on his or her own free will. On the other hand, heteronomy understood that actions were based upon external forces and obligations, like a principled Christian ethic. Neither of these worldviews was, for Bonhoeffer, an accurate interpretation of reality. Rather, reality was in Jesus Christ, and so individuals and societies were finally liberated and free to be with-one-another, for-one-another, and over-against-one-another. The divine mandates existed to manifest this reality of freedom.[99] Ulrich Nissen provides helpful commentary here. He reminds us that throughout *Ethics* Bonhoeffer remained critical of any attempt to establish a moral reality apart from the will of God. Indeed, ethics for Bonhoeffer *is* following the will of God.[100] Any attempt to follow a strictly autonomous will denied the actual reality of life in Jesus Christ. Yet an equal danger occurred when the "profane" was ignored in favor of a limited Christian ethic; principles in and of themselves could not communicate the will of God. Bonhoeffer's notion of Christonomy as the source of ethics was "an attempt to move beyond both an 'autonomous' ethic and a specific 'Christian' ethic,"[101] toward a higher unity in Jesus Christ.

Freedom, which had its source outside of the autonomous self and was not found in some specific Christian principle, was being in accordance with the will of God. Christonomy was a way to understand that the basic reality of Jesus Christ was in fact what moved and motivated Christian ethical actions. It affirmed that, just as Christ exists-for-others, the divine mandates operated in their potential when they existed with and for-one-another. Christonomy was then not just a personal ethical principle, but was a vision for God's ordering of society. There was freedom and liberation for the church when it existed with, for, and over-against the state. Likewise, the state flourished when it could support culture, be in culture, and yet receive and incorporate culture's critique. All four mandates—church, state, family, and culture—and thus the major structures of society, reached their full potential when they operated in the reality of Jesus Christ, who was with, for, and over-against the world.

Both Kuyper and Bonhoeffer recognized a positive potential for the structure and ordering of society based on Christian convictions. Kuyper,

---

99. Note the crucial difference here, that Kuyper does not have this christological basis for the orders of creation.

100. See Bonhoeffer, *DBWE* 6:47.

101. Nissen, "Disbelief and Christonomy," 95.

with his *Lectures on Calvinism*, drew on the implications of sphere sovereignty and common grace in Reformed thought to offer a Christian worldview that was radically in and for the world. Likewise, Bonhoeffer came to the concept of Christonomy in order to communicate the freedom that existed in a society that lived into the reality of Jesus Christ. Both Kuyper and Bonhoeffer realized that the individualistic autonomy inherent in modernism, while promoting certain forms of freedom, in actuality only isolated and constrained. God's sovereignty and reign in Jesus Christ alone offered true liberation. This reality and mode of interaction within and between the various spheres of life set the Christian, and society as a whole, free to experience the fullness of God's grace.

It must also be noted that, for all of these similarities, Kuyper and Bonhoeffer did make significantly different practical choices in their lives—choices that were, at least to some extent, the result of the key differences in their theology and in their historical contexts. For example, Kuyper's Calvinism equipped him not only for life as a Christian minister, but also was the driving force in his involvement in politics, education, and news media. Bonhoeffer, on the other hand, struggled in his defined role as a theologian and pastor to enact effective resistance against the Nazi state. In many ways, his Lutheran heritage proved a liability because, practically speaking, the church relied on the state for its legitimate existence. Interestingly, it was only when Bonhoeffer finally released himself from participation as a pastor in the Confessing Church that he felt able to join the conspiracy to overthrow Hitler. While Bonhoeffer worked to explicate theologically the relationship between the church and the state in new and Christ-centered ways, the Lutheran church remained too wedded to its German national identity to spark widespread resistance against the Nazi regime. In some ways, like the Barmen Declaration (penned largely by the Reformed theologian Karl Barth), the Reformed church could speak much more directly than the Lutheran church to the Christians in German churches about the lordship of Jesus Christ. It may well have been these Reformed cues that helped Bonhoeffer articulate (but not simply repeat) an emerging theology of the reality of Christ's sovereignty. Bonhoeffer's theology, in turn, would have challenged Kuyper to keep Christ's cross at the center of the notion of sovereignty. Christ is indeed Sovereign over creation, but the character of Christ's sovereignty is in how he is with, for, and over-against the world. Repentance and the decision to enter into another's place of suffering is a particular aspect of Bonhoeffer's theology of the cross that could provide a balance to Kuyper's emphasis on Christ's sovereignty in creation.[102]

---

102. Stassen provides an interesting treatment of Bonhoeffer's understanding of the

Discipleship for the Common Good

Kuyper and Bonhoeffer provide hope for a way forward in Christian public discourse, which is one of the most pressing issues in our society today. Based on their similar (though not dogmatically identical) christological foundations, both offer a profound mediating perspective. The polar extremes of either releasing the world to modernistic autonomy or Christian-principled flight from the world need not be the only options. Instead, there is hope for the world because of God's very presence and grace in it through Jesus Christ. On the one hand, Kuyper's Christology, which reaches its height in sphere sovereignty and common (and particular) grace, affirms the continuing work of God in all areas of human life and recognizes the inherent beauty and potential of God's good creation. On the other hand, Bonhoeffer's Christology identifies Jesus Christ as the central defining factor of reality, and thus the affirmation of humanity. Taken together, then, there is a common foundation for human life because all of humanity comes to itself in Christ, and is affirmed in the reconciliation of Christ.[103] In the broadest sense, Kuyper and Bonhoeffer both recognize that God is reconciling all things to himself through Jesus Christ (Col 1:15–20), and so they seek to affirm structures and orders in society that mediate this reality. Kuyper's spheres and Bonhoeffer's mandates, while distinct theological concepts, both speak to God's work and grace in all areas of human life. They offer the call of Christian discipleship to each unique sector of human endeavor, and they provide creative, productive, and promising possibilities for Christian influence and witness that is in and for the world.

At its culmination, discipleship, then, explores areas of potentiality and possibility that are ultimately for the common good. By remaining grounded in the four movements of discipleship that have been established throughout this study, we can now assess a way forward for Christian engagement with the world. The Christian tradition is ripe for this discussion, particularly as it relates to the notion of the "common good." David Hollenbach, for example, provides a robust treatment of the concept of the common good throughout human history, from Cicero to Aristotle, and then through Augustine, Aquinas, and Ignatius.[104] He demonstrates that the common good is not just a Christian (or Catholic) concept, but that, in

---

cross as "incarnational representation" in *Thicker Jesus*, 150–53. However, a Reformed perspective would view the incarnation as an event, and would argue that when we follow—if we follow—then this is due to the work of the Holy Spirit. See Van der Kooi, "This Incredible Benevolent Force."

103. See Nissen, "Disbelief and Christonomy," 103.

104. See Hollenbach, *Common Good*.

its nature, it supports a practice of dialogic universalism by the pursuit of deep intellectual and cultural exchanges of practices and ideas. The common good is defined by the diversity of both local and global society, and, as such, one historical or intellectual tradition cannot hold a monopoly on defining or practicing it. Recently, there seems to be if not a resurgence, then at least a renewed appreciation of the necessity of the common good, which Christians can acknowledge by their efforts to mediate positive exchanges in the public sphere. The common good, as Hollenbach asserts, is not a concept that can be monopolized by one constituency. Indeed, affirming the diversity of its use provides a common entry point for multiple traditions and groups to discuss and take action on pertinent issues. Just a sampling of some of the recent literature that explains and models this commitment includes significant works from a wide variety of authors and traditions.[105] These studies provide critical supplementary support to Christian understanding and practice of the common good. But this project approaches the issue from a specific point of view: what does engagement with the common good look like from the particular perspective of *discipleship*?

In Western evangelical culture, an inherent tendency to disconnect personal discipleship from the call to public engagement can often be found. But we learn from Kuyper and Bonhoeffer that such a divide is far removed from the holistic concept of what it means to follow-after Jesus Christ. Recall the definition of discipleship that was provided at the beginning of this chapter: *Discipleship is the response to the call to follow-after Jesus Christ in all aspects of human life and endeavor, from the inner personal disciplines to the deliberate shaping of culture—in the very midst of the world.* From Kuyper and Bonhoeffer it is clear that their engagement with the world—whether as prime minister or prisoner—is intimately related to a person's experience of discipleship. It would even be fair to suggest that Kuyper and Bonhoeffer could not have enjoyed such influence apart from their theological convictions and practice of discipleship. So, in acknowledging the long and diverse Christian tradition of the common good, we must add—*via* Kuyper and Bonhoeffer—that discipleship reaches a culmination when it builds through the four movements of revelation, reality, action, and possibility. The possibility of a discipleship that is grounded in God's self-revelation, sees reality in and through Jesus Christ, and acts in faithful belief-obedience, is full of potential—when it remains fixed on the eschatological promise of Jesus Christ. In this freedom, discipleship led Kuyper to the highest political office in the Netherlands, while for Bonhoeffer it led to the lowest public existence.

105. Recent publications relating to Christianity and the pursuit of the common good include authors such as Walter Brueggemann, Andy Crouch, David Gushee, Charles Gutenson, James Davidson Hunter, Marcia Pally, Miroslav Volf, and Jim Wallis.

Our lives—and the lives of most Christians—will likely not encounter such extreme circumstances. But the point is that these circumstances do exist, in history and in contemporary life. Consequently, we must consider if our theology and practice of discipleship will be able to sustain God's calling on our lives—whatever that may be. Is our discipleship ready for any such possibility? Only by God's grace.

Conclusion

The Culmination of Discipleship

Again Jesus spoke to them, saying, "I am the light of the world. Whoever follows me will not walk in darkness, but will have the light of life."

—John 8:12

THE CALL OF JESUS Christ is not to a static conclusion; Jesus calls to places and experiences we can hardly imagine. Discipleship, then, gets its form in a process of interchange between context and content. As the historical, theological, or ethical context changes, it challenges, shapes, and ultimately culminates in a rich theology *and* practice of discipleship. Abraham Kuyper understood this, as did Dietrich Bonhoeffer.

Through a focus on Kuyper's life and thought during the years 1894–1905, we begin to see the implications of such a holistic theological practice of discipleship. Kuyper's *Encyclopedia of Sacred Theology* reveals how the four movements of discipleship—revelation, reality, action, and possibility—take root in theological thinking. The series "Dienst des Woords" encourages a culture of learning for discipleship among both ministers and congregants—historically for the newly formed Gereformeerde Kerken in Nederland (GKN), and also for us today. Kuyper addresses very real questions of belief and obedience with his study on the Sermon on the Mount in *Christ and the Needy*, and his Stone Lectures continue to challenge our own understanding of the possibility of discipleship in a myriad of cultural spheres. With Kuyper's rise to the office of prime minister, we see how the experience of discipleship impacts pressing political issues of war and international affairs, a volatile national labor strike, and education reform. Kuyper processed these issues through his various writings, such as "The South African Crisis," *The Work of the Holy Spirit*, and *To Be Near Unto God*. These diverse works give us insight into the spiritual and theological grounding that is so necessary for life in the public sphere. Additionally, Kuyper's work on "Common Grace," his speech on the concept of "sphere sovereignty," and his further meditations upon the death of his wife, all provide a compelling context for grappling with a holistic understanding and practice of discipleship.

Bonhoeffer too helps us establish a holistic framework for discipleship through his writings, reflections, work, and ministry. As we have seen, the four theological movements emerge in *Discipleship*, and Bonhoeffer lived out this theology particularly during the time of theological education between 1935 and 1940—first in Zingst and Finkenwalde, and then "underground" after the closing of the seminaries by the Gestapo in 1937. His unique approach to seminary education, like the House of Brethren and the seminary's practice of meditation, helps us see how theology connects to lived practice in a particular context. Investigating his understanding of the Sermon on the Mount provides further clarity to the commitment to a discipleship of simple obedience, and as Bonhoeffer continued his journey, we see the nuances of how discipleship is a continual process of discernment and action.

For example, by 1937 the legal question was pressing further on the conscience of the Confessing Church, threatening to undermine its purpose and structure. It was only with the approaching outbreak of war during the summer of 1939, that Bonhoeffer, out of necessity, let the issue fade. By this time, he was more caught up in the potential repercussions of his own decisions and actions on the viability of the Confessing Church. In June of 1939, Bonhoeffer traveled to America in order to avoid conscription into the German military. But rather than remaining in the safe haven of the United States, he quickly realized that faithfulness to God's call on his life demanded his immediate return to Germany. In simple obedience he returned, and in simple obedience he joined the conspiracy against Hitler and the Nazi regime. Bonhoeffer's writings and correspondence during the critical years of 1943 to 1945 (especially those contained in *Ethics* and *Letters and Papers from Prison*) were crucial in describing the momentum that he experienced in his own personal and theological understanding of discipleship. His interaction with intellectuals such as Dilthey, Ortega y Gasset, and Weizsäcker, help to describe the nuances of this emerging theology, while, at the same time, connecting it to a clear, continuous, and holistic concept

The Culmination of Discipleship

of discipleship. With the failure of the July 21, 1944 assassination attempt on Hitler, Bonhoeffer's fate was sealed. But even here, at the end of his life, he approached discipleship with a sense of hope and purpose. He continued to affirm life—in all its possibility and potentiality—in and through Jesus Christ.

On their own, Kuyper and Bonhoeffer provide compelling studies of discipleship; taken together, we have the opportunity to develop and explore a wider and more comprehensive theology of discipleship that is for the church. Comparing Kuyper and Bonhoeffer was a key test for the validity and usefulness of the four-movement framework of discipleship set out in this book. In order for the theological concepts of revelation, reality, belief-obedience, and possibility to hold lasting significance within an understanding of discipleship, it was important to show that these characteristics did not act in historical or theological isolation. Exploring the four movements of discipleship in diverse—and sometimes divergent—historical and theological settings, suggests the possibility of an on-going usefulness in contemporary questions of ethics and discipleship. This is where the notion of the common good becomes a launching point for further theological and historical implications of discipleship. When concepts such as revelation, creation, Jesus Christ, the church, the Holy Spirit, personal disciplines, and ethical actions are investigated, both within and beyond particular theological traditions, we find our own conceptions—as robust and systematic as they may be—have room for the mysteries of God. This is a critical point. Discipleship must culminate in possibility for the common good, because God is still revealing the mysteries of creation, redemption, and the eschaton. So, by placing the practice of discipleship within the sphere of the common good, we commit to a further exploration of God's mysteries. Revelation, reality, belief-obedience, and possibility keep a person grounded in Jesus Christ, all the while releasing them simply to pursue his call in all its mystery and abundance.

This conversation between Kuyper and Bonhoeffer, then, allows us to advance the contemporary question of discipleship far beyond the scope of a particular theological tradition. It is one task to explicate a Dutch Reformed perspective of discipleship, for example, but by claiming that there is continuity (while affirming the differences) between figures as diverse as Kuyper and Bonhoeffer, the conversation on discipleship can move beyond the walls of a particular church tradition and into the realm of wider society. This is crucial. As demonstrated, discipleship is incomplete—indeed unfulfilled—apart from its potential to influence the common good of society. No longer should discipleship be limited to a list of personal disciplines. In the lives of Kuyper and Bonhoeffer, the personal disciplines made up just part of one of the four movements of discipleship—they make their appearance most fully (but not exclusively) in the movement of belief-obedience. But discipleship is theologically and practically holistic—it must envelop all of one's life and thought. A way to express this inclusive understanding is through the movements of revelation, reality, action, and possibility. Certainly there are other formulations to describe a holistic understanding of discipleship, but the present framework affords a creative opportunity specifically to compare and nuance the critical factors of the call to follow Jesus Christ.

Recall, for example, how revelation is the critical foundation of theology—and thus of a theological conception of discipleship. Kuyper emphasized God's self-revelation in creation and in the subsequent divine mandates to create and cultivate organizing structures in society. He understood the decisive nature of the lordship of Jesus Christ in creation, but this did not cause him to view creation from an explicitly christological perspective. Bonhoeffer, on the other hand, favored the concept of the call of Jesus Christ above the creation mandates in his theology of revelation. In part due to the pressing historical and theological climate of his day, Bonhoeffer was exceedingly cautious about any talk of natural theology that emphasized the structures of creation. Instead, an emphasis on Jesus Christ elevated the concept of christological lordship over creation to the extent that Christology became a defining characteristic of his theological system (such as it was). Kuyper, while thoroughly "christological," did not labor under the contextual burden of Bonhoeffer's time, and so his theology of revelation is more in line with the traditionally Reformed emphasis on creation. Context alone, however, cannot explain away the importance of these theological differences. The uniting factor between Kuyper and Bonhoeffer is their agreement that revelation is the foundation of discipleship, while the contemporary question concentrates on the substantive differences and implications of an emphasis on creation (or Christology) in understanding the meaning of revelation. While this question was addressed in the present study, additional exploration of this issue remains important. Such theological differences must be thoroughly examined and explored, for they make a profound difference in how we understand the world. Taken together, Kuyper's and Bonhoeffer's concept of revelation encourages an affirmation of creational structures while emphasizing the sovereignty of Jesus Christ; and this sovereignty includes the crucified Christ's posture of humility in the world. Such a juxtaposed understanding of revelation is not meant to minimize the substantive differences between the two foundational concepts; but by placing aspects of Kuyper's and Bonhoeffer's theology of revelation side-by-side, it is possible to press deeper into the theological mystery and profound practicality of God's self-revelation.

There is room for similar—and nuanced—exploration in the concepts of reality, action, and possibility. This study makes a significant start, but there remains considerable potential for multiple comparative studies of each of these theological concepts. Even with further investigation into their similarities and differences, the possible impact of a theology of discipleship on the common good would, undoubtedly, be substantial. Taken together, revelation, reality, action, and possibility lead to a broadening of our conception of discipleship from the limits of personal piety to the opportunities for significant societal change. Such a call to public action would not be divorced from a dynamic personal faith; indeed, as in Kuyper and Bonhoeffer, it would be the result. Further scholarship in the historical, theological, and ethical conceptions of a holistic understanding and practice of discipleship have the potential to contribute to a renewed expectation that following-after Jesus Christ demands our entire heart, soul, mind, and strength.

It will no longer be acceptable to conceive of the call to discipleship outside of an engagement with all of life. Surely, the potential for this engagement will take on countless forms—that is the beauty and mystery of Jesus Christ's call to simple obedience. But unless discipleship is rightly conceived *theologically*, it will not be able to sustain the work that God is setting before us *practically*. Revelation is foundational; apart from it stands only human-centered religion. Reality as understood in and through Jesus Christ guards against the fragmentation of life into disconnected pieces. Action marks the life of belief-obedience because faith is not a mental proposition. Possibility demands a daily posture of discernment-for-action in the world; but it cannot provide faithful results apart from its movement in revelation, Jesus Christ, and belief-obedience. There is hope in the world because of God's faithful work in the unfolding of history. Discipleship is not the path of least resistance, nor is it the path devoid of hardship, turmoil, and tragedy. Discipleship is, however, the joyous response to the sustaining work of God, in our life and for the world.

Perhaps the greatest challenge of all is to move this nuanced theology of discipleship into the fellowship halls, small groups, and sermons of our churches. Within these places, there is often a thin *practice* of discipleship that is the outworking of an equally thin *theology* of discipleship. For example, if discipleship programs are created only for the development of personal spiritual disciplines, notice the theological lesson: discipleship is limited to the disciplines of prayer, Bible study, meditation, and fasting. That is, discipleship is about what I do in my own time with God. By implication, discipleship is thus removed from the much larger work of God in and for the world. This is not to downplay the personal disciplines, but rather to realize they are just one part of a comprehensive theology of the Christian life. This shift towards holistic discipleship will not be easy, but it is the calling set before us and is an all-encompassing endeavor. If we think in terms of one or two discipleship programs or curricula, chances are we are thinking much too narrowly. Ultimately, discipleship is our entire theology in action; and if we have little theology, we will have little action. By God's grace, in Jesus Christ and through the power of the Holy Spirit, there is the potential for ever so much more.

Bibliography

Dietrich Bonhoeffer Primary Source Material

Bonhoeffer, Dietrich. *Dietrich Bonhoeffer Works* [*DBWE*]. 17 vols. Minneapolis: Fortress, 1996–2014.

———. *DBWE* 1: *Sanctorum Communio*. Translated by Reinhard Krauss and Nancy Lukens. Edited by Clifford J. Green. Minneapolis: Fortress, 1998.

———. *DBWE* 2: *Act and Being*. Translated by Martin H. Rumscheidt. Edited by Wayne Whitson Floyd and Hans-Richard Reuter. Minneapolis: Fortress, 1996.

———. *DBWE* 3: *Creation and Fall: A Theological Exposition of Genesis 1–3*. Translated by Douglas Stephen Bax. Edited by John W. de Gruchy. Minneapolis: Fortress, 1997.

———. *DBWE* 4: *Discipleship*. Translated by Barbara Green. Edited by Geffrey B. Kelly and John D. Godsey. Minneapolis: Fortress, 2001.

———. *DBWE* 5: *Life Together* and *Prayerbook of the Bible*. Translated by James H. Burtness and Daniel W. Bloesch. Edited by Geffrey B. Kelly. Minneapolis: Fortress, 1996.

———. *DBWE* 6: *Ethics*. Translated by Reinhard Krauss, Charles C. West, and Douglas W. Stott. Edited by Clifford J. Green. Minneapolis: Fortress, 2005.

———. *DBWE* 8: *Letters and Papers from Prison*. Translated by Reinhard Krauss, Nancy Lukens, Lisa E. Dahill, and Isabel Best. Edited by John W. de Gruchy. Minneapolis: Fortress, 2010.

———. *DBWE* 11: *Ecumenical, Academic, and Pastoral Work: 1931–1932*. Translated by Douglas W. Stott, Isabel Best, Anne Schmidt-Lange, Nicholas S. Humphrey, and Marion Pauck. Edited by Victoria J. Barnett, Mark S. Brocker, and Michael Lukens. Minneapolis: Fortress, 2012.

———. *DBWE* 12: *Berlin: 1932–1933*. Translated by Douglas W. Stott, Isabel Best, and David Higgins. Edited by Larry L. Rasmussen. Minneapolis: Fortress, 2009.

———. *DBWE* 13: *London, 1933–1935*. Translated by Isabel Best. Edited by Keith W. Clements. Minneapolis: Fortress, 2007.

———. *DBWE* 14: *Theological Education at Finkenwalde: 1935–1937*. Translated by Douglas W. Stott. Edited by H. Gaylon Barker and Mark S. Brocker. Minneapolis: Fortress, 2013.

———. *DBWE 15: Theological Education Underground: 1937–1940*. Translated by Claudia D. Bergmann, Scott A. Moore, and Peter Frick. Edited by Victoria J. Barnett. Minneapolis: Fortress, 2012.

———. *DBWE 16: Conspiracy and Imprisonment: 1940–1945*. Translated by Lisa E. Dahill. Edited by Mark S. Brocker. Minneapolis: Fortress, 2006.

Abraham Kuyper Primary Source Material

Kuyper, Abraham. "Aan den schrijver van Van dag tot dag." *Algemeen Handelsblad*, 20967, October 24, 1895.

———. *Christ and the Needy*. Edited by Harry Van Dyke. Translated by Herbert Donald Morton. *Journal of Markets & Morality* 14 (2011) 647–83.

———. "Common Grace." In *Abraham Kuyper: A Centennial Reader*, edited by James Bratt, 165–201. Grand Rapids: Eerdmans, 1998.

———. *Common Grace*. Vol. 1, *The Historical Section, Part 1: Noah-Adam*. Edited by Jordan J. Ballor and Stephen J. Grabill. Translated by Nelson D. Kloosterman and Ed M. van der Maas. Grand Rapids: Christian's Library, 2013.

———. *Common Grace*. Vol. 1, *The Historical Section, Part 2: Temptation-Babel*. Edited by Jordan J. Ballor and Stephen J. Grabill. Translated by Nelson D. Kloosterman and Ed M. van der Maas. Grand Rapids: Christian's Library, 2014.

———. "Common Grace in Science." In *Abraham Kuyper: A Centennial Reader*, edited by James Bratt, 441–60. Grand Rapids: Eerdmans, 1998.

———. *De Gemeene Gratie*. Leiden: D. Donner, 1902–5.

———. "Dienst des Woords." *Gereformeerde Stemmen uit vroeger en later tijd* 2de Serie No. 2. Rotterdam: A. ter Weeme, 1895–96.

———. *Eenige Kameradviezen uit de jaren 1874 en 1875*. Amsterdam: J. A. Wormser, Koninklijke Nederlandsche Stoomdrukkerij, 1890.

———. *Encyclopedia of Sacred Theology: Its Principles*. Translated by J. Hendrik De Vries. New York: Charles Scribner's Sons, 1898.

———. *Het sociale vraagstuk en de christelijke religie*. Amsterdam, 1891.

———. *Kuyper in America: This Is Where I Was Meant to Be*. Edited by George Harinck. Translated by Margriet Urbanus. Sioux Center, IA: Dordt College Press, 2012.

———. *Lectures on Calvinism*. New York: Cosimo, 2007.

———. *Ons program*. Amsterdam: J. A. Wormser, 1891.

———. *Pro Rege: of het koningschap van Christus*. 3 vols. Kampen: J. H. Kok, 1911–1912.

———. "The South African Crisis." In *Abraham Kuyper: A Centennial Reader*, edited by James Bratt, 323–60. Grand Rapids: Eerdmans, 1998.

———. "Sphere Sovereignty." In *Abraham Kuyper: A Centennial Reader*, edited by James Bratt, 461–90. Grand Rapids: Eerdmans, 1998.

———. *To Be Near Unto God*. Translated by J. H. De Vries. Grand Rapids: Eerdmans Sevensma, 1918.

———. "Uniformity: The Curse of Modern Life." In *Abraham Kuyper: A Centennial Reader*, edited by James Bratt, 19–44. Grand Rapids: Eerdmans, 1998.

———. "When What Is Mortal Is Swallowed Up by Life." In *Abraham Kuyper: A Centennial Reader*, edited by James Bratt, 408–15. Grand Rapids: Eerdmans, 1998.

———. *The Work of the Holy Spirit*. Translated by Henri De Vries. New York: Funk & Wagnalls, 1900.

Secondary Source Material

Altizer, Thomas J. J., and William Hamilton. *Radical Theology and the Death of God*. Indianapolis: Bobbs-Merrill, 1966.

Anderson, Ray S. *The Shape of Practical Theology: Empowering Ministry with Theological Praxis*. Downers Grove: IVP Academic, 2001.

Augsburger, David. "Discipleship." In *Global Dictionary of Theology*, edited by William A. Dyrness and Veli-Matti Kärkkäinen, 235–37. Downers Grove: IVP Academic, 2008.

Bacote, Vincent. "Abraham Kuyper's Rhetorical Public Theology with Implications for Faith and Learning." *Christian Scholars Review* 37 (2008) 407–25.

———. *The Spirit in Public Theology: Appropriating the Legacy of Abraham Kuyper*. Grand Rapids: Baker Academic, 2005.

Barth, Karl. *Church Dogmatics* III/4. Peabody, MA: Hendrickson, 2010.

Best, S. Payne. *The Venlo Incident: A True Story of Double-Dealing, Captivity, and a Murderous Nazi Plot*. London: Hutchinson, 1950.

Bethge, Eberhard. *Dietrich Bonhoeffer: A Biography*. Revised ed. Minneapolis: Fortress, 2000.

Bezner, Steven. "Understanding the World Better than it Understands Itself: The Theological Hermeneutics of Dietrich Bonhoeffer." PhD diss., Baylor University, 2008.

Bolt, John. *A Free Church, a Holy Nation: Abraham Kuyper's American Public Theology*. Grand Rapids: Eerdmans, 2001.

———. "The Imitation of Christ as Illumination for the Two Kingdoms Debate." *Calvin Theological Journal* 48 (2013) 6–34.

Boone, Christophe, et al. "Religious Pluralism and Organizational Diversity: An Empirical Test in the City of Zwolle, the Netherlands, 1851–1914." *Sociology of Religion* 73 (2012) 150–73.

Bowlin, John, ed. *The Kuyper Center Review*. Vol. 2, *Revelation and Common Grace*. Grand Rapids: Eerdmans, 2011.

———. *The Kuyper Center Review*. Vol. 4, *Calvinism and Democracy*. Grand Rapids: Eerdmans, 2014.

Bratt, James. *Abraham Kuyper: Modern Calvinist, Christian Democrat*. Grand Rapids: Eerdmans, 2013.

———. "Editor's Introduction to 'Common Grace.'" In *Abraham Kuyper: A Centennial Reader*, edited by James Bratt, 165–66. Grand Rapids: Eerdmans, 1998.

———. "In the Shadow of Mt. Kuyper: A Survey of the Field." *Calvin Theological Journal* 31 (1996) 51–66.

Brueggemann, Walter. *Journey to the Common Good*. Louisville: Westminster John Knox, 2010.

Brunner, Emil, and Karl Barth. *Natural Theology: Comprising "Nature and Grace" by Emil Brunner and the Reply "No!" by Karl Barth*. Eugene, OR: Wipf and Stock, 2002.

Calvin, John. *Commentarii in Quatuor Euangelistas*. Vol. 6, *Opera omnia*. Amsterdam: Joannem Jacobi Schipper, 1667.

Conradie, Ernst M. *Creation and Salvation: Dialogue on Abraham Kuyper's Legacy for Contemporary Ecotheology*. Leiden: Brill, 2011.

Covolo, Robert. "Faith in a Fashionable Age: Abraham Kuyper and Charles Taylor on the Secular Nexus Between Mode and Modernité." *International Journal of Public Theology* 7 (2013) 297–314.

Crouch, Andy. *Culture Making: Recovering our Creative Calling*. Downers Grove: InterVarsity, 2008.

De Bruijn, Jan. *Abraham Kuyper: A Pictorial Biography*. Grand Rapids: Eerdmans, 2014.

De Gruchy, John W. *Bonhoeffer and South Africa: Theology in Dialogue*. Grand Rapids: Eerdmans, 1984.

———. *The Church in South Africa*. Grand Rapids: Eerdmans, 1979.

Dejonge, Michael P. *Bonhoeffer's Theological Formation: Berlin, Barth, and Protestant Theology*. Oxford: Oxford University Press, 2012.

De Marval-McNair, Nora. "Preface: José Ortega y Gasset: *Espectador universal*." In *Jose Ortega y Gasset: Proceedings of the Espectador Universal International Interdisciplinary Conference*, edited by Nora de Marval Mc-Nair, xi–xii. New York: Greenwood, 1987.

De Savornin Lohman, Witsius H. "Dr. Abraham Kuyper." *The Presbyterian and Reformed Review* 36 (1898) 561–609.

Dilthey, Wilhelm. *Gesammelte Schriften (Collected Works)*. Volume 8, edited by B. Groethuysen. Göttingen: Vandenhoeck & Ruprecht, 1968.

———. *Gesammelte Schriften (Collected Works)*. Volume 19, edited by H. Johach R. Rodi. Göttingen: Vandenhoeck & Ruprecht, 1982.

———. *Hermeneutics and the Study of History*. Edited by Rudolf A. Makkreel and Frithjof Rodi. Selected Works 4. Princeton: Princeton University Press, 1996.

———. *Leben Schleiermachers (The Life of Schleiermacher)*. Volume 13 of *Gesammelte Schriften (Collected Works)*. Göttingen: Vandenhoeck & Ruprecht, 1970.

———. *Pattern and Meaning in History*. Edited by H. P. Rickman. New York: Harper & Row, 1962.

———. *Poetry and Experience*. Edited by Rudolf A. Makkreel and Frithjof Rodi. Selected Works 5. Princeton: Princeton University Press, 1985.

———. *Selected Works*. Edited by Rudolf A. Makkreel and Frithjof Rodi. 6 vols. Princeton: Princeton University Press, 1991–2010.

———. *Von deutscher Dichtung und Musik*. Leipzig und Berlin: B. G. Teubner, 1933.

———. *Weltanschauung und Analyse des Menschen seit Renaissance und Reformation (Worldview and Analysis of Humanity Since the Renaissance and Reformation)*. Vol. 2 of *Gesammelte Schriften (Collected Works)*. 7th ed. Göttingen: Vandenhoeck & Ruprecht, 1964.

Dramm, Sabine. *Dietrich Bonhoeffer and the Resistance*. Translated by Margaret Kohl. Minneapolis: Fortress, 2009.

Du Toit, André. "No Chosen People: The Myth of the Calvinist Origins of Afrikaner Nationalism and Racial Ideology." *American Historical Review* 88 (1983) 920–52.

Editorial. "Van dag tot dag." *Algemeen Handelsblad*, 20596, October 13, 1895.

Ericksen, Robert P. *Theologians Under Hitler: Gerhard Kittel, Paul Althaus, and Emanuel Hirsch*. New Haven: Yale University Press, 1985.

Eto, Naozumi. "Bonhoeffer's Idea of Religion: A Study of Dietrich Bonhoeffer's Idea of Religion and 'Religionlessness' with Some Implications for the Interpretation of the Christian Faith in Japan Today." ThD diss., Lutheran School of Theology at Chicago, 1985.

Feil, Ernst. *The Theology of Dietrich Bonhoeffer*. Translated by Martin Rumscheidt. Chicago: Fortress, 1985.

Flipse, Ab. *Christelijke wetenschap: Nederlandse rooms-katholieken en gereformeerden over de natuurwetenschap, 1880–1940*. Hilversum: Uitgeverij Verloren, 2014.

Frank, Charles. *Operation Epsilon: The Farm Hill Transcripts*. Berkeley: University of California Press, 1993.

Gerber, John P. *Anton Pannekoek and the Socialism of Workers' Self Emancipation, 1873–1960*. Dordrecht: Kluwer, 1989.

Godet, F. L. *Commentar zu dem Evangelium des Lucas*. Hannover: Meyer, 1869–72.

———. *A Commentary on the Gospel of St. Luke*. Vol. 1. Translated by E. W. Shalders. Edinburgh: T&T Clark, 1875.

Godsey, John D. *The Theology of Dietrich Bonhoeffer*. Philadelphia: Westminster, 1960.

Graham, Gordon, ed. *The Kuyper Center Review*. Vol. 1, *New Essays in Reformed Theology and Public Life*. Grand Rapids: Eerdmans, 2010.

———. *The Kuyper Center Review*. Vol. 3, *Calvinism and Culture*. Grand Rapids: Eerdmans, 2013.

Graham, John T. *A Pragmatist Philosophy of Life in Ortega y Gasset*. Columbia: University of Missouri Press, 1994.

———. *The Social Thought of Ortega y Gasset: A Systematic Synthesis in Postmodernism and Interdisciplinarity*. Columbia: University of Missouri Press, 2001.

———. *Theory of History in Ortega y Gasset: "The Dawn of Historical Reason."* Columbia: University of Missouri Press, 1997.

Green, Clifford. *Bonhoeffer: A Theology of Sociality*. Revised ed. Grand Rapids: Eerdmans, 1999.

———. "Editor's Introduction." In *DBWE 6: Ethics*, edited by Clifford Green, 1–44. Minneapolis: Fortress, 2005.

Gushee, David, ed. *A New Evangelical Manifesto: A Kingdom Vision for the Common Good*. St. Louis: Chalice, 2012.

Gutenson, Charles. *Christians and the Common Good: How Faith Intersects with Public Life*. Grand Rapids: Brazos, 2011.

Hamilton, William. "The Letters Are a Particular Thorn." In *World Come of Age*, edited by Ronald Gregor Smith, 131–60. Philadelphia: Fortress, 1967.

———. "Questions and Answers on the Radical Theology." In *The Death of God Debate*, edited by Jackson Lee Ice and John Jesse Carey. Philadelphia: Westminster, 1967.

Harinck, George. "Abraham Kuyper, South Africa, and Apartheid." *The Princeton Seminary Bulletin* 23 (2002) 184–87.

———. "Abraham Kuyper's Historical Understanding and Reformed Historiography." *Fides et Historia* 37 (2005) 71–82.

———. "Being Public: Abraham Kuyper and His Publications." In *Abraham Kuyper: An Annotated Bibliography, 1857–2010*, by Tjitze Kuipers, vii–xxi. Leiden: Brill, 2011.

———. "For Humanity's Sake: Abraham Kuyper, the Spanish-American War of 1898 and His Calvinist View on International Relations." In *Dutch Americans and War:*

United States and Abroad, edited by Robert P. Swierenga, Nella Kennedy, and Lisa Zylstra. Holland, MI: Van Raalte, 2014.

———. "Neo-Calvinism and Democracy: An Overview from the Mid-Nineteenth Century till the Second World War." In *The Kuyper Center Review*. Vol. 4, *Calvinism and Democracy*, edited by John Bowlin, 1–20. Grand Rapids: Eerdmans, 2014.

Harinck, George, and Gerard Dekker. "The Position of the Church Institute in Society: A Comparison Between Bonhoeffer and Kuyper." *The Princeton Seminary Bulletin* 28 (2007) 86–98.

Harinck, George, and Gerrit Schutte, eds. *De school met de bijbel: Christelijk onderwijs in de negentiende eeuw*. Zoetermeer: Uitgeverij Meinema, 2006.

Hastings, Adrian. "Discipleship." In *The Oxford Companion to Christian Thought*, edited by Adrian Hastings, Alistair Mason, and Hugh Piper, 169. Oxford: Oxford University Press, 2000.

Haynes, Stephen R. *The Bonhoeffer Phenomenon: Portraits of a Protestant Saint*. Minneapolis: Fortress, 2004.

Heemskerk, T., ed. *Gedenkboek, opgedragen door het feestcomité aan Prof. Dr. A. Kuyper, bij zijn vijf en twintigjarig jubileum als hoofdredacteur van 'De Standaard', 1872–1897*. Amsterdam: Herdes, 1897.

Heidegger, Martin. "Wilhelm Dilthey's Research and the Struggle for a Historical Worldview (1925)." Translated by Charles Bambuch. In *Supplements: From the Earliest Essays to Being and Time and Beyond*, edited by John van Buren, 147–76. Albany: State University of New York Press, 2002.

Heslam, Peter. *Creating a Christian Worldview: Abraham Kuyper's Lectures on Calvinism*. Grand Rapids: Eerdmans, 1998.

Himes, Brant. "A Better Worldliness: Discipleship for the Common Good." *Verbum Incarnatum: Peace and Social Justice* 6 (2014) 38–61.

———. "Discipleship as Theological Praxis: Dietrich Bonhoeffer as a Resource for Educational Ministry." *Christian Education Journal* 8 (2011) 263–77.

———. "Distinct Discipleship: Abraham Kuyper, Dietrich Bonhoeffer, and Christian Engagement in Public Life." In *The Kuyper Center Review*. Vol. 4, *Calvinism and Democracy*, edited by John Bowlin, 147–70. Grand Rapids: Eerdmans, 2014.

Hix, Duane E. "Discipleship in a World Come of Age: 'Representation' in the Theology of Dietrich Bonhoeffer." PhD diss., McMaster University, 1981.

Holder, Rodney. "Science and Religion in the Theology of Dietrich Bonhoeffer." *Zygon* 4 (2009) 115–32.

Hollenbach, David. *The Common Good and Christian Ethics*. New York: Cambridge University Press, 2002.

Hopper, David H. *A Dissent on Bonhoeffer*. Philadelphia: Westminster, 1975.

Huntemann, Georg. *The Other Bonhoeffer: An Evangelical Reassessment of Dietrich Bonhoeffer*. Grand Rapids: Baker, 1993.

Hunter, James Davidson. *To Change the World: The Irony, Tragedy, and Possibility of Christianity in the Late Modern World*. Oxford: Oxford University Press, 2010.

International Committee of the Red Cross. "Final Act of the International Peace Conference, The Hague, July 29, 1899." Treaties and States Parties to Such Treaties. https://www.icrc.org/ihl/INTRO/145?OpenDocument.

Jackson, Timothy. "Church, World, and Christian Charity." In *Bonhoeffer and King: Their Legacies and Import for Christian Social Thought*, edited by Willis Jenkins and Jennifer McBride, 91–106. Minneapolis: Fortress, 2010.

Jenkins, Willis, and Jennifer McBride, eds. *Bonhoeffer and King: Their Legacies and Import for Christian Social Thought.* Minneapolis: Fortress, 2010.

Kaemingk, Matthew. "Mecca and Amsterdam: Christian Ethics Between Islam and Liberalism." PhD diss., Fuller Theological Seminary and Vrije Universiteit Amsterdam, 2013.

Kamphuis, Barend. *Boven en beneden: het uitgangspunt van de christologie en de problematiek van de openbaring, nagegaan aan de hand van de ontwikkelingen bij Karl Barth, Dietrich Bonhoeffer en Wolfhart Pannenberg.* Kampen: Kok, 1999.

Kantzenbach, F. W. *Programme der Theologie: Denker, Schulen, Wirkungen von Schleiermacher bis Moltmann.* Munich: Claudius-Verlag, 1984.

Kilcrease, Bethany. "Protestant Paranoia and Catholic Conspiracies: Protestant Perspectives on the Second Anglo-Boer War." *Fides et Historia* 44 (2012) 30–52.

Koopman, Nico. "The Reception of the Barmen Declaration in South Africa." *The Ecumenical Review* 61 (2009) 60–71.

Kossmann, E. H. *The Low Countries: 1780–1940.* Oxford: Clarendon, 1978.

Kuiper, Dirk Th. "Theory and Practice in Dutch Calvinism on the Racial Issue in the Nineteenth Century." *Calvin Theological Journal* 21 (1986) 51–78.

Kuipers, Tjitze. *Abraham Kuyper: An Annotated Bibliography, 1857–2010.* Leiden: Brill, 2011.

Kuitenbrouwer, Vincent. *War of Words: Dutch Pro-Boer Propaganda and the South African War (1899–1902).* Amsterdam: Amsterdam University Press, 2012.

Kuyper, H. S. S., and J. H. Kuyper. *De levensavond van dr. A. Kuyper.* Kampen: J. H. Kok, 1921.

Langley, McKendree R. *The Practice of Political Spirituality: Episodes from the Public Career of Abraham Kuyper, 1879–1918.* Jordan Station, Ontario, Canada: Paideia, 1984.

Marsh, Charles. *The Beloved Community: How Faith Shapes Social Justice from the Civil Rights Movement to Today.* New York: Basic, 2005.

———. *A Strange Glory: A Life of Dietrich Bonhoeffer.* New York: Alfred A. Knopf, 2014.

McBride, Jennifer. *The Church for the World: A Theology of Public Witness.* Oxford: Oxford University Press, 2012.

McGoldrick, James. *God's Renaissance Man: The Life and Work of Abraham Kuyper.* Auburn, MA: Evangelical, 2000.

Molendijk, Arie. "Neo-Calvinist Culture Protestantism: Abraham Kuyper's Stone Lectures." *Church History and Religious Culture* 88 (2008) 235–52.

———. "A Squeezed Out Lemon Peel: Abraham Kuyper on Modernism." *Church History and Religious Culture* 91 (2011) 397–412.

Moltmann, Jürgen, and Jürgen Weissbach. *Two Studies in the Theology of Bonhoeffer.* New York: Charles Scribner's Sons, 1967.

Mouw, Richard. *Abraham Kuyper: A Short and Personal Introduction.* Grand Rapids: Eerdmans, 2011.

———. *The Challenges of Cultural Discipleship: Essays in the Line of Abraham Kuyper.* Grand Rapids: Eerdmans, 2012.

———. *He Shines in All That's Fair: Culture and Common Grace.* Grand Rapids: Eerdmans, 2001.

Müller, Hanfried. "The Problem of the Reception and Interpretation of Dietrich Bonhoeffer." In *World Come of Age*, edited by Ronald Gregor Smith, 182–213. Philadelphia: Fortress, 1967.

———. *Von der Kirche zur Welt*. Leipzig and Hamburg, 1961.

Muller, Richard A. "A Note on 'Christocentrism' and the Imprudent Use of Such Terminology." *Westminster Theological Journal* 68 (2006) 253–60.

Nation, Mark. *Bonhoeffer the Assassin? Challenging the Myth, Recovering His Call to Peacemaking*. Grand Rapids: Baker Academic, 2013.

Naylor, Wendy Fish. "Abraham Kuyper and the Emergence of the Neo-Calvinist Pluralism in the Dutch School Struggle." PhD diss., University of Chicago, 2006.

Nielson, Paul. "The Concepts of Responsibility and Vocation in the Theological Ethics of Dietrich Bonhoeffer." PhD diss., University of Chicago, 1998.

Nissen, Ulrich. "Disbelief and Christonomy of the World." *Studia Theologica* 60 (2006) 91–110.

Ortega y Gasset, José. "Author's Forward." In *History as a System, and Other Essays Toward a Philosophy of History*, 11–12. New York: Norton, 1961.

———. "History as a System." In *History as a System, and Other Essays Toward a Philosophy of History*, 165–236. New York: Norton, 1961.

———. *Obras Completas*. 12 vols. Madrid: Reviste de Occidente, 1946–1983.

Osmer, Richard. *The Teaching Ministry of Congregations*. Louisville: Westminster John Knox, 2005.

Ott, Heinrich. *Reality and Faith: The Theological Legacy of Dietrich Bonhoeffer*. London: Lutterworth, 1971.

Pally, Marcia. *The New Evangelicals: Expanding the Vision of the Common Good*. Grand Rapids: Eerdmans, 2011.

Pangritz, Andreas. *Karl Barth in the Theology of Dietrich Bonhoeffer*. Grand Rapids: Eerdmans, 2000.

Patte, Daniel. "Discipleship." In *The Cambridge Dictionary of Christianity*, edited by Daniel Patte, 326–27. Cambridge: Cambridge University Press, 2010.

Pfeifer, Hans. "Learning Faith and Ethical Commitment in the Context of Spiritual Training Groups: Consequences of Dietrich Bonhoeffer's Post Doctoral Year in New York City 1930/31." In *Dietrich Bonhoeffer Jahrbuch 3 (Dietrich Bonhoeffer Yearbook 3, 2007/2008)*, edited by Clifford J. Green, Kirsten Busch Nielsen, Hans Pfeifer, and Christiane Tietz, 251–79. Gütersloh, 2008.

Phillips, John A. *Christ for Us in the Theology of Dietrich Bonhoeffer*. New York: Harper & Row, 1967.

Pugh, Jeffrey C. *Religionless Christianity: Dietrich Bonhoeffer in Troubled Times*. New York: Continuum, 2009.

Rasmussen, Larry L. *Dietrich Bonhoeffer: Reality and Resistance*. Revised ed. Louisville: Westminster John Knox, 2005.

Ratzsch, Del. "Abraham Kuyper's Philosophy of Science." *Calvin Theological Journal* 27 (1992) 277–303.

Rauschning, Hermann. *The Revolution of Nihilism: Warning to the West*. New York: Alliance Book Corporation, 1939.

Rickman, H. P. *Dilthey Today: A Critical Appraisal of the Contemporary Relevance of His Work*. New York: Greenwood, 1988.

———. "General Introduction." In *Pattern and Meaning in History: Thoughts on History and Society in Wilhelm Dilthey*, edited by H. P. Rickman, 11–63. New York: Harper & Row, 1962.

Rochelle, Jay C. "Gospel in a Secular World: Mystery and Relationship." In *Reflections on Bonhoeffer: Essays in Honor of F. Burton Nelson*, edited by Geffrey B. Kelly and C. John Weborg, 315–33. New York: Covenant, 1999.

Romein, Jan. "Abraham Kuyper: De Klokkenist van de Kleine Luyden." In *Erflaters van Onze Beschaving*, by Jan and Annie Romein. Amsterdam: Querido, 1971.

Rüter, A. J. C. *De Spoorwegstakingen van 1903*. Leiden, 1935.

Schlingensiepen, Ferdinand. *Dietrich Bonhoeffer 1906–1945: Martyr, Thinker, Man of Resistance*. New York: T&T Clark, 2010.

Schmitz, Florian. *"Nachfolge" Zur Theologie Dietrich Bonhoeffers*, Forschungen zur systematischen und ökumenischen Theologie Bd. 138. Göttingen: Vandenhoeck & Ruprecht, 2013.

———. "'Only the Believers Obey, and Only the Obedient Believe.' Notes on Dietrich Bonhoeffer's Biblical Hermeneutics with Reference to *Discipleship*." In *God Speaks to Us: Dietrich Bonhoeffer's Biblical Hermeneutics*, edited by Ralf K. Wüstenberg and Jens Zimmermann, 169–86. International Bonhoeffer Interpretations 5. Frankfurt: Peter Lang, 2013.

———. "Reading Discipleship and Ethics Together." In *Interpreting Bonhoeffer: Historical Perspectives, Emerging Issues*, edited by Clifford J. Green and Guy C. Carter, 147–53. Minneapolis: Fortress, 2013.

Spykman, Gordon. *Reformational Theology: A New Paradigm for Doing Dogmatics*. Grand Rapids: Eerdmans, 1992.

Stackhouse, Max L. "Public Theology and Ethical Judgment." *Theology Today* 54 (1997) 165–79.

Stassen, Glen Harold. "Healing the Rift Between the Sermon on the Mount and Christian Ethics." *Studies in Christian Ethics* 18 (2005) 89–105.

———. *A Thicker Jesus: Incarnational Discipleship in a Secular Age*. Louisville: Westminster John Knox, 2012.

Strecker, Georg, and Ekkehard Starke. "Discipleship." In *The Encyclopedia of Christianity*, Vol. 1, A-D, edited by Erwin Fahlbusch et al., 851–53. Grand Rapids: Eerdmans, 1999.

Ten Hooven, Marcel, and Theo de Wit, eds. *Ongewensten goden: de publieke rol van religie in Nederland*. Amsterdam: SUN, 2006.

Tuttle, Howard N. *Human Life Is a Radical Reality: An Idea Developed from the Conceptions of Dilthey, Heidegger, and Ortega y Gasset*. New York: Peter Lang, 2005.

Vandenbosch, Amry. *Dutch Foreign Policy Since 1815: A Study in Small Power Politics*. The Hague: Martinus Nijhoff, 1959.

Van der Kooi, Cornelis. "This Incredibly Benevolent Force: The Holy Spirit in Reformed Theology and Spirituality." Warfield Lectures, Princeton Theological Seminary, Princeton, NJ, March 31–April 3, 2014.

VanDrunen, David. *Natural Law and the Two Kingdoms: A Study in the Development of Reformed Social Thought*. Grand Rapids: Eerdmans, 2010.

Van Dyke, Harry. "Abraham Kuyper and the Continuing Social Question." *Journal of Markets & Morality* 14 (2011) 641–46.

Van Egmond, A. "Kuyper's Dogmatic Theology." In *Kuyper Reconsidered: Aspects of His Life and Work*, edited by Cornelis van der Kooi and Jan de Bruijn. Amsterdam: VU Uitgeverij, 1999.

Van Koppen, Chris A. J. "Abraham Kuyper en Zuid-Afrika." ThD diss., Rijksuniversiteit te Utrecht, 1981.

Veenendaal, A. J. *Railways in the Netherlands: A Brief History, 1834-1994*. Stanford: Stanford University Press, 2001.

Veenhof, Jan. "Hondred jaar theologie aan de Vrije Universiteit." In *Wetenschap en Rekenshcap, 1880-1980: Een eeuw wetenschapsbeoefening en wetenschapsbeschouwing aan de Vrije Universiteit*. Kampen: J. H. Kok, 1980.

Volf, Miroslav. *A Public Faith: How Followers of Christ Should Serve the Common Good*. Grand Rapids: Brazos, 2011.

Wallis, Jim. *On God's Side: What Religion Forgets and Politics Hasn't Learned About Serving the Common Good*. Grand Rapids: Brazos, 2013.

Wannenwetsch, Bernd. "The Whole Christ and the Whole Human Being: Dietrich Bonhoeffer's Inspiration for the 'Christology and Ethics' Discourse." In *Christology and Ethics*, edited by F. LeRon Shults and Brent Waters, 75-98. Grand Rapids: Eerdmans, 2010.

Weizsäcker, Carl Friedrich von. "Thoughts of a Non-Theologian on Dietrich Bonhoeffer's Theological Development." *Ecumenical Review* 28 (1976) 156-73.

―――. *The World View of Physics*. Chicago: University of Chicago Press, 1952.

Williams, Reggie. *Bonhoeffer's Black Jesus: Harlem Renaissance Theology and an Ethic of Resistance*. Waco, TX: Baylor University Press, 2014.

―――. "Christ-Centered Emphatic Resistance: The Influence of Harlem Renaissance Theology on the Incarnational Ethics of Dietrich Bonhoeffer." PhD diss., Fuller Theological Seminary, 2011.

Wolterstorff, Nicholas. "Abraham Kuyper (1837-1920)." In vol. 1 of *The Teachings of Modern Christianity on Law, Politics, and Human Nature*, edited by John Witte Jr. and Frank S. Alexander, 289-94. New York: Cambridge University Press, 2006.

―――. "Abraham Kuyper (1873-1920): Commentary." In *The Teachings of Modern Protestantism on Law, Politics, and Human Nature*, edited by John Witte Jr. and Frank S. Alexander, 29-69. New York: Columbia University Press, 2007.

Wood, John Halsey, Jr. "Covenant Theology for a Secular Society: Abraham Kuyper's *De Leer der Verbonden* (1880) as an Experiment in Modern Theology." In *The Kuyper Center Review*, Vol. 1, *New Essays in Reformed Theology and Public Life*, edited by Gordon Graham, 83-92. Grand Rapids, Eerdmans, 2010.

―――. *Going Dutch in the Modern Age: Abraham Kuyper's Struggle for a Free Church in the Nineteenth-Century Netherlands*. Oxford: Oxford University Press, 2013.

Wüstenberg, Ralf K. "The Influence of Wilhelm Dilthey on Bonhoeffer's *Letters and Papers from Prison*." In *Bonhoeffer's Intellectual Formation: Theology and Philosophy in His Thought*, edited by Peter Frick, 167-73. Tubingen: Mohr Siebeck, 2008.

―――. *A Theology of Life: Dietrich Bonhoeffer's Religionless Christianity*. Translated by Doug Stott. Grand Rapids: Eerdmans, 1998.

Zehnpfund, Dieter. *Die Familie Bonhoeffer und Friedrichsbrunn*. Katalog zur Austellung, 2006.

www.ingramcontent.com/pod-product-compliance
Lightning Source LLC
Chambersburg PA
CBHW062023220426
43662CB00010B/1449